CW00407812

A Dictionary
of
European Land Battles

From the Earliest Times to 1945

A DICTIONARY
OF EUROPEAN
LAND BATTLES

FROM THE EARLIEST TIMES TO 1945

by

John Sweetman

SPELLMOUNT
Staplehurst

British Library Cataloguing in Publication Data:
A catalogue record for this book is available
from the British Library

Copyright © John Sweetman 1984, 2004

ISBN 1-86227-234-4

First published in the UK in 1984 by
Robert Hale Ltd

This edition published in the UK in 2004 by
Spellmount Limited
The Old Rectory
Staplehurst
Kent TN12 0AZ

Tel: 01580 893730
Fax: 01580 893731
E-mail: enquiries@spellmount.com
Website: www.spellmount.com

1 3 5 7 9 8 6 4 2

Printed in Great Britain by
TJ International Ltd, Padstow, Cornwall

Contents

Introduction   7

Explanatory Notes   10

Battles   11

List of Wars and Battles   257

Select Bibliography   269

Index of Persons   271

Postscript   311

Introduction

Throughout the ages war has continually, fundamentally and often dramatically scarred the face of Europe from the Atlantic to the Urals and the Mediterranean to the Arctic Ocean. Its conduct, course and outcome have determined the geographical limits of the different countries and political systems which govern them, the cultural opportunities enjoyed and the religious affiliations practised by their inhabitants. The turbulent fortunes of Poland, from mediaeval dominance via eighteenth-century obliteration and twentieth-century revival to contemporary Soviet subordination, starkly demonstrate the power of the battlefield.

The spread of classical learning – in science, medicine, philosophy, art and architecture – postdated military conquest; and its revival after the dark era of barbarism during the Renaissance relied to a considerable extent upon the favourable results of armed conflict. Advance of the Reformation, and specifically the seventeenth-century division of central Europe into Protestant north and Catholic south, hinged as much on the sharpness of the sword as the persuasion of theological argument. So, too, did evolution of the nation-state depend on effective armies, as the rise of Prussia, the unification of Italy and the disintegration of the Austrian and Turkish empires graphically illustrate. The way of life and the very existence of individual Europeans have derived, and still do derive, from the consequences of a vast multitude of encounters, varying from the passing skirmish to prolonged set-piece epic, decided on all manner of disparate and far-flung, famous and anonymous, locations across the length and breadth of the continent.

As the development of European civilization can be related to Greece and Rome and the fate of their military ventures, so also has Europe closely affected the wider world through the military aspirations of its rulers: the eighteenth-century War of the Austrian Succession and Seven Years' War gave rise to global confrontations far beyond the original, narrow limits of territorial dispute in the heart of Europe. In an earlier age the Spanish *conquistadores* and, later, the procession of explorers, adventurers and generals who vied with one another to colour the map of Africa with their own national hues, underline the reality of this phenomenon. Many new colonies, and eventually new countries, owed their origin to religious bigotry or political persecution in Europe. Thus internecine, national disputes, such as the English Civil War and French Wars of Religion, assumed a much greater measure of international significance even remote from the shores of Europe.

Undeniably sea battles, like Lepanto (1572), Trafalgar (1805), Jutland (1916) and the more prolonged and diffuse Atlantic campaigns during two world wars have played an important, at times crucial, role in European conflicts. More recently airpower has had a keen impact upon the European battlefield, although the decisiveness of its independent contribution in terms of 'strategic bombing' remains a matter of debate. Whatever the relative merits of seapower and airpower, however, unquestionably wars in Europe have hitherto in the last resort been decided by armies and the occupation of territory. Since the close of the Second World War, no battles in the traditional sense of armed confrontation between two or more organized bodies have been fought in Europe. Arguably, with the emergence of so-called superpowers, their close involvement in the post-war alliance structure and the creation of powerful armouries capable of traumatic, widespread destruction, European states (the USSR apart) will never again individually or collectively deploy the military strength or exercise the associated political command that they have in the past.

Hence it is worth chronicling those European battles from the earliest times to 1945 which have directly or indirectly, to a greater or lesser degree, influenced the course of history. Inevitably the records for some battles are more thorough and more reliable than for others. However, lack of precise or lengthy detail does not necessarily gainsay a battle's importance: uncertainty about its duration, varying in different accounts from two to seven days, cannot obscure the crucial consequence of Charles Martel's victory over the Moors in 732. Casualty figures, almost invariably presented in convenient tens of thousands, are frequently suspect, but they do at least convey an impression of the scale of engagement.

Many military dictionaries (even those confined to a limited period of time) seek to provide comprehensive cover of battles on land, at sea and, latterly, in the air, and usually for the entire globe. In some cases, battles are listed alphabetically with land, sea and air intermingled; in others, subdivision occurs either by continent or according to the element in which each battle was fought. Quick reference is not, therefore, always easy.

This volume deals only with European land battles and aims to identify the more significant ones, where possible giving brief details of participants, commanders, action, casualties and military outcome together with an indication of the broader political implications. Entries are intended to provide a simple, factual check, although the appended select bibliography of texts and atlases does suggest sources for amplification and further research. An alphabetical list of wars and battles and an index of persons included in the work are also appended.

Explanatory Notes

1. For simplicity, to avoid distinguishing between divisional, corps, army or independent commands during the same battle or battles chronologically close together which could confuse, military personnel are simply described as 'commander'. The dates ascribed to sovereigns and rulers are the years during which they were in power, not their life span.

2. Throughout the text and appendices, with very occasional exceptions where specifically necessary, the generic terms 'Marshal', 'Field-Marshal' and 'General' are used. Thus no distinction is made, for instance, between 'Marshal of France' and 'Marshal of the Empire'; nor are the terms 'Major-General', 'Colonel-General' or 'Lieutenant Field-Marshal' employed.

3. For names of people and places which are best recognized in their English form this has been used; in other cases the original foreign spellings have been retained. Most titles have been anglicized on the grounds, for example, that 'Baron' is more meaningful than 'Freiherr'. The English designations for wars are also used: so, 'First World War' not 'World War I'.

Battles

Abensberg *(Napoleonic Wars)*, 1809

After Austria declared war on France in 1809 for the fourth time since 1792, Archduke Charles Louis, brother of Emperor Francis I, crossed the Inn river with a large army. Marching into Bavaria, he hoped to trap Marshal Davout's III French Corps at Ratisbon (Regensburg) but, aware of this danger, Davout fought his way eighteen miles south-west to link up with Marshal Lefebvre's VII Corps at Abensberg on 19 April. The next day Napoleon, now in personal command, attacked the Austrians with 25,000 men under Marshal Lannes. The Archduke's right wing was forced to pull back to Eckmühl (Eggmühl), and his left retreated south-east towards Landshut. The French and Bavarians lost 3,000 dead and wounded, the Austrians 2,700 plus 4,000 prisoners. Napoleon thus checked the resurgence of Austrian opposition which had been encouraged by French military reverses in Spain.

Aclea *(Danish Invasions of England)*, 851

Increasingly deep raids by the Danes into England brought about the battle of Aclea (Ockley), south of the Thames on the slopes of the North Downs five miles from modern Dorking. Here Ethelwulf, King of Wessex, repelled the invaders and so helped to establish his kingdom as the most important in England: but this was the only major victory which he would win over the Danes.

Acragas *(Carthaginian Invasion of Sicily)*, 406 BC

In 406 BC the Carthaginians laid siege to Acragas (Agrigentum), on the south-west coast of Sicily, whose defenders were commanded by the Spartan Dexippus. When an epidemic swept through the Carthaginian camp killing the commander, Himilco assumed control and pressed the siege. Arrival of 35,000 Syracusans under Corinthian command to relieve the city caused a pitched battle outside the walls of Acragas. The Carthaginians suffered severe losses but were not dislodged and the relief attempt failed. Disputes now broke out among defenders in the city, and many mercenaries deserted. Eight months later, after the entire garrison had abandoned it, Himilco occupied Acragas. However, further Carthaginian progress in Sicily would depend upon the outcome of struggles within Greece, notably between Athens and Sparta.

Adrianople I *(Civil Wars of the Roman Empire)*, 323

After nine years of uneasy peace Constantine I, the Western Roman Emperor, marched into Thrace with over 50,000 men and met an army of similar size under the Eastern Emperor, Licinianus Licinius, at Adrianople (modern Edirne), 130 miles north-west of Byzantium (from 330, Constantinople). On 3 July Constantine manœuvred the eastern army out of its entrenched position, and in the open his veterans overwhelmed Licinius' inexperienced troops. Licinius lost a large number of his men and was forced to retreat into Byzantium. This victory extended the influence of the Western Emperor into the Balkans, then under threat from the Goths; and the following year Constantine reunited the Empire under him.

Adrianople II *(Gothic Invasions of the Roman Empire)*, 378

Valens, the joint Roman Emperor, decided to suppress Goths whom he had allowed to settle in Thrace, because fighting had broken out between them and resident Romans. On 9 August 378 he attacked massed Gothic forces ten miles from Adrianople without waiting for reinforcements, whilst the enemy cavalry was away on a foraging expedition. Quickly driving the Goths back, Valens seemed on the point of victory when the absent cavalry returned. The legions were then virtually annihilated: 20,000 out of 30,000 infantry, including Valens, were killed. Although the Goths were unable to take Adrianople itself, this victory demonstrated their ability to defeat Romans within the imperial frontiers.

Adrianople III *(Wars of the Byzantine Empire)*, 972

Under Sviatoslav I, Prince of Kiev, Russians crossed the Balkan Mountains, seized Philippopolis (Plovdiv) in 969 and pressed on towards Constantinople. From the capital John Zimisces marched out with 30,000 infantry and cavalry to confront twice that number of Russians near Adrianople. Veteran Byzantine foot archers riddled the enemy ranks with arrows, then the cavalry put in several telling charges and, with the aid of Byzantine ships on the Danube, Zimisces drove the invaders completely out of Bulgaria.

Adrianople IV *(Fourth Crusade)*, 1205

After sacking Constantinople in 1204, Crusaders under Baldwin I and the Venetian doge Enrico Dandolo marched north-west towards Bulgaria, where Kaloyan (Yoannitsa) had refused to acknowledge Baldwin's supremacy. When the two armies met at Adrianople on 15 April 1205, the Bulgarian cavalry feigned retreat and, as the Crusaders rode in hot pursuit, suddenly wheeled about to charge and rout them. Louis, Comte de Blois, and a large number of Crusaders fell; Baldwin was captured (and later died in captivity). Kaloyan then proceeded to devastate Thrace and Macedonia.

Adrianople V *(Greco–Turkish Wars)*, 1365

The Turks, who had established themselves at Gallipoli in 1354, began to overrun Thrace and in 1365, under Murad I, they seized the historic crossroads town of Adrianople. A year later it replaced Bursa, east of the Sea of Marmara in Asia Minor, as the Ottoman capital.

Adrianople VI *(First Balkan War)*, 1913

By the terms of the armistice signed on 3 December 1912, Turkey agreed to cede Adrianople to Bulgaria. But a *coup d'état* in Constantinople overthrew the ministry of Mohammed V, and nationalists led by Enver Bey determined to retain Adrianople. The war resumed on 3 February 1913; Bulgarians invested the city forcing its surrender on 26 March, and its loss to Turkey was confirmed in the Treaty of London signed on 30 May.

Adwalton Moor *(English Civil War)*, 1643

When a Parliamentarian army led by Lord Fairfax failed to take York, the Earl of Newcastle determined to press home the Royalists' advantage, and the two armies met on Adwalton Moor, five miles east of Bradford, on 30 June 1643. Due mainly to a spirited infantry attack late in the day, Newcastle's 10,000 defeated the 4,000 Parliamentarians, who suffered some 2,000 casualties. This victory left Charles I's supporters in control of the whole of Yorkshire except Hull.

Agendicum *(Gallic Wars)*, 52 BC

When Julius Caesar moved south from Avaricum (Bourges) in central France with six Roman legions, he sent Titus Labienus north to the Seine with four legions. Labienus had just crossed to the north side of the Seine when he learnt of Caesar's defeat by the Arverni at Gergovia (Clermont). A large force of Gauls under Camulogenus, sensing victory, took up position south of the river to cut off the Romans from their base at Agendicum (Sens) seventy miles south-east of Paris, and another Gallic tribe began to assemble north of Labienus. Abandoning all thought of taking Paris, Labienus recrossed the Seine and attacked Camulogenus' larger army. The legionaries cut their way through the Gauls, killing a large number including Camulogenus, to regain their base, where they were joined by Caesar. The Romans then moved towards the Gallic stronghold of Alesia, near Dijon.

Agincourt *(Hundred Years War)*, 1415

Marching from Harfleur towards Calais with 1,000 cavalry and infantry and 5,000 archers, Henry V found his path blocked by a French army of 20,000 under the Constable d'Albret. Forced to fight, Henry chose a position between two woods, which narrowed the front to 1,200 yards, near Agincourt, thirty-three miles north-west of Arras. Sending the cavalry to the rear, Henry deployed his infantry in three divisions with archers on each flank. In front lay ploughed fields, heavy with mud after a week of rain. The vast numerical superiority of the French, who deployed in three lines, was nullified by the narrow front. At 11 a.m. on 25 October 1415 the English opened the battle with their archers' longbows (effective at 250 yards). The French first line moved forward with a cavalry spearhead but was hampered by muddy ground and severely affected by the English arrows. Nevertheless, it reached the English position, only to be repulsed, and the second line fared no better. At this point French camp-followers attacked the English camp, seeking plunder. Henry, fearing an attack in the rear and an assault from the untested third French line in front, ordered that all prisoners be massacred. The threat to the camp was quickly dealt with, however, and the third line did not attack. The battle thus ended in under three hours with the defeat of the superior French force, which suffered 7,000 casualties (including d'Albret, who was killed). At an estimated cost of under 1,600 English casualties Henry had cleared the way to Calais; but hopes of rapid progress through northern France proved premature.

Aisne I *(First World War),* 1914

Having lost the first battle of the Marne early in September 1914, the Germans withdrew to high ground north to the Aisne river, a tributary of the Oise. Three German armies – from west to east First, Seventh and Second – under the new German commander General von Falkenhayn faced the Allied left (west) wing comprising the French Sixth Army, the British Expeditionary Force and the French Fifth Army. The Allies crossed the Aisne on 13 September and attacked prepared German positions the next day, making little progress in the face of heavy resistance. Arrival of German reinforcements produced effective stalemate, and on 18 September General Joffre halted the attack. The transition from open combat to trench warfare had begun.

Aisne II *(First World War),* 1917

On 16 April 1917 General Nivelle, French commander on the Western Front, attacked on a fifty-mile front on the Aisne between Soissons and Reims with the French Sixth Army on the left and Fifth Army on the right. Forewarned by a prolonged bombardment, the Germans were well prepared. Heavy fire from the entrenched Seventh and First armies caused severe French casualties and, although reinforced by the Tenth Army on 20 April, after a month the French had not reached their first day's objectives. On 9 May the offensive finally petered out. Six days later Nivelle, who had predicted a decisive breakthrough, was replaced by General Pétain, who had to deal with widespread mutinies among French troops, for which failure of Nivelle's offensive was partly responsible.

Aisne III *(First World War),* 1918

Having reinforced the German First and Seventh armies secretly, on 27 May 1918 General Ludendorff opened a massive artillery bombardment shortly after midnight and at dawn attacked the French Sixth Army (General Duchêne). Seventeen out of forty-one available divisions attacked Duchêne on a nine-mile front and captured bridges over the Aisne intact. By evening the Germans had advanced thirteen miles (the furthest single day's advance on the Western Front in nearly four years) between Soissons and Reims. Soissons, fifty miles north-east of Paris, fell on 28 May, and two days later German troops were on the Marne, less than forty miles from the capital. Vigorous counter-attacks by American, British and French troops on the Marne and elsewhere along the line slowed down the enemy advance, however, which ended on 6 June after a penetration of thirty-five miles.

Alarcos *(Spanish–Moslem Wars)*, 1195

With the Moors in control of southern Spain, on 18 July 1195 at Alarcos, just west of Ciudad Real, al-Mansur at the head of a Moorish army met a strong Christian force commanded by Alfonso VIII of Castile. Alfonso's army was decisively beaten. Only the King and a handful of survivors escaped thirty miles north to Calatrava, leaving 30,000 casualties or prisoners behind. Two years later Calatrava fell, and Alfonso agreed to a humiliating peace settlement.

Albuera *(Peninsular War)*, 1811

On 16 May 1811 Marshal Soult, with 25,000 French troops, attacked an allied force of some 35,000 Spanish, Portuguese and British under the command of Sir William Beresford at Albuera, fifteen miles south-east of the fortress of Badajoz, as it sought to penetrate Spain in the south while Viscount Wellington marched on Madrid further north. Only 7,000 of Beresford's men were British, but these stood firm, despite losing 5,000 killed, wounded or captured, as many of their allies fled. Soult incurred 8,000 casualties before retiring to Badajoz, having successfully checked Beresford's invasion attempt.

Alcantara *(Spanish Conquest of Portugal)*, 1580

In 1580 Philip II of Spain despatched the Duke of Alva with an army into Portugal to claim the throne, left vacant when the King died without issue. On 25 August at Alcantara on the Tagus river and close to the border, Alva defeated an untrained horde of peasants and townspeople led by the other claimant, Dom Antonio. For the next sixty years Portugal was ruled from Madrid.

Alcolea *(Deposition of Isabella II),* 1868

Rebelling against Isabella II's harsh rule in Spain, forces under Francisco Serrano crushed the royal army on 28 September 1868 at Alcolea on the Guadalquivir river east of Cordoba. Isabella fled the country next day, and a provisional government ruled until she formally abdicated and Amadeo I came to the throne in 1870.

Alesia *(Gallic Wars),* 52 BC

In 52 BC Julius Caesar besieged the strongly fortified town of Alesia (just north of modern Dijon) in Gaul with some 50,000 troops. Inside were 80,000 infantry and cavalry under the Arvernian leader Vercingetorix. Caesar constructed works stretching nine and a half miles round the town, which were attacked from the rear by another enemy force of 100,000 infantry and 8,000 cavalry. This huge body was driven off with heavy loss and a night breakout by the besieged Gauls also foiled. Yet another attempt was made to raise the siege by Vercassivellaunus, son-in-law of Vercingetorix, who attacked from the heights of Mont Rea to the north. Due to the personal intervention of Caesar in the threatened area, this relief attempt failed too. In despair, Vercingetorix then surrendered Alesia, and a year later Caesar completed his conquest of Gaul. Meanwhile Vercingetorix had been taken to Rome, where he was later beheaded.

Alford *(English Civil War),* 1645

On 2 July 1645, having crossed the Don river, Scottish Covenanters led by General Baillie attacked a Royalist force under the Marquis of Montrose, believing it to be in full retreat. In reality Montrose led them up to a well-prepared position at Alford, where they were routed with heavy loss. This encounter was not decisive, however, and the Covenanters soon rallied to challenge the Royalists again.

Alghero *(Aragonese Conquest of Sardinia)*, 1353

In 1353 Pedro IV of Aragon invaded Sardinia and defeated the Genoese so decisively at Alghero on the shore of La Loiera in the west, that the island remained in Aragonese hands for almost 400 years.

Alhama *(Spanish–Moslem Wars)*, 1482

On 28 February 1482 the Marquis of Cadiz led a Spanish army against the Moorish fortress of Alhama and so opened a campaign to recover Granada. A party managed to scale the ramparts undetected and open the gates, but the Spanish needed to fight hard to secure the town. Once in possession of it, however, Cadiz found himself besieged by 50,000 Moors under Abdul Hassan, who withdrew on 29 March before the approach of Ferdinand, King of Castile and Aragon, with a large relieving force. Thus the drive to recover Granada from the Moors had begun well.

Aljubarrota *(Spanish–Portuguese Wars)*, 1385

When Ferdinand I of Portugal died in 1383, his illegitimate half-brother John became Regent, though the throne was claimed by John of Castile on behalf of his wife Beatrice, Ferdinand's daughter. John of Castile invaded Portugal with 18,000 men to support the claim of Beatrice and was met by the Regent's 7,000 troops (which included English and Gascon veterans) at Aljubarrota, fifty miles north of Lisbon. The Castilians were routed on 14 August 1385, and Beatrice was forced to abandon her claims to the kingdom. The Regent was then crowned John I, the first of the Aviz dynasty which ruled Portugal for 200 years.

Alkmaar I *(Revolt of the Netherlands)*, 1573

Having recaptured Haarlem from the rebels, Don Frederick of Toledo attacked Alkmaar, twenty miles north-west of Amsterdam, with 16,000 Spaniards on 21 August 1573. The 2,000 defenders, comprising soldiers and armed citizens, repulsed the attackers, who then settled down to mount a siege. After the dykes had been opened to flood the surrounding land, a Spanish fleet under Comte Bossu was defeated in the Zuider Zee trying to bring up supplies for Don Frederick. On 8 September the Spaniards abandoned the siege, and Alkmaar thus became the first town to resist the Duke of Alva's troops.

Alkmaar II *(French Revolutionary Wars)*, 1799

On 2 October 1799 30,000 British and Russian troops under the command of the Duke of York met a French army of similar size led by General Brune before Alkmaar. An outflanking movement allowed the British to drive back the French left, and the allies went on to capture the town. But Brune quickly recovered to besiege them in Alkmaar, and sixteen days later the Duke of York was obliged to sign a convention, by which French prisoners were released in return for safe conduct for British troops out of the country. This ill-planned and ill-conceived attempt to free the Low Countries from French rule therefore ended in abject failure.

Allia River *(Gallic Invasions of Italy)*, 390 BC

As the Gauls under Brennus swept southwards, 40,000 Romans led by Quintus Sulpicius tried to halt them on the Allia river, eleven miles north of Rome. On 18 July, however, Brennus crushed the defenders and hurried on to sack the city, although the Capitol held out. Eventually after several months the Gauls withdrew from Rome on payment of an estimated 1,000 pounds of gold to them.

Alma *(Crimean War)*, 1854

Between 14 and 18 September 1854 approximately 60,000 British, French and Turkish troops landed at Calamita Bay on the Crimean peninsula, some thirty miles north of Sevastopol, and next day began to advance towards the Russian Black Sea naval base. On 20 September they found their way barred by a strong Russian force under Prince Menshikov, which was drawn up on heights south of the Alma river. The Russians failed to cover an accessible path close to the sea, and the French manœuvred cannon onto the heights to enfilade Menshikov's position. Meanwhile the British doggedly crossed the river further inland and, despite withering fire, took two important redoubts. The Russians retreated to Sevastopol, leaving 5,709 dead, wounded or captured behind. The combined allied casualties were about 2,200, including 362 British dead. The allies now went on to besiege Sevastopol, but a more efficient Russian commander might well have stopped them on the Alma and ended the Crimean War before it really got under way.

Almansa *(War of the Spanish Succession)*, 1707

Having proclaimed Archduke Charles of Austria as King of Spain in Madrid, the Earl of Galway moved eastwards with a force of 15,000 English, Dutch and Portuguese troops. On 25 April 1707 he encountered a superior French and Spanish army under the Duke of Berwick at Almansa, sixty miles south-west of Valencia. Galway was so thoroughly beaten that the attempt to put Charles on the Spanish throne failed.

Alnwick *(Anglo–Scottish Wars)*, 1092

Dispute between England and Scotland over the border between the two countries led to fierce but intermittent fighting, until William Rufus advanced English territory by capturing Carlisle and colonizing the surrounding area to the Tweed-Cheviot line early in 1092. Malcolm III of Scotland reacted by marching an army south and laying siege to Alnwick Castle in Northumberland. On 13 November 1092 an English relief force heavily defeated the Scots, killing Malcolm and his son and raising the siege. The English position in the north was thus consolidated and Scotland now experienced a period of internal dissension over the accession to the throne.

Amiens *(First World War)*, 1918

On 8 August 1918 Marshal Foch, the Allied Commander-in-Chief, launched an offensive under immediate direction of Sir Douglas Haig, which aimed to eliminate the enemy salient jutting towards Amiens and free the Amiens–Paris railway from interdiction by German artillery. The British Fourth Army, supported by 400 tanks, advanced on a ten-mile front behind a creeping artillery barrage, and by nightfall a nine-mile penetration had been achieved during a day called 'the Black Day' of the German Army by General Ludendorff. To the south General Debeney had made progress with the French First Army, and more Allied troops now joined the advance. On 10 August the French Third Army under General Humbert attacked further south; in the north the British Third and First armies also advanced. By 15 August General Rawlinson's British Fourth Army had control of the Lassigny massif, and shortly afterwards Ludendorff ordered a strategic withdrawal. The salient had therefore been erased, the Amiens–Paris railway freed for uninterrupted traffic. The Germans had suffered 75,000 losses, including over 30,000 prisoners, the Allies 46,000. Not only did this defeat seriously weaken the German forces, but it further undermined Austrian political faith in ultimate victory.

Amphipolis *(Great Peloponnesian War)*, 422 BC

In March 422 BC Cleon with 1,500 Athenians advanced to recover Amphipolis in eastern Macedonia, which had been occupied by 2,000 Spartans under Brasidas. The Spartans, unwilling to undergo a siege, surged out of the city as the Athenians approached. Quickly Cleon's left wing gave way, and soon his whole force was in flight, pursued by the Spartans. During the pursuit both Cleon and Brasidas fell, and the following year Sparta and Athens made peace.

Antwerp I *(Revolt of the Netherlands)*, 1584–5

Attacked by Spanish troops of the Duke of Parma, the citizens of Antwerp cut important dykes in 1584 and initially resisted attempts to storm the city. But Parma built a fortified bridge over the Scheldt river and cut off the defenders' supplies, so that eventually after fourteen months they were forced to surrender. With Brussels already in Spanish hands and Dutch morale low following the assassination of William the Silent, Parma now threatened to crush the revolt. However, diversion of his resources to aid the Spanish Armada and to attack north-eastern France prevented him from doing so.

Antwerp II *(First World War)*, 1914

After the invading German armies had taken Liège and Namur in August 1914, the main body of the Belgian Army, numbering 150,000, fell back to Antwerp. After the front had stabilized along the Aisne, the Germans turned their attention to the untaken port on 28 September. Three days later heavy siege guns began to demolish the surrounding forts and, covered by a small British naval brigade which continued to hold the city, on 6 October the Belgians withdrew along the Flemish coast to join other Allied forces. Four days after this, German troops occupied Antwerp.

Anzio *(Second World War)*, 1944

Halted by the Gustav Line defences, which included Monte Cassino, in their northward advance along the Italian peninsula, on 22 January 1944 Allied forces launched Operation Shingle. Designed to draw off German troops from the Gustav Line, thus weakening it for a breakthrough, it entailed landing 50,000 men of VI Corps (British First and American Third infantry divisions) under General Lucas at Anzio, seventy miles behind the enemy lines. Instead of pushing forward to secure the Alban Hills, the landing force dallied near Anzio and allowed the Germans to bring up reinforcements from their reserves without weakening the Gustav Line. More Allied troops were sent to Anzio, but the primary concern now was to protect the beachhead (fifteen by seven miles) rather than attack the enemy. Not until after the Gustav Line had crumbled did the troops break out of their confined area around the port: Operation Shingle was not therefore a success.

Aquileia I *(Germanic Invasions of Italy)*, 166–7

In 166 Germanic tribes swept into northern Italy. Leaving a force to besiege Aquileia at the head of the Adriatic, they moved south, but at the Piave river the invaders were halted by Marcus Aurelius, who then pursued them northwards to raise the siege of Aquileia. The Romans were too weak to establish a firm ascendancy over the Germanic tribes at this time, however, and Marcus Aurelius set an unhappy precedent by allowing them to settle within the Empire.

Aquileia II *(Civil Wars of the Roman Empire)*, 394

In 394, for the second time in six years, Theodosius, Emperor of the Eastern Roman Empire, went to Italy to deal with a usurper. On 5 September, just east of Aquileia, he met the pagan Eugenius, who had assumed control of the western Empire. During the first day's fighting Theodosius made little progress, but the desertion of part of the enemy force to him on 6 September led to a crushing defeat for Eugenius. The usurper himself was captured, and later beheaded; his general Abrogastes committed suicide. Pagan worship was forbidden and temporarily the two parts of the Roman Empire were reunited.

Aquileia III *(Wars of the Western Roman Empire)*, 452

In 452 Huns led by Attila invaded Italy, stormed and sacked Aquileia and moved south to threaten Rome. Pope Leo I bought off the invaders, and Aquileia was reoccupied, but meanwhile some of its refugee citizens had founded Venice. Attila died the following year.

Arcis-sur-Aube *(Napoleonic Wars)*, 1814

During the allied advance on Paris in 1814, Napoleon faced 90,000 troops under Prince von Schwarzenberg at Arcis-sur-Aube, fifteen miles north of Troyes. Despite an inferiority of 3–1, he attacked, causing Schwarzenberg 2,500 casualties. But Napoleon incurred, 1,700 casualties which he could ill afford, and was forced to withdraw without halting the threat to his capital.

Arcole *(French Revolutionary Wars)*, 1796

In November 1796 Napoleon was anxious to prevent the union of the main Austrian body in northern Italy of 24,000 men under General Alvintzy and another column approaching from the Tyrol under General Davidovich, as he himself had only 18,000 troops. The French attacked on 15 November, and the critical feature of the battlefield soon became the bridge over the Alpone river at Arcole, fifteen miles south-east of Verona. Not until 17 November did General Augereau's division cross the bridge and take Arcole, forcing Alvintzy to give ground. The Austrian lost 6,000 men and, at a cost of 4,600 casualties, the main French aim of preventing union of the two Austrian forces had been achieved.

Ardennes *(Second World War)*, 1944–5

On December 16, 1944 Field-Marshal Model launched Operation Watch on the Rhine against the area held by General Middleton's American VIII Corps between Monschau, fifteen miles south-east of Aachen, and Echternach, twenty miles north-east of Luxembourg. Twenty German divisions of the Sixth Panzer (General Dietrich), Fifth Panzer (General Manteuffel) and Seventh (General Brandenberger) Armies attacked in dense fog with the primary aim of splitting the Allied armies by a drive to capture Liège and Antwerp. Once this had been achieved, the American Ninth and First, British Second and Canadian First Armies, north of the breakthrough, were to be annihilated. To assist the attack, a special unit disguised as Americans would penetrate the Allied lines to cause chaos in the rear, and a paratroop drop on Malmédy in the north would prevent reinforcements driving south. The main axis of the advance was the Sixth Panzer Army in the north, but little progress was made here due to stubborn American defence in the St Vith region. Model, therefore, switched his major effort in support of the Fifth Panzer Army, in the centre of the attack. Manteuffel reached Bastogne on 20 December, but the American 101st Airborne Division hurried forward to its defence, and the Germans were forced to mask the town with infantry, whilst armour drove on westwards. For ease of command in the confused situation on 20 December the American Ninth and First armies, north of the bulge which had appeared in the Allied line, were put under Field-Marshal Montgomery, and at the same time General Patton's American Third Army was ordered to turn north and attack the Germans from the south. On 23 December the weather lifted, allowing Allied aircraft to take part in the battle with decisive effect on the Germans surrounding Bastogne, and to attack the enemy supply lines. Next day Manteuffel was checked four miles from the Meuse and sixty miles from his start line. On Christmas Day the American 2nd Armoured Division counter-attacked at Celles; next day Patton's 4th Armoured Division relieved Bastogne, and on 3 January 1945 Montgomery launched a major assault with the British XXX and American VII Corps. In desperation Model tried a last attack in the south, then on 8 January began a strategic withdrawal. Five days later British and American patrols made contact at St Hubert, and on 11 January the American 2nd (from the north) and 11th (from the south) Armoured Divisions linked up at Houffalize. Thereafter the Germans were gradually driven back until the original front was restored on 25 January. The Battle of the Bulge had cost Hitler some 200,000 casualties, 600 tanks and 1,500 aircraft. His gamble had failed in the west, but of more importance it had used up reserves which might have been used against Russian troops in the east. In all the battle had delayed the invasion of the Rhineland by six weeks and cost the Allies 75,000 in casualties and prisoners.

Argentoratum (*Alemanni Invasions of the Roman Empire*), 357

Worried by barbarian pressure on the Empire's Gallic frontier, Emperor Constantius II appointed his cousin Julian to take aggressive action. In August 357 Julian with 13,000 men encountered some 40,000 Alemanni near Argentoratum (Strasbourg). He attacked the superior enemy force and despite initial setbacks eventually drove it from the field, capturing the Alemanni king Chnodomar and causing 6,000 enemy casualties for the loss of 250 men himself. This victory helped to eliminate the threat from the Rhine Valley.

Arnhem (*Second World War*), 1944

In a bid to outflank the northern part of the Siegfried Line, Operation Market Garden planned that the British XXX Corps should advance to link up with the American 101st, American 82nd and British 1st Airborne Divisions, which were to drop on 17 September 1944 and secure vital bridges between Eindhoven and Arnhem in Holland. Despite initial difficulties the Americans secured their objectives, but the British could not take the bridge at Arnhem. Dropped too far west and unexpectedly faced by the 9th SS Panzer Division, they were further hampered by bad weather which prevented accurate dropping of supplies and reinforcements. When it was clear that success could not be achieved, in the early hours of 26 September 2,323 survivors were withdrawn by boat across the lower Rhine river by troops which had fought their way forward from Nijmegen. 1,130 British casualties had been incurred and a further 6,450 men became prisoners. Bridges over the Waal and Maas (Meuse) rivers had been captured, but a breakthrough into northern Germany had not been gained. Whether such a penetration could have been made with the allocation of greater resources to the operation would remain contentious for many years to come.

Arques *(French Wars of Religion)*, 1589

When Henry III of France was assassinated in July 1589, Henry of Navarre, the Huguenot leader, claimed the throne – a move hotly disputed by the Catholic League. At Arques, five miles south-east of Dieppe, Henry's force of 9,000 men was attacked by a much stronger Catholic army led by the Duke of Mayenne. The marshy nature of the ground meant that Mayenne could commit his troops only in relatively small numbers, and the Huguenots were able to beat back a succession of assaults with heavy loss. Eventually Henry was left master of the field, when the enemy withdrew, and Navarre had won an important victory on the way to being accepted by Protestants and Catholics as Henry IV of France.

Arras I *(Franco–Spanish Wars)*, 1654

Two years after he deserted France for Spanish service, the Great Condé laid siege to the French town of Arras, eighty miles south-west of Brussels and a hundred miles north of Paris. However, during the night 24–25 August 1654, a force under the Vicomte de Turenne attacked the siege lines and routed the Spanish. Having suffered 3,000 casualties, Condé fell back towards Cambrai, leaving the French in command of the territory north-east of Paris.

Arras II *(First World War)*, 1917

On 9 April 1917, preceded by a five-day bombardment of 2,800 guns, Sir Douglas Haig launched an attack in the area of Arras. His primary aim was to draw German troops away from the sector in which General Nivelle was to make his offensive a week later. In the north the Canadians took Vimy Ridge, and to the south General Allenby's Third Army advanced over three miles. But British exuberance was short-lived as German Sixth Army reserves counter-attacked. In the far south, beyond Allenby, General Gough's Fifth Army was also committed. Nivelle's offensive failed and by 3 May any hope of further British advance near Arras had disappeared. For their modest gains along a twenty-mile front, Haig's forces had incurred 84,000 casualties but had inflicted 75,000 on the enemy, captured some 20,000 prisoners and taken a considerable amount of equipment.

Artois *(First World War)*, 1915

On 9 May 1915, preceded by a heavy bombardment, the French attacked on a six-mile front north of Arras in the Pas de Calais. Rapidly advancing three miles, they seized part of Vimy Ridge, but German counter-attacks threw them back. The battle developed into one of attrition, and when it came to a halt on 18 June the French had suffered almost 100,000 casualties, the Germans 75,000; and, yet once more, no significant territorial advantage had been gained.

Asculum I *(Rise of Rome)*, 279 BC

At Asculum (Ascoli Satriano), eighteen miles south of Foggia, the Epirot commander Pyrrhus with 40,000 men encountered a similar force of Romans under Publius Sulpicius, who were trying to relieve the city. In furious fighting Pyrrhus' cavalry proved decisive, and the Romans retreated with the loss of 6,000 men. Pyrrhus lost only 3,500, but he realized that the Romans could more easily make good their losses. Pyrrhus therefore turned his attention to Sicily, and his success at Asculum gave rise to the term 'Pyrrhic victory'.

Asculum II *(Roman Social War)*, 90–89 BC

During 90 BC discontent at the rights granted by Rome led allied tribes to band together in revolt, during which Asculum was captured and its Roman citizens massacred. The following year the allies (Socii) were besieged and overwhelmed in Asculum by

Roman legionaries, and at length an offer of Roman citizenship ended the conflict.

Ashdown *(Danish Invasions of England)*, 871

The Danes penetrated the Thames as far as Reading, then moved on westwards early in 871. At Ashdown on 8 January, however, they were checked by West Saxons led by Ethelred I and his brother Alfred (later the Great). Alfred was obliged to charge uphill but succeeded in routing the Danes, who retreated to Reading with heavy loss. Although this victory did not eject the invaders from Wessex, it gave hope that they could be contained and was important for Saxon morale.

Ashingdon *(Rise of England)*, 1016

On 18 October 1016 Edmund II (Ironside) and Canute, the Dane, fought a decisive battle at Ashingdon in Essex in a struggle for the English throne. Due to the desertion of his brother-in-law Edric, Edmund was beaten and agreed that Canute should rule the whole of England except Wessex. Shortly afterwards Edmund died, however, and Canute became ruler of Wessex also.

Aspern *(Napoleonic Wars)*, 1809

Having constructed a bridge to Lobau Island, near the far bank of the Danube and four miles below Vienna, on 20 May 1809 Napoleon began to pass troops across. By noon on 21 May, with the bridge extended to the far bank, 23,000 French troops were on the other side of the river in possession of Aspern and Essling. During the afternoon Archduke Charles Louis with some 95,000 Austrian troops attacked but could not dislodge the French who were reinforced during the night to 48,000 infantry, 7,000 cavalry and 144 guns. On 22 May Marshal Lannes attacked the Austrian centre, and Archduke Charles Louis, realizing that the enemy could not be ejected, resorted to a steady bombardment with his 264 guns. At nightfall the French withdrew to Lobau Island, having lost almost 20,000 men including Lannes and suffered Napoleon's largest setback so far, although in the fighting the Austrians had over 23,000 casualties. Napoleon now concentrated on rebuilding his army before launching another, more successful assault across the river.

Aspromonte *(Italian Wars of Independence)*, 1862

Early in 1862 Giuseppe Garibaldi organized a force in Sicily with the aim of marching on Rome, still garrisoned by French troops. In defiance of the Italian government, which feared major intervention by France if Rome should be attacked, he crossed to the mainland. On 29 August Victor Emmanuel II's royal army met and defeated Garibaldi in Aspromonte, the mountainous region in the toe of Italy immediately east of the Straits of Messina, so avoiding a potentially dangerous international situation. Garibaldi and several hundred of his supporters were captured but later freed under an amnesty, which enabled them to continue the fight for Italian independence.

Astrakhan I *(Conquests of Ivan the Terrible)*, 1554–6

Marching southwards after securing the area around Kazan on the upper Volga, in 1554 Ivan the Terrible laid siege to the Tatar stronghold of Astrakhan at the head of the river delta. So fierce was the defence that not until 1556 did Ivan capture the town and so gain control of the entire course of the Volga with its access to the Caspian Sea.

Astrakhan II *(Russo–Turkish Wars)*, 1569

The Sultan of Turkey, Selim II, planned to dig a canal between the Don and Volga rivers to give the Ottoman Black Sea fleet access to the Caspian. He therefore sent an army to take Astrakhan in 1569, but the defenders held out until a Russian relief force arrived, forcing Selim to raise the siege and abandon the canal project.

Auerstadt, see *Jena*

Aughrim *(Irish Rebellion against William III)*, 1691

On 12 July 1691, during the struggle to eliminate opposition to William III in western Ireland, having captured Athlone General

Ginkel crossed the Shannon and came upon a force of Irish and French troops under the Earl of Lucan and Marquis de St-Ruth at Aughrim, thirty miles east of Galway. The rebels fought strongly, and it was some time before English cavalry successfully turned their flank. St-Ruth was killed, Lucan took refuge in Limerick and over 6,000 Irish and French perished in the rout which followed. Ginkel's leisurely pursuit meant that the surrender of Limerick, the last rebel stronghold, was ultimately secured in October by negotiation not military action.

Auldearn *(English Civil War)*, 1645

On 9 May 1645 at Auldearn east of Nairn, despite being heavily outnumbered, 2,200 Royalists under the Marquis of Montrose successfully attacked and defeated a strong force of Covenanters led by Sir John Hurry, which was marching north to raid the lands of the Gordons. This victory strengthened Charles I's hold on Scotland, at a time when his cause was waning south of the border.

Auray *(Hundred Years War)*, 1364

There were two rival claimants to the dukedom of Brittany in 1364: John de Montfort of England and the Frenchman Charles de Blois. Supporters of de Montfort, led by John Chandos, were besieging Auray on the Gulf of Morbihan when a French army under Blois and Bertrand du Guesclin attacked them on 29 September. The French were repulsed, Guesclin captured and Blois killed. In the following year de Montfort was recognized as Duke of Brittany.

Austerlitz *(Napoleonic Wars)*, 1805

Late in November 1805 85,000 Russian and Austrian troops led by the veteran Russian general Kutuzov occupied the Prazen plateau and planned to cut off Napoleon's path to Vienna. At daybreak on 2 December they launched an attack against the 70,000 French troops just west of Austerlitz. An attempt to turn the French right flank held by Marshal Davout's III Corps failed, and a counter-attack by Marshal Soult drove the allies off the plateau. In turn a

Russian counter-attack in the centre failed to recover ground, and meanwhile Marshals Lannes and Bernadotte struck from the French left. The allies gave ground all along the line, but the French were too exhausted to pursue vigorously. The Russians and Austrians lost 15,000 casualties and 11,000 prisoners and the French suffered 9,000 casualties. This encounter is often referred to as the Battle of the Three Emperors, for the emperors of France, Austria and Russia were present with their armies. Its outcome had important political repercussions in the short term, for the Third Coalition against France collapsed, with Russian forces retiring east, Austria making peace immediately and Prussia the following year.

Avaricum *(Gallic Wars)*, 52 BC

In 52 BC serious opposition to Roman occupation of Gaul arose and centred on the Arvernian leader, Vercingetorix. Considerable destruction of life and property took place, so when Julius Caesar arrived to restore order, the revolutionaries could expect little mercy. He laid siege to Avaricum (Bourges), eighty miles south-east of Tours, beat off all attempts at relief and, having successfully stormed the walls, massacred the garrison and inhabitants.

Azov *(Russo–Turkish Wars)*, 1696

The Turkish fortress of Azov, at the head of the Sea of Azov and commanding the outlet to the Black Sea, was an important objective for Peter I (later the Great) in his plans to expand Russia. Having failed to take it in 1695, the following year he mounted a more thorough siege by land and sea, achieving success at length on 28 July. Russian access to the Black Sea had therefore been gained, but it was lost once more to Turkey before the end of Peter's reign.

Badajoz *(Peninsular War)*, 1812

Advancing from Portugal in March 1812, Viscount Wellington invested the fortress of Badajoz, strategically situated 200 miles south-west of Madrid, near the border, to bar an invasion of Spain, with its 5,000 garrison of French, German and Spanish troops. On

5 April, with the walls breached, he launched an assault which succeeded only after terrible slaughter and at a cost of 3,500 casualties. For two days after the capture of the fortress his troops were out of hand but, after order had been restored on threat of capital punishment, Wellington was ready to take advantage of the way into Spain which now lay open.

Balaclava *(Crimean War)*, 1854

During the siege of Sevastopol, British supplies came through the port of Balaclava, some eight miles south-east of the besieged naval base. North of Balaclava lay a plain, divided into South and North Valleys by a low range of hills known as the Causeway Heights. On 25 October 1854 three actions took place on this plain which have become known collectively as the Battle of Balaclava. Firstly Russian cavalry converged on Balaclava across the South Valley and were repulsed by the 93rd Highlanders under Sir Colin Campbell (the 'thin red line'), then another body of cavalry was charged off the Causeway Heights by the Heavy Brigade under Brigadier-General Scarlett. Finally came the famous 'Charge of the Light Brigade' up the North Valley. Led by Lord Cardigan, the Brigade attacked Russian guns and massed troops at the head of the valley, instead of preventing the enemy towing captured cannon from redoubts on the Causeway Heights. Although some support was given by French cavalry on the way back, of the 673 who started the attack 113 were killed and many others wounded or made prisoner. However, the three actions that day removed any immediate threat to the British supply port.

Balathista *(Wars of the Byzantine Empire)*, 1014

Seeking to curb the growing power of Bulgaria, in 1014 Basil II, the Byzantine emperor, trapped a large force of Bulgarians at Balathista in the Struma valley. The Bulgarians were overwhelmed and 15,000 taken prisoner. According to legend Basil ordered that the captives should be blinded, except for a few who would be allowed one eye to lead the others back to their capital. The Bulgarian tsar, Samuel, is reputed to have dropped dead at the sight of his mutilated warriors returning home.

Bannockburn *(Anglo–Scottish Wars)*, 1314

When Scottish forces under Robert Bruce threatened the English-held castles of Berwick and Stirling, Edward II led an army of 15,000 (including 2,000 cavalry) north. Bruce deployed 8,000 men on a rise overlooking Bannockburn, five miles south of Stirling, with 500 cavalry in reserve. On 24 June 1314, as the English struggled through the river, the Scots attacked. An attempt to outflank them was defeated by Scottish cavalry, and eventually the English fled. Edward II escaped but many of his men were drowned or slaughtered in the surrounding marshes. For the loss of some 4,000 men, the Scots had ended immediate English hopes of conquering their land.

Bapaume *(Franco–Prussian War)*, 1871

On 3 January 1871 a French force under General Faidherbe attempted to relieve Péronne, thirty miles east of Amiens, which was under siege by the Prussian General von Goeben, but was checked at Bapaume, fifteen miles short of its objective. Despite initial tactical success, the French were at length compelled to retreat. Six days later Péronne fell, and before the end of the month Paris also surrendered.

Barcelona I *(War of the Spanish Succession)*, 1705

In August 1705 the Earl of Peterborough landed with 6,000 English troops north of Barcelona and proceeded to invest the city, which was held in the name of Philip V. By a bold night march Peterborough captured the dominant Montjuich feature south of Barcelona and shortly afterwards, on 9 October, the city surrendered. Peterborough's success encouraged Catalonia to recognize the Austrian Archduke Charles as King of Spain, but the bulk of the Spanish still favoured Philip V, grandson of Louis XIV of France.

Barcelona II *(Spanish Civil War)*, 1938–9

A determined advance by six Nationalist armies, including four Italian divisions, in Catalonia during December 1938 drove disorganized Republican troops back to Barcelona, then under air attack. Only token resistance was offered, however, before Republican leaders, the Government, some 250,000 troops and 200,000 civilians fled into France; and on 26 January 1939 Generalissimo Franco's troops occupied the almost-deserted city. On 10 February Nationalist troops closed the border with France, leaving Madrid as the last important centre in Republican hands.

Barletta *(Franco–Spanish Wars in Italy)*, 1502

Outside the walls of Barletta, on Italy's Adriatic coast, seventy miles north-west of Taranto, Spanish troops under Gonzalo de Córdoba clashed with French forces, which included Swiss pikemen. Relying on infantry to get to close quarters and nullify the effectiveness of the pikemen, the Spaniards attacked and defeated the French. Their success laid the foundations for the development of Spanish infantry formations, which were to be most effective in the years to come.

Barnet *(Wars of the Roses)*, 1471

On 14 April 1471 Lancastrian forces led by the Earl of Warwick (known as 'the Kingmaker') met an army under Edward IV outside Barnet, twelve miles north of London. In poor visibility due to fog, Edward turned the Lancastrian left and then fell upon the centre. Warwick's men fled and he himself was killed. Within a month Edward IV would defeat other Lancastrian forces in southern England and enter London in triumph to reclaim the throne from Henry VI.

Bautzen *(Napoleonic Wars)*, 1813

Thirty miles north-east of Dresden, 100,000 Russian and Prussian troops took up a defensive position around Bautzen with their front protected by the Spree river. Napoleon with 115,000 men came up and on 20 May 1813 forced a passage across the Spree, capturing Bautzen itself the next day. Then on 22 May, in conjunction with 84,000 men under Marshal Ney, who attacked the enemy right, he overran the whole position but could not prevent the Russian and Austrian troops from carrying out an orderly retreat. During this indecisive battle both sides suffered some 15,000 casualties, and the allies fell back into Silesia before agreeing to an armistice. In August, however, hostilities recommenced; and, following reverses in central Europe and the Iberian peninsula, nine months later Napoleon would abdicate for the first time.

Baza *(Spanish–Moslem Wars)*, 1489

In his drive to clear the Moors from Granada, in June 1489 Ferdinand of Castile and Aragon besieged the fortress of Baza, fifty miles north-east of the Moorish capital, with a Spanish force of 90,000 men. Not until 4 December did the garrison surrender, leaving the capital of Granada effectively isolated.

Beaugé *(Hundred Years War)*, 1421

Pursuing to the south of Normandy French and Scottish forces, which had raided English territory in defiance of the Treaty of Troyes (1420), the Duke of Clarence and a body of cavalry charged ahead of the main English column. At Beaugé on 21 March 1421 they were suddenly confronted with a superior enemy force, which slaughtered them to a man. Although the English infantry later drove off the victors and recovered Clarence's body, this remained one of the few defeats sustained by the English during this phase of the war.

Bedriacum *(Civil Wars of the Roman Empire)*, AD 69

Early in AD 69 legionaries and auxiliaries who supported the claim of Aulus Vitellius to the imperial throne advanced into northern Italy from Gaul, and at Bedriacum, outside Cremona, on 19 April they encountered other legions led by Emperor Otho. After inconclusive fighting Otho withdrew; the next day he committed suicide, and shortly afterwards Vitellius was proclaimed Emperor.

Belgrade I *(Ottoman Wars)*, 1456

Advancing into southern Europe with a large Turkish army, Mohammed II laid siege to Belgrade in 1456. Hungarian forces under János Hunyadi attacked the besiegers, and after forty days Mohammed was obliged to raise the investment. This defence of Belgrade, an important stronghold at the junction of the Danube and Sava rivers which barred the way into Hungary, Austria and central Europe, delayed a Turkish advance on Vienna until the following century.

Belgrade II *(Ottoman Wars)*, 1521

In 1521 the Ottomans, now led by Suleiman the Magnificent, again advanced on Belgrade. A regular siege, culminating in the walls being breached by mines, resulted in the capture of the city, and the way was open for a further penetration into Europe.

Belleau Wood *(First World War)*, 1918

On 6 June 1918 General Bundy's 2nd Division attacked four German divisions in the mile-square Belleau Wood, close to Vaux on the Paris–Metz road north-east of the capital, which marked the limit of German forward movement during their spring offensive. Not until 1 July was the wood cleared after heavy fighting against strong enemy formations in the first major American battle of the war. The Americans lost 9,777 casualties (1,811 killed) but took over 1,600 prisoners, and on 1 July also Vaux was re-captured.

Benevento *(French Wars in Italy)*, 1266

At the request of the Pope a French army went to southern Italy to deal with Manfred, illegitimate son of the Holy Roman Emperor Frederick II, who had proclaimed himself King of the Two Sicilies. On 26 February 1266 Manfred was defeated and slain at Benevento, thirty-five miles north-east of Naples, and Charles I of Anjou, commander of the French army, became the acknowledged sovereign of Sicily and Naples.

Beneventum *(Rise of Rome)*, 275 BC

Returning to Italy from Sicily in 275 BC, four years after his 'Pyrrhic victory' at Asculum, Pyrrhus attacked Roman forces under Manius Curius Dentatus at Beneventum, 130 miles south-east of Rome, in a night assault. He was repulsed with the loss of eight elephants, and shortly afterwards the legions attacked him on a nearby plain. The first Roman attack failed, but during the second Pyrrhus' own elephants were stampeded back through his lines. In the ensuing confusion the Roman legionaries drove the enemy troops from the field, and Pyrrhus never again threatened the Republic.

Beresteczko *(Polish–Cossack War)*, 1651

Faced by demands for a separate Ukrainian state, on 1 July 1651 a large force of Poles under John I met some 250,000 Cossacks led by Bogdan Chmielnicki at Beresteczko, thirty miles south of Lutsk in north-west Ukraine. In a fierce encounter the Cossacks were defeated, and hopes of Ukrainian independence vanished when they subsequently allied with Russia, which formally secured their territory from Poland in 1667.

Berezina River *(Napoleonic Wars)*, 1812

In its retreat from Moscow, Napoleon's Grand Army reached the Berezina river in bitter winter weather to find the Russians controlling the bridge of Borisov. Near Studenka, eight miles north, French engineers constructed a temporary bridge, and during 27 and 28 November the bulk of Napoleon's troops crossed, leaving Marshal Victor's IX Corps as rearguard on the other bank. Victor was attacked by a strong enemy force and on 29 November also crossed to the west bank, destroying the bridge behind him with 10,000 French stragglers still on the wrong side of the river, in addition to some 20,000 casualties during the three-day action. Many more were drowned in the icy waters during the various crossings, and the Russians later claimed to have recovered 36,000 bodies from the river. Ahead lay Vilna and the Niemen river, which the exhausted French still had to negotiate before completing a truly disastrous retreat from Moscow: of 655,000 who had set out in the summer, only 93,000 recrossed the Vistula. The myth of French military invincibility had been convincingly shattered.

Bergen-op-Zoom I *(War of the Austrian Succession)*, 1747

The conflict, which followed the accession of Maria Theresa to the Austrian Empire in 1740, concerned most European countries in an eight-year land and sea war involving three continents: Europe, America and Asia. Thus, in the Low Countries on 15 July 1747, 25,000 French troops under Count von Löwendal invested Bergen-op-Zoom on the Scheldt estuary. The Anglo–Dutch garrison made frequent sorties to inflict losses on the attackers, but on 18 September the French gained a lodgement and captured the town. In the course of the siege they had suffered over 20,000 casualties to 4,000 among the garrison. With his rear now secure, however, Löwendal marched east once more to join Marshal Saxe in the unfulfilled hope of permanently securing the Low Countries for France.

Bergen-op-Zoom II *(French Revolutionary Wars)*, 1799

In 1799, 35,000 British and Russian troops under the Duke of York advanced down the Helder peninsula in the Netherlands. Outside Bergen-op-Zoom on 19 September they were met by a French force of 30,000 under General Vandamme. When Vandamme attacked, the British held their ground, but Russians guarding one flank gave way, forcing the Duke of York to retreat. The French suffered 3,500 casualties, the Russians a similar number and the British 500. This optimistic allied expedition now had no realistic hope of success and shortly afterwards came to an inglorious end.

Berlin *(Second World War)*, 1945

In April 1945 Russian army groups, commanded from north to south by marshals Rokossovski, Zhukov and Konev, were poised on the Oder–Neisse line. On 16 April, preceded by an air and artillery bombardment, Zhukov's troops in the centre broke out of the bridgehead west of the Oder and attacked General Heinrici's forces. Although Zhukov initially made slow progress, the other two army groups advanced so that on 25 April their units met west of Berlin, thus encircling the city. The following day 464,000 Russian troops, supported by 12,700 guns and mortars, 21,000 multiple rocket-launchers and 1,500 tanks, began the final assault. Fanatical German resistance meant that individual buildings had to be cleared at great cost, but on 1 May the Red Flag was placed on the ruined Reichstag building. Next day the senior German officer, Lieutenent-General Weidling, surrendered the capital and its remaining 135,000 defenders. The battle for Berlin cost the Soviets over 300,000 casualties.

Berwick-on-Tweed *(Anglo–Scottish Wars)*, 1296

In 1296 Edward I marched north to subdue the Scots, who had made an alliance with France, then at war with England. He stormed the border town of Berwick, massacred the bulk of its citizens and sacked its buildings. The town was then fortified as an English military base. The Scots recaptured it in 1318 but were ejected once more fifteen years later.

Bibracte *(Gallic Wars)*, 58 BC

Marching northwards to subdue Gaul in 58 BC, at Bibracte Julius Caesar encountered a large force of Helvetii. Posting his six legions on high ground, Caesar resisted determined enemy attacks for several hours before his experienced legionaries were able to move onto the offensive. By nightfall the battle had been won, with the transport and camp of the Helvetii in Roman hands, and Caesar now resumed his northward march.

Bilbao *(Spanish Civil War)*, 1937

After a steady advance from north of Madrid, on 11 June 1937 50,000 Nationlist troops led by General Davila laid siege to the Basque stronghold of Bilbao, where 40,000 defenders had established a so-called Ring of Steel. Next day, under cover of artillery, Davila's troops breached this defensive line, then gradually moved forward until surviving Basque units withdrew on 17 June, allowing Nationalists to occupy the city two days later. This defeat proved a major setback not only for the Republicans but also for the cause of Basque independence.

Blenheim *(War of the Spanish Succession)*, 1704

Following his march south from the Netherlands and victory at Donauwörth, with inferior numbers the Duke of Marlborough supported by Prince Eugène found himself faced by two French armies under marshals Tallard and Marsin together with Bavarian troops totalling 60,000 men. Marlborough attacked Tallard's troops defending Blenheim on the River Danube on 13 August and was initially held, while Eugène tackled Marsin on the French left. By mid-afternoon need to reinforce Marsin weakened Tallard, so that a British cavalry charge divided the two French armies and gave the allies a resounding victory for the loss of 12,000 men. The enemy lost 40,000 as either casualties or prisoners, and Tallard was captured. This battle saved Vienna and forced Bavaria out of the war.

Borodino *(Napoleonic Wars)*, 1812

Advancing further into Russia after the capture of Smolensk in mid-August 1812, Napoleon's cavalry screen discovered that Field-Marshal Kutuzov had established a defensive position with 100,000 infantry and cavalry and 640 guns on high ground close to the village of Borodino. On 6 September Napoleon deployed his 114,000 troops and 587 guns ready for an assault. The following day he attacked on both wings and, although fighting fluctuated during the morning, by late afternoon the Russians withdrew from the battlefield after losing a crucial earthwork in the centre, the Great Redoubt, and suffering 45,000 casualties. The French incurred 30,000 casualties, including twelve generals, but were too weary to mount a serious pursuit. Capturing Moscow unopposed a week later, nevertheless they were severely harassed during their later withdrawal by Russian troops who had survived Borodino and since been reinforced.

Bosworth Field *(Wars of the Roses)*, 1485

On 22 August 1485 with 10,000 men, Richard III faced 5,000 rebels under Henry Tudor, Earl of Richmond, who had advanced from Wales. Shortly after battle commenced, 6,000 additional cavalry led by Lord Stanley and his brother, who were in the vicinity, joined the rebels. Richmond then secured victory in this, the last battle of the Wars of the Roses, and with it the Crown of England as Henry VII.

Bouvines *(Anglo–French Wars)*, 1214

Although faced by a superior force of English, Imperial and Flemish troops, on 27 July 1214 with an army of 10,000 Philip Augustus of France attacked and won a decisive victory at Bouvines near Lille, which put an end to King John's hopes of regaining lost English territory in north-east France and weakened baronial support for him in England.

Boyne, The *(Irish Rebellion against William III)*, 1690

On 1 July 1690 the deposed James II with a French army of 25,000 occupied a defensive position south of the River Boyne covering Dublin against 35,000 troops led by William III. Sending the Duke of Schomberg to cross the river further west and attack the French flank, William overwhelmed the enemy centre and drove James II from the field. Although casualties were light – 1,500 French and 500 English – this battle forced James II to flee to France.

Breitenfeld I *(Thirty Years War)*, 1631

After crossing the River Elbe, a Protestant army of 26,000 Swedes, commanded by Gustavus Adolphus, and 16,000 Saxons encountered an inferior Catholic force under the Comte de Tilly at Breitenfeld, north of Leipzig. Nevertheless, on 18 September Tilly attacked on both flanks, quickly putting Saxons on the allied left to flight. Gustavus Adolphus deployed Swedish infantry to prevent an outflanking movement, however, and throughout the morning and afternoon repeated Catholic attacks were repulsed. Late in the day Gustavus launched his reserve cavalry against Tilly's line, which broke. Tilly was wounded and an utter rout prevented only by a stout rearguard action from Count zu Pappenheim. Nevertheless Tilly lost nearly 20,000 men and all his artillery and was forced to abandon Leipzig. This was the first major Protestant victory in the war, establishing the Swedish

King's military reputation and halting the immediate Habsburg threat to the Baltic coastline.

Breitenfeld II *(Thirty Years War)*, 1642

Threatened by the advance of a strong Imperial army under Archduke Leopold William, Swedish troops commanded by Field-Marshal Torstensson abandoned the siege of Leipzig and retired north. At Breitenfeld on 2 November 1642 the Swedes prepared to stand and, as the enemy began to advance under cover of artillery fire, suddenly launched cavalry against the Austrian left, which gave way. Quickly exploiting this success, the Swedish cavalry wheeled to attack the centre, as Torstensson sent the bulk of his army against Leopold William's right flank. The Imperial troops fell back into Bohemia, leaving 10,000 on the field as either casualties or prisoners.

Breslau *(Seven Years War)*, 1757

Although a major advance by their French allies failed, 70,000 Austrians under Prince Charles of Lorraine penetrated Silesia and attacked 20,000 Prussian troops outside Breslau (Wroclaw) on the Oder 180 miles south-east of Berlin. On 22 November 1757 the Prussians were defeated with the loss of 8,000 men, and two days later Breslau itself fell. Hurrying backing from Saxony to meet the new threat that this defeat posed, Frederick the Great met and defeated another Austrian force at Leuthen early in December, which redressed the military balance.

Busaco *(Peninsular War)*, 1810

As Viscount Wellington retired towards prepared lines at Torres Vedras, twenty-five miles north of Lisbon, he deployed a combined British and Portuguese force of 50,000 men on the heights of Busaco (Buçaco) 120 miles north-east of the capital and close to Coimbra. On 27 September 1810 Marshal Masséna attacked the position in poor visibility with 60,000 troops and by mid-morning was repulsed with the loss of 4,600. Wellington suffered 1,250 casualties but held up the enemy advance long enough for most of his army to reach safety.

Calais I *(Hundred Years War)*, 1346–7

In August 1346 English troops under Edward III laid siege to Calais, which finally surrendered on 4 August 1347. During the course of the siege the lives of six burghers, who had offered themselves as hostages, were spared after Queen Philippa had interceded on their behalf. Calais would remain English for over 200 years.

Calais II *(Anglo–French Wars)*, 1558

Following a siege of a mere seven days, on 6 January 1558 French troops under the Duke of Guise captured Calais, the last English foothold on the Continent. The news reputedly caused Queen Mary to declare that 'Calais' would be engraved on her heart.

Calatafimi *(Italian Wars of Independence)*, 1860

After landing with his celebrated Thousand Red Shirts in Sicily, together with Sicilian recruits to his cause, Giuseppe Garibaldi attacked a Neapolitan army at Calatafimi on the north-west of the island on 15 May 1860. Garibaldi's victory opened the way to Palermo, conquest of the island and eventual success on the Italian mainland.

Cambrai *(First World War)*, 1917

On 20 November 1917, achieving tactical surprise, 381 British tanks moved forward against the German Second Army south-west of Cambrai, signalling the first massed use of this new weapon in battle. The gap which they created in the enemy line was swiftly exploited by British infantry, but mechanical problems and failure to bring up infantry reinforcements allowed the enemy to stabilize his line, eventually counter-attack on 30 November and by 4 December recapture the lost ground. Overall the battle cost the British 43,000 men and 158 guns, the Germans 41,000 men and 138 guns, but, for all the tank's evident shortcomings, it signalled the dawn of mechanized land warfare.

Cannae *(Second Punic War)*, 216 BC

Eight Roman legions commanded by Varro crossed the Apennines and on 3 August 216 BC attacked 50,000 Carthaginians under Hannibal on the plain outside Cannae close to modern Barletta on the Adriatic coast of Italy. Hannibal allowed the centre of his line to be pushed back by the Romans, then as it appeared about to collapse launched cavalry from both flanks to trap the enemy in a double-envelopment manœuvre. 55,000 Romans (including twenty-nine tribunes and eighty senators) were killed or captured against only 5,700 Carthaginian casualties. Effectively Roman forces outside the capital had now been crushed. However, Hannibal lacked the infantry and heavy siege equipment to invest Rome.

Caporetto *(First World War)*, 1917

At dawn on 24 October 1917, following a heavy artillery bombardment, fifteen German and Austrian divisions of the Fourteenth Army under General Otto von Bülow attacked the Italian Second Army at Caporetto, which was part of a defensive position along the Isonzo river. The Italian line broke between Zaga and Auzza, and next day Austrian advances against the right and left forced a general Italian retreat to the Piave river, seventy miles away. This defeat and subsequent retreat cost the Italians an estimated 250,000 prisoners, 45,000 casualties and over 2,000 guns. It had a lasting psychological, as well as military, effect upon Italy.

Castillon *(Hundred Years War)*, 1453

Early in 1453 three French armies converged on Bordeaux, intent on ejecting the English from Gascony. The central French army laid siege to Castillon, thirty miles east of Bordeaux, and, yielding to Gascon civilian pressure against his military judgement, on 17 July 1453 the Earl of Shrewsbury attacked the besiegers before Castillon with an English force. Misled by reports of French panic, Shrewsbury launched a frontal attack against a fortified camp, encountered heavy artillery fire and was utterly routed by a vigorous flank attack. Shrewsbury and his son died in this, the last battle of the Hundred Years War, as a result of which Gascony fell to the French.

Cerignola *(Franco–Spanish Wars)*, 1503

During the struggle for southern Italy, French and Spanish armies respectively under the Duke of Nemours and Gonzalo de Córdoba clashed at Cerignola, twenty miles inland from Barletta on the Adriatic coast, on 28 April 1503. The French infantry suffered heavy casualties at the hands of the Spanish musketeers in its initial attack. This opened the way for a Spanish counter-attack which carried the day, captured the French artillery train and forced the defeated troops to fall back westwards across the Italian peninsula. Although French reinforcements soon arrived, Naples had to be abandoned to the Spanish on 13 May.

Châlons-sur-Marne I *(Alemanni Invasions of the Roman Empire)*, 366

Advancing deep into Gaul under Vadomair, in July 366 the Alemanni were checked ninety miles east of Paris at Châlons-sur-Marne by a Roman army under Emperor Valentinian. The invaders lost 10,000 in casualties and prisoners, the Romans 1,200. The following year Valentinian pursued the Alemanni across the Rhine and effectively quelled their threat to Gaul for almost a generation.

Châlons-sur-Marne II *(Wars of the Western Roman Empire)*, 451

In June 451 combined Roman and Visigoth forces under Flavius Aëtius and Theodoric I fought a fierce battle with invading Huns led by the legendary Attila on open ground near Châlons-sur-Marne. As the allied line repulsed Attila's opening attack, Visigoth cavalry counter-attacked to rout the enemy right, causing the Huns to withdraw with heavy loss. Theodoric fell on the field, Aëtius failed to follow up the victory, and Attila succeeded in re-crossing the Rhine with the remnants of his force.

Chippenham *(Danish Invasions of England)*, 878

While Saxons under King Alfred were celebrating Twelfth Night in January 878, Danish troops led by Guthrum, who had never previously changed quarters in mid-winter, surprised and routed them at Chippenham. Alfred went into hiding amid inaccessible forests west of Selwood, leaving Guthrum in control of southern England and giving rise to romantic accounts of Alfred's activities before he successfully engaged the Danes once more later in the year.

Ciudad Rodrigo *(Peninsular War)*, 1812

Advancing on Madrid via Leon, Viscount Wellington found his way barred by the fortress of Ciudad Rodrigo, 100 miles due south of the capital, where Marshal Marmont commanded a French garrison of 2,000 equipped with 150 guns. After a ten-day siege, at a cost of 1,300 men, the British successfully stormed the walls on 19 January 1812, and Wellington could now concentrate on Badajoz further south, which lay astride his way into Andalusia.

Clontarf *(Danish Invasion of Ireland)*, 1014

On 23 April 1014 an Irish army under Boromha (Brian Boru) defeated a strong invading force of Danes at Clontarf on the coast just east of Dublin and drove them out of the country with an estimated loss of 6,000 men. Boromha and his son fell during the battle, but the Danes now turned their attention once more to England.

Constantinople I *(Wars of the Byzantine Empire)*, 717–18

On 15 August 717 the Byzantine Emperor found himself besieged in Constantinople by 50,000 Saracens under Maslama. The besiegers suffered severe loss on land and among their supporting fleet through casualties and disease, so that after a year Maslama lifted the investment, having lost over half his force, and retired to Asia Minor. Saracen troops from Arabia would never again seriously threaten Constantinople, despite later attacks on south-eastern Europe.

Constantinople II *(Wars of the Byzantine Empire)*, 1453

At the head of 80,000 Ottoman troops with seventy cannon, Mohammed II laid siege to Constantinople on 6 April 1453. After several damaging bombardments, the walls were decisively breached and on 29 May Mohammed carried the defences. Thousands of citizens and military defenders were put to the sword in three days of pillage which followed, and the Byzantine Empire had been conquered. Militarily the success of heavy artillery against Constantinople boded ill for fortress strongholds, and its fall erased the last outpost of Christian government in south-eastern Europe.

Copenhagen *(Napoleonic Wars)*, 1807

In conjunction with a fleet of warships, during August 1807 18,000 British and Hanoverian troops under Sir William Cathcart invested Copenhagen. On 28 August a relief force was beaten off but when, after a naval bombardment, the Danish fleet surrendered and the object of the expedition had been achieved, Cathcart lifted the siege and re-embarked his troops.

Coronea *(First Peloponnesian War)*, 447 BC

When part of Boeotia rebelled against Athenian rule, Tolmides gathered an army to restore order. But he was defeated by a rebel force near Coronea in western Boeotia north of the Gulf of Corinth, and, to secure the release of prisoners taken in this battle, Athens abandoned claims to Boeotia.

Corunna *(Peninsular War)*, 1809

After a 250-mile retreat across the Cantabrian Mountains in biting conditions and harassed continuously by the enemy, 14,000 British troops preparing to embark at Corunna in northern Spain were attacked on 16 January 1809 by a superior French force under Marshal Soult. The French lost 2,000 men but although 1,000 fell, including Sir John Moore, its commander, the bulk of the British force escaped.

Courtrai *(Franco–Flemish Wars)*, 1302

In spring 1302 a French force under the Comte d'Artois, reinforced by Genoese archers and German cavalry, moved into Flanders to suppress a revolt against Philip IV. The Flemings deployed skilfully near Courtrai (Kortrijk) fifteen miles north-east of Lille, and their pikemen made short work of impetuous French attacks, especially after cavalry became bogged down in soft ground. Artois and several nobles were killed, and the French were routed. This victory showed that unsupported cavalry could not match determined infantry, and 800 gilt spurs from the enemy were hung in Courtrai cathedral to celebrate the Flemish triumph.

Coutras *(French Wars of Religion)*, 1587

The Protestant leader, Henry of Navarre, positioned 6,500 men, interspersing musketeers and cavalry, on wooded heights near Coutras in south-west France, twenty-five miles north-east of Bordeaux. On 20 October 1587 they were attacked by 10,000 Catholics under the Duke of Joyeuse, who were beaten back by the musketeers and routed by a cavalry counter-attack. Joyeuse and some 3,500 of his men perished, while Protestant casualties were minimal. This established Navarre's military reputation and widened support for his claim to the French throne.

Crécy *(Hundred Years War)*, 1346

As Edward III's army of 10,000 men marched north, after landing at Sluys, it was pursued by 12,000 French under Philip VI. The English halted, turned and took up a defensive position with longbowmen on the wings at Crécy, ten miles north of Abbeville. The French attacked on 26 August 1346 and were driven back by the archers, a fate also suffered by their cavalry. Repeated French assaults were repulsed and by nightfall 4,000 French lay dead on the battlefield. English losses were reported as a mere 100, and Edward III resumed his advance on Calais in relative safety. During this encounter the English used primitive artillery, a development which would ultimately change the whole face of warfare.

Crefeld *(Seven Years War)*, 1758

Pursued over the Rhine by a Prussian army of 30,000 under the Duke of Brunswick, 50,000 Frenchmen commanded by the Comte de Clermont made a stand at Crefeld, where they were utterly routed with heavy loss by the Prussians on 23 June 1758. This left Brunswick free to campaign in Hanover, which through George II of England was allied to Prussia.

Cremona *(War of the Spanish Succession)*, 1702

Moving west with an Imperial army, on 1 February 1701 Prince Eugène launched a night attack on Cremona on the River Po, catching the French garrison by surprise. Although several officers were captured (including the Duke of Villeroi) and 1,000 defenders killed, the French retained the citadel and held out until arrival of a relief force, when Eugène retired. A summer of desultory campaigning ensued, including the indecisive battle of Luzzara, before Eugène left Italy; and relative stalemate occurred for another three years.

Crimisus River *(Carthaginian Invasion of Sicily)*, 341 BC

During the struggle between Carthage and Syracuse for Sicily, a force of 2,500 Carthaginians moved eastwards towards the Crimisus River in 341 BC. Although outnumbered, a Syracusan army under its Corinthian commander Timoleon attacked as they were crossing the river in heavy rain and drove them back. An estimated 10,000 Carthaginians were killed or drowned and another 15,000 taken prisoner; nevertheless, Carthage managed to retain a hold on Sicily into the next century.

Culloden *(Second Jacobite Rebellion)*, 1746

After Scottish Jacobite forces under the Young Pretender, Prince Charles Edward, had occupied Inverness, the Duke of Cumberland marched north with an English army of 10,000 and brought them to battle at Culloden on 16 April 1746. The English beat off repeated Jacobite attacks, then Cumberland used his cavalry to counter-attack and ruthlessly cut down the fleeing enemy. For the loss of only 300, he thus crushed the rebellion but earned the nickname 'Butcher'.

Custozza I *(Italian Wars of Independence)*, 1848

Following the expulsion of Austrian troops from Milan in March 1848, Charles Albert (King of Sardinia and Piedmont) joined Lombardy and Venetia in their bid to end Austrian rule in northern Italy. Meanwhile Field-Marshal Radetsky had withdrawn into a strong defensive position bounded by the fortresses of Verona, Peschiera, Legnano and Mantua known as 'The Quadrilateral'. Rebel forces attacked the western side of this at Custozza, ten miles south-west of Verona, where the octogenarian Radetsky won an overwhelming victory on 25 July. Austria then quickly recovered Lombardy, and serious dissension between the allied rebels led to an armistice.

Custozza II *(Italian Wars of Independence)*, 1866

On 24 June 1866 80,000 Italians under the Marchese di La Marmora crossed the Mincio and advanced over rugged country towards the Austrian army of 74,000 commanded by the Archduke Albert, which was covering Verona. The Austrians caught La Marmora's men before they could reorganize after emerging from the hills and drove them back across the Mincio. The Italians lost 8,000 in casualties and prisoners, the Austrians 4,600. However, the decisive victory by her Prussian ally over Austria at Sadowa on 3 July resulted in Venetia's being ceded to Italy.

Cynoscephalae I *(Wars of the Greek City-States)*, 364 BC

Vying for control of Thessaly, in 364 BC armies under Alexander of Pherae and the Theban Pelopidas fought a stern battle on the heights of Cynoscephalae in the south-east. Despite an initial cavalry reverse, Alexander's infantry gained control of the heights. The Thebans then fought bitterly to dislodge them and at length put them to flight. Pelopidas fell in the battle, but Theban control over Thessaly had been secured.

Cynoscephalae II *(Second Macedonian War)*, 197 BC

Seeking to defeat Philip V of Macedonia, Titus Quinctius Flamininus marched into Greece with 20,000 legionaries. On the heights of Cynoscephalae the two armies, roughly equal in strength, clashed. Although the Macedonians made early progress against the Roman left, their own left wing gave way and allowed Flamininus to wheel his troops behind the Macedonian line to win an overwhelming victory. Roman losses were small, but Philip lost 10,000 men and, after paying a large indemnity, was obliged to quit Greece, thus ending the war.

Danzig I *(War of the Polish Succession)*, 1733–4

Acting in support of Augustus III, a claimant to the Polish throne, in October 1733 a Russian army under Count von Münnich laid siege to Danzig at the mouth of the River Vistula, whose garrison was commanded by the rival claimant, Stanislas Leszczynski, Louis XV's father-in-law. French attempts to reinforce Danzig were frustrated and the city capitulated on 2 June 1734, with Leszczynski escaping to Prussia. The war, effectively between France and Austria, continued for another five years, mainly in Italy. Eventually the Treaty of Vienna (1739) settled Lorraine on Leszczynski and thus secured it for France.

Danzig II *(Napoleonic Wars)*, 1807

After defeating Prussia in 1806, Napoleon moved east against Russia, masking Danzig. But on 19 March 1807 Marshal Lefebvre with 18,000 French troops besieged the city, which was garrisoned by 14,000 Prussians and 4,000 Russians under Count von Kalkreuth, and completed its investment on 1 April. A Russian attempt to relieve the city by probing westwards along the Baltic coast was foiled on 15 May, and Danzig finally capitulated on 26 May, when the garrison had been reduced to 7,000 effectives.

Delium *(Great Peloponnesian War)*, 424 BC

In 424 BC Athens planned a two-pronged attack on Boeotia. Demosthenes' advance was quickly checked, but Hippocrates pressed on to confront a combined Boeotian and Theban force under Pagondas near Delium. Both armies were about 17,000 strong, but after an early, bitter struggle, cavalry put the Athenians to flight, and Hippocrates fell in the battle. Ultimately Sparta would defeat Athens in the war and establish its own dominance in Greece.

Denain *(War of the Spanish Succession)*, 1712

In the summer of 1712 Prince Eugène, then in command of the allied Dutch, Prussian and Austrian forces, concentrated a large army under the Earl of Albemarle at Denain on the River Scheldt, thirty miles east of Arras, where it was attacked by 24,000 French under the Duke of Villars. Eugène made valiant attempts at relief but was unable to get sufficient numbers across the river, and Villars won a resounding victory, killing or capturing 8,000 of the allies in the last major battle of the war.

Dennewitz *(Napoleonic Wars)*, 1813

Marching through Dennewitz in column, forty miles south-west of Berlin, on 6 September 1813 a French army under Marshal Ney was attacked by the Prussian army of Baron von Bülow. Despite stubborn resistance, the French lost 10,000 men and forty-three guns against 7,000 Prussian casualties, and they were driven back to the River Elbe, away from Berlin. This set-back persuaded Napoleon to concentrate beyond the Elbe around Leipzig.

Dessau *(Thirty Years War)*, 1626

Learning of a planned advance into the bishopric of Magdeburg by Count von Mansfeld's Protestant mercenary army of 12,000, General von Waldstein (Wallenstein) massed 20,000 Catholic troops at Dessau commanding a bridge over the River Elbe thirty miles south-east of Magdeburg. Repeated charges by Mansfeld on 25 April 1626 failed, and he eventually retired, leaving 4,000 of his troops in the field. This was Mansfeld's last battle.

Dettingen *(War of the Austrian Succession)*, 1743

Retiring westwards before strong Austrian forces, French troops under the Duke of Noailles encountered a hostile army intent on driving a wedge between them and their Bavarian allies. Having trapped 40,000 English, Hanoverian and Hessian troops between

Aschaffenburg and Hanau on the River Main, however, Noailles deployed 28,000 men under the Comte de Grammont at one end of the valley near the village of Dettingen as he himself prepared to attack the allied rear. On 27 June 1743, however, French cavalry impetuously charged the allied left near Dettingen, were held and counter-attacked by determined infantry under the command of George II. Before Noailles could intervene, Grammont's line broke and suffered 5,000 casualties, leaving the allies victorious and driving the French to retreat beyond the Rhine. This was the last time that a British monarch led troops in battle.

Donauwörth *(War of the Spanish Succession),* 1704

Following his advance up the Rhine valley from the Netherlands and subsequent march south-eastwards, with an allied army of 52,000 men the Duke of Marlborough reached Donauwörth on the Danube between Ulm and Ratisbon (Regensburg) on 1 July 1704 to find 12,000 French and Bavarians under the Comte d'Arco in possession of rising ground at Schellenberg to the north-east. The following day Marlborough carried the fortified position, incurring 5,400 casualties, drove the enemy out of Donauwörth and prepared to move on Augsburg.

Dornach *(Swiss–Swabian War),* 1499

In a drawn-out dispute over its frontier with the Holy Roman Empire, the Swiss confederation clashed with Swabian forces on 22 July 1499, five miles south of Basle (Basel). The Swiss infantry won the day and virtually ensured Swiss independence.

Douai *(War of the Spanish Succession),* 1710

Prince Eugène laid siege to Douai, twenty miles south of Lille and garrisoned by 8,000 French under General d'Albergotti, with a superior Imperial force on 25 April 1710. The defenders made several damaging sorties but, when repeated attempts at relief failed, were forced to surrender on 26 June. Eugène lost an estimated 8,000 men, although this gain, together with the towns of Béthune, Aire and St Venant, secured the Low Countries for the allies and prompted an advance on Paris.

Dresden *(Napoleonic Wars)*, 1813

Noting that Dresden was defended by a single French corps, Prince von Schwarzenberg marched a Prussian and Austrian army of 158,000 men northwards across the Bohemian mountains towards it in August 1813. Realizing the danger, Napoleon force-marched three additional corps to raise the garrison to 70,000 by 26 August, the day that Schwarzenberg opened his attack. With both flanks secured on the River Elbe, north and south of the city, the allies advanced and steadily gained ground until Napoleon counter-attacked in early evening to drive the attackers back to their start line by nightfall. The following day Napoleon attacked the enemy flanks, where his cavalry achieved considerable success, allowing infantry in the centre also to move forward. During the night the allied army retired, having suffered 38,000 casualties to Napoleon's 10,000, but it was the last victory that the French Emperor would gain on German soil.

Drogheda *(Cromwell in Ireland)*, 1649

Determined to crush Royalist resistance in Ireland, with 10,000 men on 3 September 1649 Oliver Cromwell laid siege to Drogheda on the River Boyne, garrisoned by 3,000 English and Irish royalists. After several bombardments, on 12 September Cromwell's men stormed the defences and put every defender and inhabitant to the sword, killing an estimated 4,000.

Dunbar *(Cromwell in Scotland)*, 1650

Aiming to crush support for the exiled Stuarts, Oliver Cromwell went north across the border with 16,000 men to be confronted by 25,000 Scots under David Leslie, who drove the English eastwards to Dunbar. There, close to the mouth of the Firth of Forth, on 3 September 1650 Leslie was foolishly persuaded by Presbyterian ministers to descend from surrounding hills and face the English. Cromwell quickly counter-attacked, broke the Scottish right and inflicted losses in casualties and prisoners of 13,000. This defeat created division among the Scots, many of whom questioned the wisdom of Kirk, whose authoritarian position now seemed weaker.

However, at the behest of the Covenanters, Charles II was crowned at Scone shortly afterwards.

Dunes, The *(Franco–Spanish Wars)*, 1658

In May 1658 a combined English and French force of 14,000 under the Vicomte de Turenne laid siege to Dunkirk, then in Spanish hands. A relief force of 15,000 led by Don John of Austria and the Great Condé advanced through the coastal dunes. On 14 June 1658 Turenne's troops turned to face the new threat and, although initially driven back by the enemy cavalry on the right, succeeded in pressing forward in the centre and on the right, eventually putting the attackers to flight and causing them 4,000 casualties. Ten days later, Dunkirk surrendered.

Dybböl *(Schleswig–Holstein War)*, 1864

Early in 1864, 16,000 Prussian troops under Prince Frederick Charles marched through Schleswig–Holstein and on 30 March besieged the fortress of Dybböl (Düppel) at the base of the Danish peninsula fifteen miles north-east of Flensburg, which was held by 22,000 men and protected by an outer defence of ten redoubts. The Prussians launched a strong attack on the redoubts after a heavy bombardment on 17 April, quickly capturing six and finally ending all resistance next day. Prussian losses amounted to 1,400, Danish some 5,500. Frederick Charles pressed on north into Denmark, which at length ceded Schleswig to Prussia at the Peace of Vienna in October.

Dyrrachium *(Wars of the First Triumvirate)*, 48 BC

In January 48 BC, aiming to defeat Pompey's main force, with 15,000 men Julius Caesar crossed the Adriatic Sea. Marching north after landing, close to Dyrrachium (Durazzo), fifteen miles west of modern Tirana, he found 40,000 Pompeian troops occupying a strong, entrenched position, which he dared not attack. Caesar waited until 10,000 reinforcements under Mark Antony arrived, but in the ensuing battle Pompey managed to outflank Caesar's army and drive it from the field with the loss of 1,000 dead, thus forcing Caesar to retreat into Thessaly.

Ebro River *(Spanish Civil War)*, 1938

Aiming to restore communications between Catalonia and the remainder of Republican territory, during the night of 24–25 July 1938 General Modesto began to pass 100,000 men over to the west bank of the Ebro. Achieving surprise, 4,000 Nationalists were captured and an advance of twenty-five miles quickly made, but a counter-attack on 1 August halted Republican progress. Subjected to constant air attack, the Republicans held on until a massive Nationalist assault on 30 November drove them back, and by 18 November the right bank of the Ebro had again been cleared. This four-month battle reputedly cost the Republicans 70,000 men in casualties and prisoners, with the Nationalists suffering 33,000 casualties.

Eckmühl *(Napoleonic Wars)*, 1809

Seeking a decisive engagement and hoping to force the Austrian commander into Bohemia via Ratisbon with a defeated army, thus leaving the road to Vienna unguarded, on 22 April 1809 with 90,000 troops Napoleon attacked 75,000 Austrians under Archduke Charles Louis who were occupying high ground above Eckmühl (Eggmühl), twelve miles south of Ratisbon. Repeated French attacks were beaten off until early evening, when the Austrian line was pierced. However, nightfall allowed the Archduke to withdraw in good order, having lost 8,000 men in casualties and prisoners as against 2,500 French. The exhausted French troops were unable to mount an immediate pursuit, and the Austrians managed to delay the French at Ratisbon long enough for the bulk of their army to reach Bohemia. But Napoleon could not ignore such a strong force still in the field before advancing on Vienna.

Edgehill *(English Civil War)*, 1642

Marching south from Nottingham, with the object of crushing rebel resistance in London, in command of some 14,000 infantry and cavalry Charles I found his way barred by a Parliamentary army of similar size under the Earl of Essex at Edgehill. The King's nephew, Prince Rupert, led a cavalry charge which broke

the enemy line, then pressed the pursuit so hard that his own infantry was exposed to a vigorous counter-attack in which seven
royal cannon were captured. Rupert returned in time to prevent
Charles' troops being overrun, but both sides claimed victory in
this opening battle of the English Civil War.

Edington *(Danish Invasions of England)*, 878

Recovering from his defeat at Chippenham, during the early
months of 878 King Alfred gathered support in his refuge on the
Isle of Atheney (in modern Somerset) and by Easter had begun to
send out raiding parties to harass the Danes. In May he at length
challenged them at Edington, fifteen miles south of Chippenham,
and drove them from the field; a fortnight later he captured
Chippenham. Under peace terms, the Danish king Guthrum was
baptized into the Christian Church, and in the autumn he and his
army moved north into Mercia, leaving Alfred in undisputed
control of Wessex.

Evesham *(Second Barons' War)*, 1265

After crossing the River Severn with a rebel army of 51,000, on 4
August 1265 Simon de Montfort advanced on Evesham, seeking to
join with another rebel formation led by his son. In poor visibility
de Montfort mistook the royal army of 8,000 under Prince Edward
for that of his son. During the rout which followed, he himself was
slain and the rebellion soon afterwards collapsed.

Eylau *(Napoleonic Wars)*, 1807

On 7 February 1807 Napoleon had 50,000 men and 200 guns
positioned at Eylau, twenty-three miles south of Königsberg.
Facing him, Field-Marshal Bennigsen deployed 70,000 Russians
and 400 guns along a range of low hills. Early next morning an
artillery duel preceded the French attack, but in blinding snow
Marshal Augereau's VII Corps was thrown back. Although Marshal Davout's III Corps did make some headway against the enemy
right, General Lestocq arrived with 7,000 Prussian troops to
prevent a French breakthrough. Night came with neither side
having gained the advantage, and next day the Russians retired

unmolested. During the fierce and costly fighting the French suffered some 20,000 casualties, the Russians about 15,000. Shortly afterwards Napoleon pulled his forces back to rest and prepare for the spring campaign.

Falaise *(Second World War)*, 1944

Breaking out of the western end of the Normandy beachhead, General Patton's American Third Army captured Avranches, then Le Mans, thus threatening German troops in the Falaise area with encirclement. As American troops approached from the south and British and Canadian armies pressed down from the north, the Germans desperately held open a ten-mile gap for five days, allowing the bulk of three armies to escape eastwards. On 19 August 1944 the Allied pincers snapped shut at Chambois, fifteen miles south-east of Falaise, and three days later all resistance within the pocket ceased. In this battle the Germans had lost a total of 60,000 in casualties and prisoners in addition to much valuable equipment.

Falkirk I *(Anglo–Scottish Wars)*, 1298

In 1298 Edward I took an army of 13,000 men north to deal with Scottish rebels led by Sir William Wallace, who had defeated an English force the previous year. At Falkirk on 22 July Edward found 10,000 Scots deployed behind marshy ground. Wallace had few cavalry or archers, but the English cavalry were hampered by conditions underfoot and suffered some loss in the opening phase of the battle. The longbowmen in Edward's ranks were decisive, however, inflicting heavy damage on the Scottish squares, and Wallace's force was scattered, with himself escaping only to become a hunted fugitive. In the battle the Scots lost 5,000 casualties, Edward's army less than 1,000. Edward I now moved west to deal with Robert Bruce but failed to bring him to battle, and after supplies ran low he turned south towards the border once more.

Falkirk II *(Second Jacobite Rebellion)*, 1746

Failing to find sufficient support in England, Charles Edward (the Young Pretender) withdrew north of the border again, where his cause still flourished. At Stirling the Jacobites turned to face their English pursuers, and on 17 January 1746 Lord George Murray, with a similar number of men, attacked a royal force of 8,000 under General Hawley. Hawley's force was routed, with 1,300 killed or captured and much of the baggage and equipment lost. Murray suffered about 150 casualties, but this proved the last Jacobite success in the field. Four months later, the Duke of Cumberland would finally crush the '45 Rebellion on Culloden Moor.

Fehrbellin *(Dutch War of Louis XIV)*, 1675

Allied with France against Brandenburg and the Netherlands, Charles XI of Sweden invaded Brandenburg and on 28 June 1675 met an army of 15,000 men under the Great Elector, Frederick William, at Fehrbellin, twenty-five miles north-west of Berlin. The Swedish army was defeated and the prestige of Brandenburg immensely enhanced, even though at the subsequent peace Brandenburg lost her conquest of Swedish Pomerania. Fehrbellin was the first important victory of the force which a hundred years later would become the formidable Prussian army.

Fleurus *(Thirty Years War)*, 1622

Learning that the Spanish under the Marquis of Spinola had besieged Bergen-op-Zoom on the North Sea coast, Count von Mansfeld and Prince Christian of Brunswick marched a Protestant army north-west from Alsace towards the Netherlands. At Fleurus, seven miles north-east of Charleroi, they were faced by another Spanish force under Gonzales de Córdoba, which had hurried across the Rhine to intercept them. On 29 August 1622 Christian led repeated cavalry charges against Córdoba's men and at the fifth attempt broke through, losing his right arm in the process. This victory cost the Protestants 7,000 men, but the way lay open to Bergen-op-Zoom, which was relieved in October.

Fleurus II *(War of the Grand Alliance)*, 1690

In June 1690 Prince George Frederick of Waldeck occupied a strong position at Fleurus with 40,000 troops from nations of the Grand Alliance stationed behind brooks and marshy ground. On

30 June, however, this allied force was attacked by 45,000 French troops under the Duke of Luxembourg. First launching a frontal assault with his infantry, Luxembourg then sent his cavalry round both enemy flanks in a double envelopment. For the loss of 2,500 casualties, he routed George Frederick's army, killing 5,000 and capturing 8,000 men, forty-eight guns and 150 colours. This was one of several victories by Luxembourg in the Low Countries during this war. Yet at the Peace of Ryswick (1697) France agreed to the Dutch right to garrison frontier towns in the Spanish Netherlands, thus effectively negating these successes.

Fleurus III *(French Revolutionary Wars)*, 1794

Moving deep into the Austrian Netherlands after taking Charleroi, with 70,000 French troops General Jourdan was attacked at Fleurus on 26 June 1794 by an Austrian force of 50,000 led by Prince Frederick Josias of Saxe-Coburg. Saxe-Coburg's column attack was unco-ordinated and stout French resistance denied him success. After six hours, although his casualties were only half those of the French, Saxe-Coburg retired across the Meuse. This victory proved of immense value to French morale and was an important step towards clearing the Austrians from the Netherlands and the break-up of the First Coalition against republican France.

Flodden *(Anglo–Scottish Wars)*, 1513

Taking advantage of the English invasion of France, James IV of Scotland crossed the border into northern England. However, the Earl of Surrey with 25,000 men outflanked the Scots and forced them to fall back to Flodden in Northumberland. Here on 9 September 1513 they were tempted into a precipitate charge from the high ground which they occupied, driven from the field in hand-to-hand fighting and scattered by pursuing cavalry. James IV, many Scottish nobles and 10,000 men perished on the field, leaving James' infant son to be proclaimed king.

Florence *(Wars of the Western Roman Empire)*, 406

Some 100,000 Germans swarmed into northern Italy in 406 and penetrated to the Arno river. A strong force under Radagaisus besieged Florence, whose defenders were encouraged to resist stoutly by the approach of a relief column under Flavius Stilicho. The Germans did not immediately retire, and Stilicho was obliged to attack. Driving the besiegers four miles north-east, he caught and routed them at Fiesole on 23 August, capturing and executing Radagaisus. Thus Florence was saved.

Focsani *(Russo–Turkish Wars)*, 1789

With the Ottoman Empire declining in strength, Catherine the Great of Russia and Emperor Joseph II sent a combined army into Bessarabia in 1789. Advancing over the Pruth river, this force invaded Moldavia and at Focsani, 120 miles west of the Danube delta and ninety miles north-east of Bucharest, overran a Turkish camp scattering the military units in it. This enabled the allies to penetrate deeper into Ottoman territory. Neither Austria nor Russia would gain a permanent foothold in the Balkans, however, although for the next hundred years Russia would continually interfere politically and militarily in the region.

Fontenoy *(War of the Austrian Succession)*, 1745

During his campaign in the Austrian Netherlands, Marshal Saxe laid siege to Tournai close to the border with a French army of some 60,000 men. Marching to the town's relief with 50,000 English, Dutch and Austrian troops, the Duke of Cumberland reached Fontenoy, five miles to the south-east. Here on high ground Saxe had prepared a strong defensive position between the Scheldt river and Gavrain Wood protected by four redoubts. On 11 May 1745 Cumberland attacked and after heavy fighting managed to carry French entrenchments in the centre of the line. But bold French counter-attacks and the failure of the Dutch troops to act decisively gradually forced the allied troops from their new positions, and Cumberland withdrew having suffered 7,000 casualties. Shortly afterwards Tournai fell, English troops were recalled to deal with the Jacobite Rebellion, and Saxe took Brussels. However, success in Flanders was balanced by Prussian victories against France's ally Austria in Germany.

Formigny *(Hundred Years War)*, 1450

Pressing northwards, the French army of Charles VII reached Formigny, twenty-seven miles north-west of Caen, where reinforcements under Thomas Kyriel had brought the English force up to 5,000 in strength. On 15 April 1450 the Comte de Clermont attacked, after artillery placed on both flanks had seriously disrupted the English line. Almost 4,000 of the English fell, and Charles VII went on to capture important centres such as Caen and Cherbourg and dominate northern France.

Fornovo *(French Wars in Italy)*, 1495

Withdrawing northwards from Naples after intervention by the Holy League to eject it from Italy, Charles VIII's French army of 8,000 men was confronted by some 30,000 Venetians and Mantuans under Francesco Gonzaga. The Italians attacked on 6 July 1495 at Fornovo, seventy miles south-east of Milan, but were decisively and swiftly repulsed by the French heavy cavalry in ten minutes. In this encounter the French suffered 100 casualties, the Italians 3,500, and Charles VIII successfully recrossed the Alps. Charles' successor, Louis XII, would invade the peninsula again four years later and in 1501 once more advance on Naples.

Frankenhausen *(Peasants' War)*, 1525

During unrest caused by the Reformation in Germany, in Thuringia Thomas Münzer led a peasant uprising which had Anabaptist associations. Troops from Saxony, Hesse and Brunswick overcame the rebels at Frankenhausen, fifty-five miles west of Leipzig, captured Münzer and summarily hanged him. This ended the uprising.

Frankfurt-am-Oder *(Thirty Years War)*, 1631

Landing on the Baltic coast in Pomerania with 13,000 men, Gustavus Adolphus augmented his army by local recruitment and advanced along the Oder river in 1631 with some 20,000 troops. On 13 April he stormed Frankfurt and, although the commander of the garrison escaped, the Imperial defenders suffered 2,500 losses in casualties and prisoners. This was the first significant Swedish success in the field of the war.

Frederikshald *(Great Northern War)*, 1718

After his return from refuge in Turkey in 1714, Charles XII of Sweden rebuilt the country's military strength. Four years later he was able to invade Norway, then under Denmark, and lay siege to the fortress of Fredrikshald (Halden), fifty miles south of Oslo. While he was inspecting forward trenches on 11 December 1718, he was killed and the Swedes promptly raised the siege. Charles' death led to a decline in Swedish military might, and at the close of the war Sweden gave up her eastern Baltic lands to Russia.

Freiburg *(Thirty Years War)*, 1644

In early August 1644 16,000 French troops under the Vicomte de Turenne and the Great Condé crossed the Rhine and approached Freiburg, eighty miles south-west of Stuttgart, which had been captured by 15,000 Bavarians under Baron von Mercy. On 3 August Turenne took 6,000 men on a long flank march to attack the enemy rear and, although the steep, wooded terrain prevented completion of this manœuvre, Condé launched a frontal assault on von Mercy's lines before the town with the remaining 10,000 troops late in the afternoon. Despite determined opposition, the French advanced gradually, and during the night the Bavarians fell back to new positions. On 5 August the attack was resumed, after French reinforcements had come up, but still the Bavarians held on to Freiburg. Three days later von Mercy did begin to retire, however, and during the following two days his retreating columns were harassed by French cavalry. Turenne thus took Freiburg, though at a cost of over 8,000 casualties to 5,000 of the enemy, and Condé was free to mop up remaining enemy forces on the upper Rhine south of Coblenz.

Friedland *(Napoleonic Wars)*, 1807

Retiring towards Königsberg (Kaliningrad), 60,000 Russians under General Bennigsen crossed to the west bank of the Alle river at Friedland (Pravdinsk), twenty miles to the south-east, to dis-

cover 26,000 French troops commanded by Marshal Lannes block-
ing their path. On 14 June, preceded by an artillery bombardment,
the Russians attacked, but Lannes resisted for nine hours until reinforcements arrived. By late afternoon the French had 80,000 on
the field and General Victor's artillery began to take a heavy toll of
Russians within Friedland itself. By 10 p.m. the French were
masters of the field, having lost some 10,500 men in casualties and
prisoners. The Russians, however, had suffered 18,000 casualties
besides countless others drowned trying to recross the Alle. This
victory was followed by French occupation of Königsberg, and by
the Peace of Tilsit with Russia signed on 25 June.

Fuentes de Onoro *(Peninsular War)*, 1811

In spring 1811 Viscount Wellington sent Sir William Beresford by
a southern route from Portugal into Spain, whilst he advanced
with some 30,000 men to besiege Almeida near the Spanish
frontier further north. Marshal Masséna hurried from Ciudad
Rodrigo with 30,000 men and thirty-six guns to relieve the fortress. Wellington took up a strong defensive position ten miles to
the south, and here Masséna attacked on 5 May. At the cost of
1,500 casualties and prisoners, Wellington held his ground, and
the French withdrew having suffered over 2,000 casualties. The
British and Portuguese then took Almeida.

Fulford *(Norse Invasion of England)*, 1066

In September 1066 Harold Hardrada, King of Norway, sailed up
the Humber with a Norse invasion force. Landing at Fulford, two
miles south of York, he was attacked on 20 September by troops
under the earls Edwin and Morcar. The English were utterly
defeated with considerable loss, and Harold II was then forced to
march north himself in an attempt to restore the situation. His
absence from the south would coincide with the Norman invasion
prior to the Battle of Hastings.

Fürth *(Thirty Years War)*, 1632

In the summer of 1632 General von Waldstein (Wallenstein) and
Maximilian I, Elector of Bavaria, joined forces and marched on

Nuremberg, held by Gustavus Adolphus with mainly Swedish troops. Not risking an attack, Wallenstein entrenched his army at Fürth, five miles north-west of the city. Calling on all available reserves, Gustavus moved out to attack on 3 September and for two days assaulted the position at Fürth. He eventually retired, having lost 2,000 men, and abandoned Nuremberg on 18 September, but Wallenstein failed to take up the pursuit.

Gaeta *(Italian Wars of Independence)*, 1860–61

Ejected from the capital, Naples, Francis II of the Two Sicilies set up his court at Gaeta on the west coast of Italy, which Piedmontese troops under Colonel Cialdini began to besiege on 3 November 1860. The French fleet offshore prevented a complete investment until its withdrawal on 19 January 1861; then Cialdini was able to press the siege more vigorously and induce surrender on 13 February. The rule of the Bourbons in southern Italy thus ended, and Cialdini was created Duke of Gaeta for his achievement.

Garigliano *(Franco–Spanish Wars)*, 1503

Falling back across the Garigliano (which runs south-west into the Gulf of Gaeta) in November 1503 after reverses in southern Italy, the French encamped north of the river. On 28 December 15,000 Spaniards commanded by Gonzalo de Córdoba crossed the river and attacked the French camp near modern Cassino. In the ensuing fight the French lost 4,000 men and most of their artillery and baggage; so decisive was this defeat that Louis XII sued for peace.

Gembloux *(Revolt of the Netherlands)*, 1578

Sent to restore order in the Spanish Netherlands, Don John of Austria ejected the Dutch from Namur on 31 January 1578. He immediately despatched a picked force of some 2,000 men to pursue the fleeing garrison, whose rearguard was caught and routed at Gembloux, ten miles north-west of Namur. The main body was then also defeated and, for the loss of less than 100, Don John had killed or captured 8,000 of the rebels. This crushing victory ensured return of the southern provinces to Spanish rule, and William the Silent had to accept foreign aid to defend the Calvinist north.

Gerberoi *(Norman Revolt against England)*, 1080

Although in England, William the Conqueror continued to rule as Duke of Normandy. His son Robert disputed this dual role and, aided by Philip I of France, raised a revolt in Normandy. Troops loyal to William forced Robert to take refuge in Gerberoi castle, outside which the two factions clashed. Robert's men were defeated and he himself was captured with the fall of the castle. He would rebel once more, unsuccessfully however, two years later.

Gergovia *(Gallic Wars)*, 52 BC

Seeking to subdue Vercingetorix, who had assumed leadership of the dissident Gauls, Julius Caesar marched six legions towards Gergovia (Clermont), capital of the Arverni, in 52 BC. Swiftly taking possession of two dominant heights overlooking the fortress, the Romans attacked in an unco-ordinated fashion and were fiercely repulsed. Only the Tenth Legion stood firm, and Caesar was obliged to withdraw, leaving forty-six centurions and 700 men dead behind him. Marching north, he joined the four legions commanded by Titus Labienus and prepared for another campaign against the Arverni.

Gibraltar I *(War of the Spanish Succession)*, 1704

Aiming to gain control of the entrance to the Mediterranean, a British and Dutch fleet under Admiral Rooke bombarded Gibraltar on 23 July 1704, after disembarking 1,800 marines for a simultaneous landward attack. Next day the fortress was secured and held for a total of 288 allied casualties, despite several Spanish counter-attacks. Possession of Gibraltar, confirmed in the Treaty of Utrecht (1714), enabled British naval domination of the Mediterranean and control of the straits between Europe and Africa.

Gibraltar II *(American War of Independence)*, 1779–83

On 24 June 1779 a combined French and Spanish naval force commenced a loose blockade of Gibraltar, which British vessels were able to evade and so take supplies in to the 7,000 defenders commanded by General Eliott. By September 1782, however, the blockading force had been reinforced to fifty ships, and ten fireproof floating barriers mounting a total 154 guns plus 33,000 troops with 300 artillery pieces on the land were also prepared for action. The land artillery opened its bombardment on 9 September, and four days later the floating batteries joined in. But the floating batteries proved particularly vulnerable to the defenders' heavy guns: nine were destroyed (with an estimated loss of 1,500 men) and the tenth was boarded by crews from British gunboats. The combined fleet then withdrew out of artillery range, hoping to starve Eliott's men into submission. In October, however, Admiral Howe forced his way through with a naval squadron to bring much-needed supplies. The garrison was therefore able to hold out until peace was signed in February 1783, and Britain thus retained Gibraltar.

Gijon *(Spanish Civil War)*, 1937

Once Bilbao and Santander had fallen, only the area of the Asturias remained to the Republicans in northern Spain. General Aranda launched an attack towards Gijon on the Bay of Biscay on 1 September, only to meet stubborn Asturian opposition in the mountain passes. At Infiesto on 15 October, however, Aranda joined with General Solchaga from Navarre, and six days later this combined force entered Gijon with little resistance. Northern Spain thus passed finally into Nationalist hands.

Giornico *(Swiss–Milanese War)*, 1478

Soon after the Burgundian threat from the west had been dealt with at Nancy in 1477, the Swiss cantons were faced with a Milanese army advancing up the Ticino river. At Giornico, north-west of Pavia, on 28 December 1478 the Swiss pikemen drove back the Italians and, in so doing, enhanced the reputation of the mountaineer infantry.

Gisors *(Anglo–French Wars)*, 1197

After his return from the Third Crusade, Richard I of England challenged Philip II of France for possession of north-western France. Thirty miles north-west of Paris, at Gisors, in 1197 the English drove the French and their king out of the town. Richard was never to taste the full fruits of victory for, not long afterwards, he was killed by the bolt from a crossbow, while besieging Chaluz castle.

Gorlice-Tarnow *(First World War)*, 1915

In preparation for a major offensive, the German Eleventh Army was secretly transferred to the eastern front and united with the Austrian Fourth Army under General von Mackensen. On 2 May 1915, preceded by a bombardment of 950 guns, Mackensen's troops attacked the Russian Third Army in the Gorlice-Tarnow sector, south-east of Cracow (Kracow). Within two days the Russian army was annihilated (120,000 prisoners being taken), and the Allied force pressed on rapidly to take Lvov on 22 June. Then, reinforced by further German and Austrian troops, it swept north towards Brest-Litovsk, 120 miles east of Warsaw. The German Twelfth Army now marched on Warsaw from the north, and by the end of August both the Polish capital and Brest-Litovsk had fallen. When the fighting petered out in September, the Russians had been pushed back some 600 miles for the loss of two million men in casualties and prisoners. Events in the Gorlice-Tarnow area had therefore resulted in major gains, for the Dual Alliance powers had seriously weakened the Russian forces. This would have critical long-term implications for the Romanov dynasty.

Gothic Line *(Second World War)*, 1944–5

By August 1944, following their rapid advance after the break-through at Cassino and the capture of Rome, Allied forces had come to a halt before the Gothic Line of defences stretching across Italy from Pisa in the west to Rimini in the east. Ten divisions of the British Eighth Army attacked Rimini on 26 August 1944 and were at length successful on 20 September. Meanwhile the Fifth Army had captured Pisa on 2 September, but progress in the centre stopped on 20 October, nine miles short of Bologna. During the winter very little territory was gained, and not until 20 April 1945 did Bologna fall. Three days later the Allies crossed the Po river, causing the Germans to abandon their last positions in the line.

Granada *(Spanish–Moslem Wars)*, 1491–2

In his drive to clear the Moslems out of the Iberian peninsula, Ferdinand of Castile and Aragon besieged the Moorish capital of Granada with some 50,000 Spanish troops on 26 April 1491. The defenders under Abou Abdilehi (Boabil) resisted stoutly and even attempted several unsuccessful forays outside the walls. At length, however, with the fortress completely surrounded, the Moors surrendered, and on 2 January 1492 the Spanish took formal possession. Thus the Moslem occupation of Spain was brought to an end.

Grandson *(Swiss–Burgundian War)*, 1476

Following his conquest of Lorraine and Alsace, Charles the Bold (Duke of Burgundy) seized Grandson in the Swiss canton of Vaud with his Burgundian troops in February 1476. He was still en-camped there, on the shores of Lake Neuchâtel, when on 2 March a force from other Swiss cantons marched over Mount Aubert. Charles attacked with his 30,000 men, but the Swiss resisted successfully. As they counter-attacked, Charles withdrew the centre of his line, hoping to envelop the attackers with his cavalry as they pressed forward. At the moment that he commenced this manœuvre, Swiss reinforcements arrived and, despite their numerical superiority, the Burgundians fled. The Swiss therefore retook Grandson.

Grantham *(English Civil War)*, 1643

During the evening of 13 May 1643 Oliver Cromwell with 400 cavalry encountered a superior Royalist body near Grantham in Lincolnshire. The Royalists were driven from the field with the loss of 100 casualties and forty-five prisoners. Cromwell claimed to have lost 'two men at the most'. This minor skirmish greatly enhanced Cromwell's growing military reputation.

Gravelines *(Franco–Spanish Wars)*, 1558

Aided by the fire of an English naval squadron off-shore, the Comte d'Egmont with 10,000 Spanish troops attacked 8,500 French at Gravelines, on the coast east of Calais, on 13 July 1558. A determined cavalry charge broke the French line, and severe hand-to-hand fighting led to a Spanish victory in which some 2,000 of the enemy were killed, wounded, captured or drowned trying to escape. The following year, in the Treaty of Cateau-Cambrésis, France surrendered all her northern conquests except Calais.

Gravelotte *(Franco–Prussian War)*, 1870

With his route to Verdun blocked by the Prussian First and Second Armies following his failure at Mars-la-Tour, Marshal Bazaine made a stand with his 113,000 French troops at Gravelotte, seven miles west of Metz. On 18 August 1870 the combined Prussian armies of 187,000 men attacked, and although the French around Gravelotte held firm, the arrival of reinforcements enabled the Prussians to turn Bazaine's right flank at St Privat. The Marshal then retired into Metz, having lost 18,000 men in casualties and prisoners. The Prussians incurred 20,000 casualties but were able to besiege Metz and detach troops to assist in the destruction of another French army at Sedan. Had Bazaine shown more offensive spirit at Gravelotte, he might well have changed the whole course of the war, for his ultimate surrender of Metz would prove militarily and psychologically decisive.

Grochow *(Polish Revolt against Russia)*, 1831

Inspired by success of the revolution in Paris in 1830, patriots declared an independent Poland and prepared to defend themselves against Russia. At Grochow, on the right bank of the Vistula just east of Warsaw, 80,000 under Prince Radziwill faced a Russian army of 100,000 led by Count von Diebitsch. After a bloody engagement on 20 February 1831, fighting ceased with neither side having gained an advantage, though the Russians suffered 10,000 casualties, the Poles half that number. In fact, the battle was a Polish failure, for a decisive victory was crucial for their cause.

Grossbeeren *(Napoleonic Wars)*, 1813

Once fighting had been resumed after the Austrian declaration of war in August 1813, Napoleon despatched Marshal Oudinot with 66,000 men to capture Berlin. On 23 August he overran the advance posts of the 80,000 defenders under the Crown Prince of Sweden and captured Grossbeeren, twelve miles south of the Prussian capital. But General von Bülow launched a successful counter-attack to recapture Grossbeeren and save Berlin, for Oudinot now retired, having lost 1,500 men and eight guns.

Gross-Jägersdorf *(Seven Years War)*, 1757

In the summer of 1757 some 90,000 Russian troops under Count Apraskin invaded East Prussia and overwhelmed 30,000 Prussians commanded by General von Lehwald at Gross-Jägersdorf on 30 July. However, a breakdown in the Russian supply organization caused unrest amongst the troops, and Apraksin recrossed the frontier without exploiting his success. This enabled the Prussians to concentrate upon the French in Saxony, where Frederick the Great would soon achieve one of his most famous victories at Rossbach.

Guadalajara *(Spanish Civil War)*, 1937

With the object of completely encircling Madrid, on 8 March 1937, 22,000 Nationalist troops under General Moscardo and 30,000 Italians under General Roatta attacked towards Guadalajara, situated thirty-four miles from the Spanish capital. After a week the Nationalist advance slackened in the face of determined resistance, and on 16–17 March, aided by Soviet tanks and aircraft, Republican defenders counter-attacked. The Italians were quickly pushed back, then Moscardo retired, so relieving pressure on Madrid. Italian casualties were estimated at 6,000 in addition to 300 taken prisoner.

Gumbinnen *(First World War)*, 1914

On 17 August 1914 General Rennenkampf's Russian Second Army invaded East Prussia and, advancing on a thirty-five-mile front, swept aside weak German opposition at Stallupönen. Three days later, however, Rennenkampf's 200,000 men were attacked by the German Eighth Army before Gumbinnen, sixty-eight miles east of Königsberg. One corps, led by General von François, made progress on the Russian right, but the German centre was checked by heavy Russian artillery fire, and an assault on the Russian left also failed. François was therefore obliged to retire to avoid being outflanked, and by evening the entire German Eighth Army was in retreat, with the Russians in possession of Gumbinnen. Discouraged by this reverse, the German commander, General von Prittwitz, decided to pull back beyond the Vistula river, but on learning of his intention the General Staff recalled General von Hindenburg to replace Prittwitz. With the assistance of Major-General Ludendorff as Chief of Staff, Hindenburg was soon to restore the position for Germany in East Prussia.

Gustav Line *(Second World War)*, 1943–4

Late in 1943 Allied troops in Italy came to a halt before strong German defences, manned by a total of eighteen divisions, which stretched across the peninsula from the mouth of the Garigliano river on the west coast to a point north of Ortona on the Adriatic Sea. Although the Allies had overwhelming air superiority, the broken ground and wintry conditions caused considerable difficulty for their Fifth and Eighth Armies. On 17 January 1944 the British X Corps established a bridgehead over the lower Garigliano, but the dominant monastery and enemy positions on the heights at Cassino were the crucial features in the Line. Three attacks in this area failed between early February and the middle of March. General Alexander, the Allied commander, then transferred the bulk of the Eighth Army from the Adriatic coast for a major assault on Cassino, which commenced on 11 May. Six days later, after bitter fighting, the Polish II Corps took Cassino, and the Gustav Line had been broken. The Fifth and Eighth armies soon afterwards overran the secondary Hitler Line and on 4 June entered Rome.

Haarlem *(Revolt of the Netherlands)*, 1572–3

With 30,000 troops Don Frederick, natural son of the Duke of Alva, laid siege to Haarlem, twelve miles west of Amsterdam, on

11 December 1572. Although the town was defended by only 4,000 troops, three major assaults were repulsed, and on 25 March 1573 the Dutch made a brief sortie to capture a Spanish supply train. Eventually, however, on 12 July 1573 Haarlem was forced to surrender for lack of supplies, and the surviving 1,800 of the garrison and 400 citizens were executed, in reprisal for publicly hanging their prisoners. The siege cost the Spaniards an estimated 12,000 men, lost in combat or through disease, and their action after the surrender underlined the current Spanish reputation for cruelty towards the rebels.

Haliartus *(Wars of the Greek City-States)*, 395 BC

Marching a Spartan army against Haliartus in Boeotia in 395 BC, Lysander did not wait for reinforcements to arrive before launching his attack. The defenders, however, came out to meet the Spartans, whilst a Theban force attacked them from the rear. Lysander's force was routed, and he himself was killed.

Halidon Hill *(Anglo–Scottish Wars)*, 1333

In 1333 Edward III of England laid siege to Berwick, fifteen years after it fell to Robert Bruce. Coming to the town's aid, Sir Archibald Douglas with a Scottish column attacked the strong English position close by at Halidon Hill on 19 July. The Scots were disorganized by English archers and cut to pieces by the pursuing cavalry, Douglas being among the slain. Berwick fell soon afterwards, and the Scots paid homage to Edward III, though in fact Scotland was by no means subdued.

Hanau *(Napoleonic Wars)*, 1813

Retreating after the Battle of Leipzig in mid-October 1813, Napoleon reached Hanau, eleven miles east of Frankfurt-am-Main, on 30 October with 95,000 men to find his way barred by 43,000 Austrian and Bavarian troops under Prince von Wrede. Attacking the enemy left, the French drove it back, so opening the road westwards. Napoleon then resumed his retreat with the main force, leaving a rearguard to cope with counter-attacks. However, next day von Wrede attacked and captured Hanau. During the fighting von Wrede was severely wounded, the French suffered some 6,000 casualties, the allied force over 10,000; thus Napoleon had preserved the bulk of his army to defend the French frontier.

Harfleur *(Hundred Years War)*, 1415

In mid-August 1415 Henry V of England landed with a force of some 10,000 men at the mouth of the Seine, and on 19 August he laid siege to Harfleur. Disease among the besiegers and stubborn defence by the garrison cost the English 3,000 casualties and prolonged the siege until 22 September, when the port finally surrendered. Henry then expelled the citizens from Harfleur and encouraged English immigration.

Harkany *(Ottoman Wars)*, 1687

Following its failure before Vienna in 1683, the Ottoman army retreated through Hungary. At Harkany, just south-west of the site of the Turkish victory at Mohacs on the Danube in 1526, the Ottomans were attacked by a force under the Duke of Lorraine on 12 August 1687. The Ottomans were utterly defeated with heavy loss, and as a result of this reverse the Sultan, Mohammed IV, was deposed.

Hastenbeck *(Seven Years War)*, 1757

In the summer of 1757 the Duke of Cumberland deployed 36,000 Hanoverians along the Weser river to protect the duchy from the French, and on 26 July he was challenged by a French army of 74,000 under the Marquis de Courtanvaux at Hastenbeck, three miles south-east of Hameln. The battle was inconclusive but, having lost several hundred men, Cumberland believed himself beaten and withdrew to the Elbe. Shortly afterwards the Convention of Kloster-Zeven was signed, by which the Hanoverian army was disbanded.

Hastings *(Norman Conquest of England)*, 1066

William the Conqueror landed near Pevensey in Sussex with some 7,000 Normans on 28 September 1066, while Harold II was in the north of England dealing with Norse invaders. Hurrying south, Harold eventually deployed over 7,000 men on Senlac Hill, eight miles north of Hastings and astride the route to London, on 13 October. Next day the Normans attacked and were thrown back by the English infantry. A bitter struggle then developed on the slopes of the hill. Late in the afternoon William feigned a general withdrawal by his cavalry, encouraging English infantry to leave their strong defensive positions in pursuit. Once the English had been drawn out, the Norman cavalry wheeled to cause great slaughter, though the decisive moment occurred when Harold was mortally wounded as an arrow pierced his eye. Both sides suffered in excess of 2,000 casualties, but the way was now open for a Norman advance on London. On the site of this conflict, William constructed Battle Abbey.

Heathfield *(Rise of England)*, 633

In the seventh century Northumbria, under its Christian king Edwin, dominated other Anglo–Saxon kingdoms in England. In 633, however, the pagan king of Mercia, Penda, allied with Cadwallon of Gwynedd (North Wales) to attack Northumbria. At Heathfield (Hatfield Chase), east of Manchester, Edwin's army was defeated and the Northumbrian king and his son were slain. Penda proceeded to devastate Northumbria, which soon disintegrated into its old divisions of Deira and Bernicia.

Heavenfield *(Rise of England)*, 634

A year after the death of Edwin the Northumbrians rallied behind his nephew Oswald. Determined to avenge their defeat at Heathfield, they caught Cadwallon's force, without the assistance of its Mercian allies, at Heavenfield, near Hadrian's Wall. The Britons were completely annihilated and Cadwallon was killed, reaffirming Northumbrian superiority in the north and reuniting Deira and Bernicia into one kingdom.

Hedgeley Moor *(Wars of the Roses)*, 1464

In yet another effort to restore Henry VI to the throne, the Duke of Somerset and Sir Ralph Percy raised a force in Northumberland.

At Hedgeley Moor near Alnwick on 25 April 1464, however, these Lancastrian rebels were utterly beaten by a Yorkist force under Lord Montagu. Somerset escaped from the field, but Percy was killed.

Heilsberg *(Napoleonic Wars)*, 1807

After failing to defeat the French in East Prussia, General Bennigsen fell back with 90,000 Russian troops to occupy high ground on the left bank of the Alle river at Heilsberg (Lidzbark Warminski), forty miles south of Königsberg. Here on 10 June 1807 30,000 French under Marshal Murat drove in the Russian outposts but could make no substantial progress. Both sides suffered about 8,000 casualties, and, although Bennigsen did not give ground immediately, two days later he withdrew to the north. Shortly afterwards at Tilsit (8 July) Napoleon imposed harsh conditions on Tsar Alexander I of Russia as the price for peace.

Hennersdorf *(War of the Austrian Succession)*, 1745

In the autumn of 1745 two Austrian armies began to march on Berlin. One numbering 40,000 men led by Prince Charles of Lorraine approached from Bohemia and was intercepted by Frederick the Great with 60,000 Prussians at Hennersdorf, now in south-west Poland, on 24 November. Catching the Austrians on the march, the Prussians scattered Prince Charles' column, drove the remnants back towards the south and removed any immediate threat to Frederick's capital.

Heraclea *(Epirot Invasion of Italy)*, 280 BC

Responding to an appeal from the inhabitants of Tarentum (Taranto) at the base of the peninsula, threatened by the southwards expansion of Roman forces, King Pyrrhus of Epirus landed with 25,000 men and twenty elephants on the western coast of Lucania in 281 BC. The following year some 35,000 Romans under Pius Laverius Laevinus crossed the Siris river to attack the invaders. With the Romans disorganized during and after the crossing, the Epirots charged and, despite fierce resistance, succeeded in driving them back over the river with the loss of 8,000 casualties. Skilful use of the elephants contributed greatly to this success.

Heraclea Propontis *(Civil Wars of the Roman Empire)*, 313

Through the Edict of Milan, Constantine I agreed that Licinianus Licinius should rule over the eastern Roman Empire in place of Galerius Valerius Maximinus. Learning this, Maximinus took possession of Byzantium with some 70,000 men and marched on Heraclea Propontis on the Sea of Marmara. With 30,000 Illyrians Licinius went to its relief and eighteen miles short of the city was attacked by Maximinus on 30 April. Initially driven back through weight of numbers, Licinius' force gradually gained the upper hand and eventually defeated the enemy, forcing Maximinus to flee to Cilicia. Constantine now ruled the western part of the Roman Empire, Licinius the eastern.

Héricourt *(Swiss–Burgundian Wars)*, 1474

When Charles the Bold, Duke of Burgundy, marched an army of 10,000 into Lorraine in 1474, the Swiss gathered 15,000 men to protect their borders. On 13 November these two forces clashed, the Burgundians were defeated with heavy losses, and the town of Héricourt, five miles south-west of Belfort, was occupied by the Swiss. This victory afforded only a temporary respite, for two years later the Burgundians invaded Swiss territory once more.

Hexham *(Wars of the Roses)*, 1464

Having escaped capture at Hedgeley Moor in April 1464, the Duke of Somerset began to organize more support for the Lancastrian cause. On 15 May he and his supporters were surprised in camp at Linnels, near Hexham in Northumberland, by a Yorkist force under the Marquis of Montagu. The rebels were quickly routed, several of their leaders captured and executed. This victory eliminated the main existing opposition to Edward IV.

Hingston Down *(Danish Invasions of England)*, 837

Joined by Britons from Cornwall, Danish invaders advanced on the kingdom of Wessex in 837. The combined force was defeated by King Egbert at Hingston Down near Callington, seven miles north-west of Plymouth. Thus the Danes were repulsed, and Cornwall was brought under Egbert's control.

Hochkirch *(Seven Years War)*, 1758

Realizing that a Prussian army under Prince Henry was threatened by a large Austrian force commanded by Count von Daun, Frederick the Great hurried into Saxony. On 13 October 1758 he encamped 30,000 men at Hochkirch, forty miles east of Dresden, planning to attack the enemy next day. Lax Prussian security during the night allowed von Daun to surround Frederick's camp with 78,000 men under the cover of darkness. At dawn he attacked and, although Frederick organized effective resistance after the initial confusion and withdrew towards Bautzen, the Prussians suffered 10,000 casualties besides losing 100 guns. Austrian casualties were some 7,500 in this, the last battle of the 1758 campaign.

Höchst *(Thirty Years War)*, 1622

In June 1622 a combined Catholic army of Spanish under Gonzales de Córdoba and Bavarians under the Comte de Tilly, numbering some 30,000, sought to prevent Prince Christian of Brunswick's 12,000 men from crossing the Main River to join Count von Mansfeld's troops. On 22 June the Catholics caught Christian as his men were crossing the bridge at Höchst, five miles west of Frankfurt. For five hours a bridgehead south of the river was most gallantly held, as Christian's troops crossed to that bank in the face of heavy enemy fire. During the crossing alone 2,000 men and most of the baggage were lost and a considerable number of others were killed or wounded as a passage was forced through to meet von Mansfeld. The Catholics claimed a victory, because their casualties were less, but Christian did link up with von Mansfeld. His depleted force raised the Protestant strength to only about 25,000, and a prudent withdrawal was therefore made west of the Rhine. The sacrifices at Höchst, therefore, seemed in vain.

Höchstädt I *(War of the Spanish Succession),* 1703

Joining with Maximilian Emmanuel, Elector of Bavaria, the Duke of Villars took a large combined force eastwards along the Danube towards Vienna. At Höchstädt, on the river between Ulm and Ingolstadt, the Bavarian and French force was confronted by Austrians in a prepared defensive position. Villars attacked on 30 September 1703 and routed the enemy, who incurred 11,000 casualties, for the loss of under 1,000 men. Although the way to Vienna was now open, Villars failed to exploit the opportunity offered by this victory to force the Holy Roman Empire out of the war.

Höchstädt II *(Napoleonic Wars),* 1800

As General Moreau advanced south with 60,000 French troops in May 1800, Baron Kray fell back towards Ulm with an Austrian army of some 70,000 men. Moreau, instead of making an attack upon Ulm, marched on Höchstädt, thirty miles to the east. Taking advantage of Kray's absence, after eighteen hours' bitter fighting the French took Höchstädt on 19 June, although casualties on neither side were large. Possession of Höchstädt gave Moreau a firm base on the left bank of the Danube, from which he crossed to take Munich the following month. Meanwhile Kray had been obliged to abandon Ulm and retire behind the Inn river, and following his successes in Italy Napoleon had opened truce negotiations with the Austrians.

Hohenfriedberg *(War of the Austrian Succession),* 1745

Determined to recover Silesia from Russia, Prince Charles of Lorraine crossed the Sudetic Mountains with 85,000 Austrian and Saxon troops. Frederick the Great commanded 65,000 Prussians in the area of Striegau (Strzegom), thirty-five miles south-west of Breslau, and on 4 June these suddenly struck the Saxons, who were in the van of Charles' force, at Hohenfriedberg. Before the Austrians could come to their assistance, the Saxons were routed and Frederick then dispersed the Austrians, driving the remnants back into Bohemia. Prussian casualties were about 2,000, and the Austrians lost some 11,000 in casualties and prisoners plus sixty-five guns. Frederick had taken another important step towards securing Austrian recognition of his claim to Silesia.

Hohenlinden *(Napoleonic Wars)*, 1800

Following its retirement from Ulm, after the battle of Höchstädt in June 1800, the Austrian army concentrated behind the Inn river. Here its strength was built up to 130,000 men, and its commander Baron Kray was replaced by Emperor Francis II's brother, Archduke John. Meanwhile General Moreau had increased his army around Munich to almost 120,000 men. When peace talks failed, Moreau began to advance towards Vienna, and Archduke John crossed the Inn to meet him. Twenty miles east of Munich, at Hohenlinden, on 3 December 70,000 Austrians advanced to attack the French, but their complicated plan broke down in the forested area. Moreau's subordinate commanders were able to defeat the enemy in detail, and the Austrians retired, having lost almost 20,000 in casualties and prisoners and eighty-seven guns. Moreau then drove forward rapidly in the direction of Vienna, but peace was signed before he could near his objective.

Holowczyn *(Great Northern War)*, 1708

Having placed his candidate, Stanislas Leszczynski, on the Polish throne, Charles XII of Sweden crossed the Vistula in January 1708 with 45,000 men, prepared to deal with Russia. The Russians made no major effort to stem the advance until the Swedes reached Holowczyn, west of Mogilev on the Dnieper river. Here Charles was challenged by a force under Prince Menshikov, which he defeated; but Menshikov fell back, carrying out a scorched earth policy. When supplies became short, Charles abandoned the pursuit and turned south into the Ukraine, hoping to link up there with Cossacks under Ivan Mazepa. This unremarkable battle was the last that Charles was to win on Russian soil: defeat at Poltava and ignominious exile in Turkey lay ahead.

Homildon Hill *(Anglo–Scottish Wars)*, 1402

While England was preoccupied with the Hundred Years War and civil unrest at home, Scots took the opportunity to raid deep into northern areas of the country. In September 1402, however, as they returned from one such foray led by the Earl of Douglas, they were waylaid by an English force under Sir Henry Percy (Hotspur). At Homildon Hill the Scots were routed with heavy loss, and Douglas was taken prisoner. This avenged an earlier incident in 1388 when Percy had been captured and ransomed by the Scots. However, Henry IV offended the Percy family by insisting that Douglas should be considered his prisoner.

Hondschoote *(French Revolutionary Wars)*, 1793

Driving into north-eastern France from the Low Countries in 1793, an Anglo–Austrian force laid siege to Dunkirk. On 6 September the besiegers were attacked by a French army of 40,000 under General Houchard at Hondschoote, ten miles south-east of Dunkirk. During a three-day battle the allied troops were gradually driven back, as the French made skilful use of low hedgerows and dykes for cover. Houchard's success raised the siege of Dunkirk and stopped the threat to Paris from this direction.

Hoxne *(Danish Invasions of England)*, 870

The increasing boldness of Danish invaders in East Anglia was challenged by a force under King Edmund in 870 at Hoxne, midway between modern Norwich and Ipswich, twenty miles from the coast. The Danes were completely victorious, and Edmund was captured and beheaded, reputedly for refusing to renounce Christianity. Later he became known as 'The Martyr', and his remains were interred at Bury St Edmunds.

Huesca *(Spanish–Moslem Wars)*, 1096

The Moors retained complete control of southern Spain in the eleventh century, but fighting broke out with Spaniards in the north-east. Here in 1096 Pedro I of Aragon and Navarre stormed Huesca, forty miles north-east of Saragossa, which had been a Moslem stronghold for three hundred years. Having driven the Moors out, Pedro made Huesca capital of his kingdom.

Ilerda *(Wars of the First Triumvirate)*, 49 BC

After Pompey had fled to Greece, Julius Caesar marched into northern Spain to subdue the province, which had been under Pompey's control. Having left a force to besiege Massilia (Marseilles), Caesar had only 40,000 to deal with 70,000 men under Pompey's lieutenants at Ilerda (Lerida), forty-five miles north-west of Tarraco (Tarragona) overlooking the Sicoris (Segre) river. Initially Caesar was driven off, but he returned to attack with the help of local recruits. By a series of counter-marches he manœuvred the enemy troops into a weak defensive position and so demoralized them that they surrendered with little resistance. Caesar thus gained control of Spain and, when Massilia capitulated, was able to return to Rome.

Ilipa *(Second Punic War)*, 206 BC

During his campaign to conquer Spain, in 206 BC Publius Cornelius Scipio (later Africanus) took up a defensive position with 48,000 men at Ilipa, sixty miles north of modern Seville. For several days he refused battle, then suddenly he launched a dawn attack against the camp of the 75,000 Carthaginians who faced him. Deploying his local Iberian troops in the centre, Scipio used Roman cavalry and infantry to drive back the Carthaginian wings and so oblige the enemy centre also to retreat. This decisive victory ended Carthaginian domination in Spain and opened the way for a Roman invasion of North Africa.

Inkerman *(Crimean War)*, 1854

In an attempt to break the Anglo–French siege of Sevastopol, the Russian commander Prince Menshikov launched some 55,000 men under generals Soimonov and Paulov against the allied right at dawn on 5 November 1854. In thick fog neither attackers nor defenders were able to carry out a co-ordinated plan of battle on the so-called Heights of Inkerman, and fighting mainly comprised fierce hand-to-hand engagements. After eight hours the Russians were at length repulsed by allied troops, who at no time during the battle numbered more than 20,000. The struggle was particularly fierce around the Sandbag Battery, where on viewing the evidence of carnage General Bosquet supposedly remarked: '*Quel abattoir!*' British casualties were 2,505, French 1,726 and Russian about 12,000. The siege lines were preserved, but allied troops now faced a bitter, debilitating winter on the exposed heights with inadequate supplies, which brought savage political criticism at home and the fall of Lord Aberdeen's Government.

Inverlochy *(English Civil War)*, 1645

With Perth and Aberdeen in his hands, the Marquis of Montrose in command of 1,500 Royalists turned west. On 2 February 1645 at Inverlochy, near the head of Loch Linnhe, he encountered 3,000 Campbells and Lowland Covenanters under the Marquis of Argyll. Argyll fled to a ship on Loch Linnhe, and his force was scattered, with about half of it killed or wounded. This defeat ended Campbell power in the Highlands for many years.

Isonzo River *(First World War)*, 1915

Hoping to gain Austrian territory, Italy declared war on the Dual Monarchy on 23 May 1915. The Italians chose to attack along a sixty-mile front on the Isonzo river at the head of the Adriatic Sea. Here on 23 June Count Cadorna attacked Field-Marshal von Hötzendorf's fourteen Austrian divisions (later increased to twenty-two) with thirty-five of his own. Cadorna made very little progress and was obliged to wage eleven battles in the same area during the next seventeen months. His total gains were about ten to twelve miles of territory, and in 1915 alone he suffered the loss of almost 270,000 men wounded, dead or captured.

Ivry *(French Wars of Religion)*, 1590

Seeking to defeat 11,000 Huguenots under Henry of Navarre at Ivry on the Eure river, forty miles west of Paris, 25,000 Catholics led by the Duke of Mayenne attacked on 14 March 1590. The Catholics were thrown into confusion by steady fire from Navarre's musketeers and the fierce counter-attacks of his cavalry and were repulsed with some 4,000 casualties to the Huguenots' 500. Navarre then marched on Paris, but failed to take the capital, as Mayenne's reorganized troops were joined by a Spanish force from the Netherlands. Three years later, after formally becoming Catholic, Henry entered the capital unopposed to be recognized as Henry IV, the first Bourbon King of France.

Jadar River *(First World War)*, 1914

On 12 August 1914 Field-Marshal Potiorek launched part of the Austrian Second Army and the Fifth and Sixth Armies across Serbia's northern frontier in a two-pronged attack. Four days later a five-day battle commenced along a thirty-mile front on the Jadar river, when the Serbs struck at the hinge between the VIII and XIII Corps of the enemy Fifth Army. With the Second and Sixth Armies failing to make progress, Potiorek withdrew his whole force, after suffering 40,000 casualties, and the first attempt to defeat Serbia had collapsed.

Jankau *(Thirty Years War)*, 1645

While peace negotiations were in progress, Field-Marshal Tor-stensson, Swedish commander on the Elbe, struck southwards towards Prague. On 6 March 1645 he was intercepted by a combined Austrian and Bavarian force at Jankau, thirty-five miles south-east of Prague. The superior numbers of the allies could not be brought to bear in wooded terrain, and the Swedes gained ascendancy in a series of minor skirmishes, during which Count von Goetz, the Austrian cavalry commander, was slain. Thorough-ly alarmed, Emperor Ferdinand III fled from Prague, though Torstensson subsequently failed to capture the city. The Battle of Jankau secured no permanent advantage for either side, but heavy casualties among its cavalry seriously weakened the Bavarian Army.

Jarnac *(French Wars of Religion)*, 1569

Worried about growing Protestant influence there, Charles IX despatched an army to south-west France, and on 13 March 1569 Catholic troops under the Duke of Anjou and Marshal Tavannes attacked a Huguenot army under Louis I, the Prince of Condé, at Jarnac on the Charante river seven miles east of Cognac. Once their cavalry had been broken, the Huguenots fled the field, leaving behind Condé, who had been killed. A series of Catholic victories followed, yet at the Peace of St Germain (August 1570), mainly through the diplomatic skill of Gaspard de Coligny, the Huguenots secured important judicial and religious concessions from the King.

Jena *(Napoleonic Wars)*, 1806

On 10 October 1806 Napoleon with 82,000 men reached a position to the left rear of 130,000 Prussians under Frederick William III, who were marching west towards Saxony. Forced to turn and meet this threat, Frederick William deployed his troops on the line Jena-Auerstadt, east of Weimar. On the right at Jena were 48,000 under the Prince of Hohenlohe, on the left the Duke of Brunswick had 63,000 at Auerstadt, eleven miles further north, and the remainder of the Prussian army was in the rear between Jena and Weimar. At daybreak on 14 October Napoleon launched his main body under Marshal Lannes against Hohenlohe, later reinforcing this with two further corps under Marshals Soult and Augereau to make a total of 56,000 men. By noon the Prussian line was wavering, and by evening it had broken. In this part of the field the French suffered 5,000 casualties, the Prussians 11,000 casualties and 15,000 prisoners. Meanwhile at Auerstadt 26,000 men of Marshal Davout's III Corps had clashed with Brunswick's troops. Brunswick himself was killed and, although Frederick William took personal command, by early afternoon the Prussians were in full retreat in the direction of Weimar. Davout suffered 8,000 casualties, but the enemy lost 15,000 in casualties and prisoners: in both actions the Prussians lost a total of some 200 guns. This decisive battle opened the way for French occupation of the whole of Prussia within a month, but it also had far-reaching political and military effects upon a country which had become used to enjoying power based upon the reputation of its army.

Kappel *(Parsons' War)*, 1531

The spread of Protestant influence due to the Reformation led the Catholic Swiss Forest Cantons, which were in alliance with the Habsburgs, into dispute with Zurich over the right of free preaching in the Common Lands. As a result in May 1531 the Forest Cantons sent an army of 8,000 men to Kappel, west of Lake Zurich, where on 11 October it routed 2,000 Protestants with heavy loss, Ulrich Zwingli (the Protestant reformer, acting as chaplain) being among the slain. The subsequent Treaty of Kappel permitted the cantons and the Common Lands to choose their own religion, effectively dividing Switzerland into two, and forbade foreign alliances.

Katzbach *(Napoleonic Wars)*, 1813

Faced by a superior French army, on 22 August 1813 General Blücher withdrew his 90,000 Prussian troops across the Katzbach river, north-west of Breslau (Wroclaw). Four days later Marshal Macdonald crossed in pursuit but allowed his force to become dispersed. He was attacked by Blücher during driving rain as his troops sought to reorganize after fording the river; then General Souham was defeated in detail as he crossed. Obliged to reford the river under heavy artillery fire, the French suffered considerable further loss. During the battle they incurred some 15,000 casualties and lost 100 guns, which considerably raised the morale of Blücher's army. This reverse, and others experienced by his subordinate commanders during the latter part of August, in effect undermined Napoleon's successful defence of Dresden and hastened French evacuation of central Europe.

Kazan *(Conquests of Ivan the Terrible)*, 1552

The Golden Horde, which had dominated most of modern Russia for nearly two hundred years, established its capital at Kazan in 1438. When Tsar Ivan IV ('the Terrible') began his policy of expansion, this city on the upper Volga became a primary objective. Thus he invested and stormed Kazan in 1552, destroying the Golden Horde's administrative centre and greatly enhancing his own prestige.

Kenilworth *(Second Barons' War)*, 1265

After Simon de Montfort, Earl of Leicester, had defeated Henry III at Lewes, disputes occurred with other barons to weaken his position, and Henry's son, Prince Edward, rallied royal support. Although de Montfort had a sizeable army, it was divided by the River Severn, and before he could cross to the east, his son's force was attacked by Prince Edward's men at Kenilworth on 31 July 1265. The town was captured, and young Simon took refuge in the castle. On 14 December the castle garrison finally surrendered, after the elder de Montfort had been defeated and killed at Evesham and the son had made good his escape to Axholme prior to reaching the Continent in January 1266.

Khotin I *(Ottoman Wars)*, 1621

Advancing towards the Ukraine in 1621, the Turkish army of Osman II was faced by a Polish force under General Chodkiewicz on the right bank of the Dniester river at Khotin east of the Carpathian Mountains. Chodkiewicz died during the battle, but despite the necessary change of command and their inferior numbers the Poles were victorious, mainly because the Janissaries broke under pressure. Osman retired to Constantinople, where he was killed by discontented Janissaries before he could rebuild his army.

Khotin II *(Ottoman Wars)*, 1673

The Ottoman Turks, supporting a Cossack revolt against Polish control, advanced into the Ukraine in 1672. When attempts to conclude peace failed, Polish forces under John Sobieski attacked and routed the Turks at Khotin in 1673 and later forced the Sultan to accept a truce. The following year Sobieski became John III of Poland.

Kiev I *(Mongol Conquests)*, 1240

Fifteen years after his victory at the Kalka river, the Mongol leader Subotai once more invaded Russia, this time accompanied by the grandson of Genghis Khan, Batu Khan. Russian defence was poor, for the separate cities were defended by ill-equipped troops and resistance was unco-ordinated. In 1240 the invaders reached the centre of Kiev and found little difficulty in storming the city on 6 December, razing it and putting the inhabitants to the sword. As the Mongols pressed westwards, the khanate of the Golden Horde was organized, based upon the Volga.

Kiev II *(Second World War)*, 1941

In August 1941 as the German advance on Moscow reached the Desna river, Hitler ordered General Guderian's Second Panzer Group south to assist in the capture of Kiev. Despite some delay, on 9 September Guderian arrived 100 miles north-east of the Ukrainian city, at a time when Field-Marshal von Kleist's troops were sixty miles to the south-east. Soviet forces in the city were thus in imminent danger of encirclement. Stalin adamantly refused to permit withdrawal until 17 September, one day after the tanks of Guderian and von Kleist had closed the trap. About 150,000 Soviet troops managed to break through weak parts of the German line, but in addition to the capture of the city, the Germans killed, captured or wounded over 600,000 Russians before 26 September, when resistance by the encircled armies ceased. However, the diversion of German forces to the Ukraine seriously delayed the advance on Moscow, which ultimately petered out in severe weather early in December short of the Soviet capital.

Killiecrankie *(Scottish Rebellion against William III)*, 1689

After the deposition of James II in England, Viscount Dundee rallied Highlanders to his support in Scotland. General Mackay then marched 4,000 troops loyal to William and Mary northwards, and on 27 July 1689 they were ambushed by 2,500 Highlanders under Dundee in the pass of Killiecrankie, twenty-eight miles north-west of Perth. Over half of Mackay's men became casualties or prisoners, and few managed to get through to Stirling. The rebels lost less than a thousand, though one of those killed was Dundee, but they failed to mount a decisive pursuit, and within a year the Highlands had been subdued by more determined government forces.

Kilsyth *(English Civil War)*, 1645

Despite Royalist reverses in England, the Marquis of Montrose was enjoying considerable success in Scotland. Marching into Stirling county, he encountered 6,000 Covenanters under General Baillie and the Marquis of Argyll at Kilsyth, ten miles north-east of Glasgow. Here on 15 August 1645 the Covenanters were utterly defeated, and Montrose for the moment stood supreme north of the border.

Kinsale *(Irish Rebellion against Elizabeth I)*, 1601

In support of an Irish insurrection against English rule led by the Earl of Tyrone, 4,000 Spanish troops seized and fortified Kinsale on the southern coast of Ireland, fifteen miles south of Cork, in September 1601. The town was then besieged by royal troops under Lord Mountjoy. When a relief column under Tyrone was defeated on 24 December, the Spaniards surrendered and were allowed to sail to Spain.

Klissow *(Great Northern War)*, 1702

Having occupied Warsaw and installed his candidate on the throne of Poland early in 1702, Charles XII of Sweden pursued the opposing Polish and Saxon army to Klissow, 110 miles north-west of Warsaw. On 13 July with 12,000 men he attacked the combined army of over 20,000, forcing first the Poles then the Saxons to give way until he had full command of the battlefield. Charles then advanced to capture Cracow on the Vistula before marching north, seeking to bring to battle Augustus II of Saxony, then also occupying the Polish throne to Charles' displeasure.

Königgrätz, see *Sadowa*

Kolin *(Seven Years War)*, 1757

In order to raise the Prussian siege of Prague, Count von Daun marched into Bohemia with some 50,000 Austrian troops. Frederick the Great detached 35,000 men to deal with this threat and led them himself to Kolin, thirty-five miles east of Prague, where von Daun was entrenched on high ground. On 18 June Frederick attacked the Austrian right, but the Prussian right in turn was severely harassed by Croatian irregulars. Despite repeated brave charges by the Prussian cavalry, Frederick was forced to withdraw from the field, having suffered 15,000 casualties to von Daun's 8,000. He then raised the siege of Prague and retired from Bohemia.

Kossovo I *(Ottoman Wars)*, 1389

In an attempt to stem Ottoman expansion, 25,000 troops from Balkan states under Lazar I, Prince of Serbia, concentrated at Kossovo (in modern Yugoslavia midway between Sofia and Dubrovnik), 130 miles inland from the Adriatic sea. On 15 June 1389 Lazar's force was annihilated by the Turkish cavalry and Janissary infantry. Lazar was killed, the Turkish leader Murad I murdered during the battle, and as a result of this victory the Turks gained control of Serbia.

Kossovo II *(Ottoman Wars)*, 1448

Recovering from a heavy defeat at the hands of the Turks four years earlier, in 1448 János Hunyadi led 24,000 Hungarians, reinforced by dissident Wallachians, into Serbia. Near Kossovo he was faced by a large Turkish army. Deploying his cavalry on the wings to deal with the Turkish cavalry and his German infantry in the centre opposite the Janissaries, Hunyadi attacked on 16 October. For two days there was no decisive development, although some of the Wallachians deserted. On the third day, however, Turkish cavalry pressed back the Hungarian wings, and Hunyadi was obliged to withdraw his infantry in the centre. The Hungarians suffered some 15,000 casualties (about 8,000 dead) and the Turks reputedly lost over 35,000 dead in the three days of fighting. Nevertheless, Hungarian resistance had been broken and the Turks could now turn their attention to Constantinople distracted only by minor guerrilla activity in the Balkans.

Kovel-Stanislav *(First World War)*, 1916

Partly to aid his French and Italian allies, who were hard pressed in mid 1916, the Tsar of Russia launched an offensive (often called the Brusilov Offensive after the general who led it) on 4 June against Austrian forces in the Ukraine. Four armies were concentrated on a 300-mile front from the Pripet Marshes south to Romania and, striking south-west, advanced rapidly. By the end of June some 700,000 German and Austrian casualties had been inflicted. But Field-Marshal von Hindenburg transferred fifteen German and eight Austrian divisions to the area, and in the north General von Linsingen halted the offensive in the area of Kovel, despite Russian reinforcements. In the south Brusilov penetrated as far as Stanislav, seventy miles south-east of Lvov (Lemberg), but by 20 September the attack had failed. Both sides suffered about one million men in losses, approximately half of these being prisoners or deserters. This was the last major battle on the Russian front, and it served to underline the inefficiency of both the Russian and Austrian armies. In Moscow the failure had serious political repercussions which contributed to the general unrest in Russia.

Kressenbrunn *(Bohemian Wars)*, 1260

Rivalry between Hungary and Bohemia reached a climax at Kressenbrunn, north-east of Vienna, in 1260. The armies of both countries led by their respective sovereigns arrived there on opposite banks of the March river. Neither had the strength to cross in the face of a hostile enemy, and Ottokar II of Bohemia allowed the Hungarians to reach the west bank from the Moravian side without challenge. The Bohemians then attacked the Hungarians, drove them back and forced their king, Bela, to surrender the province of Styria.

Kulevcha *(Russo–Turkish Wars)*, 1829

With Silistra taken, the Russian army under Count von Diebitsch marched south into the Balkans. At Kulevcha, forty miles west of Varna, it trapped 40,000 Turks under Reschid Pasha in a defile on 11 June 1829. Reschid himself and the bulk of his men managed to fight their way out of the trap, but the Turks suffered 5,000 casualties and lost all their guns. The way was therefore open for the Russians to press on to Adrianople.

Kulikovo *(Rise of Russia)*, 1380

Seeking to throw off Mongol domination, in 1380 Demetrius Donskoi, Grand Duke of Vladimir and Moscow, assembled an army with the aid of his fellow Russian princes. At Kulikovo, near the source of the Don river, the Russians won an overwhelming victory on 8 September. The myth of Mongol invincibility was therefore shattered, and Russians were encouraged to think of an organized campaign for liberation.

Kulm *(Napoleonic Wars)*, 1813

After their defeat at Dresden on 27 August 1813, Austrian and Prussian forces commanded by Prince von Schwarzenberg retreated into Bohemia. They were pursued by 32,000 French under General Vandamme, who took Kulm, twenty-five miles south of Dresden, on 29 August. Continuing his advance next day, Vandamme almost immediately found his way blocked by 45,000 of the allies under Count Ostermann-Tolstoy. Although outnumbered, Vandamme held his ground, until the arrival of 10,000 Prussians on his flank caused him to withdraw through Kulm with the loss of 11,000 casualties. This action served to restore allied morale which had been so badly affected at Dresden.

Kunersdorf *(Seven Years War)*, 1759

Early in August 1759 Frederick the Great was faced with a concentration of 90,000 Russian and Austrian troops under Count Soltikov and Baron von Laudon at Kunersdorf, four miles east of Frankfurt. Crossing the Oder with 43,000 men on 11 August, next day he attacked the enemy position, seeking a double envelopment by surrounding both flanks. But the broken ground and wooded terrain disorganized Prussian plans and, despite the gallantry of cavalry under General von Seydlitz and the desertion of some allied troops, Frederick's men were repulsed. The Austro–Russian army had 15,700 casualties in the six-hour battle; the Prussians lost 178 guns and suffered over 20,000 casualties. Disagreement between the Austrians and Russians culminating in a Russian with-drawal eastwards prevented them from following up this decisive victory over Frederick the Great, which could have been fatal to the Prussian cause if properly exploited. Crucially, the allied indecision allowed Frederick to reorganize and augment his meagre forces.

Kursk *(Second World War)*, 1943

On 5 July 1943 Field-Marshal von Kluge's Army Group Centre with thirty-seven divisions and nearly 3,000 tanks (including new Tigers) struck at the Russian salient around Kursk, 250 miles north-east of Kiev, which stretched 150 miles north to south and protruded 100 miles into the German line. In the north General Rokossovski and in the south General Vatutin defended stubborn-ly, backed by a strong force of tanks and lines of anti-tank defences. In four days the Germans advanced ten miles in the north and thirty miles in the south; two days later the Russians counter-attacked, and by 13 July the attack had failed. The number of tanks involved made this the greatest tank battle in the Second World War, and the failure of the German offensive ended prospects of any further important advance by them on the eastern front, for their losses were estimated at 70,000 killed, plus over 2,000 tanks and 1,300 aircraft lost.

Kutna Hora *(Hussite Wars)*, 1422

Taking personal charge of the drive against Jan Žižka's heretics, the Holy Roman Emperor Sigismund reached Bohemia with a large army late in 1421. Žižka had only 25,000 men, but he had mobile artillery and a system of using his baggage waggons as fortified defensive positions. At Kutna Hora, forty-five miles south-east of Prague, the two forces clashed on 6 January 1422. Due to his inferiority of numbers, Žižka took up a defensive position protected by his fortified waggons, which Sigismund's army failed to penetrate. The Bohemians then counter-attacked, and the Imperial troops were forced to retreat south-eastwards, where they soon suffered another defeat at Nemecky Brod, signall-ing the failure of the Emperor's first attempt to subdue the Hussites.

Landau *(War of the Spanish Succession)*, 1702

Crossing to the west bank of the Rhine near Speyer, on 29 July 1702 the Margrave of Baden-Baden with a force of Imperial troops, laid siege to the fortress of Landau (twenty miles north-west of Karlsruhe) held by a French garrison. The French army commander, Marshal de Catinat, was unable to send reinforcements, and the garrison was obliged to surrender on 12 September. During the siege the Comte de Soissons, elder brother of Prince Eugène, fell. However, shortly afterwards, Bavaria joined France, and Baden-Baden withdrew from the area in the face of this new twin threat.

Landeshut *(Seven Years War)*, 1760

In 1760 three enemy columns threatened to converge on Prussia from East Prussia, Saxony and Silesia. The latter was the first to take the field, under Baron von Laudon. With an Austrian army he captured Landeshut, the Silesian fortress in the Sudetic Mountains sixty-five miles south-west of Breslau (Wroclaw). Immediately Frederick the Great ordered Baron de La Motte-Fouque to recapture it. With 13,000 men he accordingly attacked on 23 June 1760, but was overwhelmed with heavy loss by Laudon's force of 31,000 men. Within a month Glatz had fallen and the Russians had advanced to the Oder. Prussian fortunes were then at a low ebb until Frederick himself defeated Laudon at Liegnitz in August.

Landshut *(Napoleonic Wars)*, 1809

Following the French victory at Abensberg on 20 April 1809, the main Austrian army fell back on Eckmühl. Meanwhile 36,000 men under Baron Hiller retired southwards to cross the Isar river and reach Landshut, thirty-five miles north-east of Munich. Napoleon believed Hiller's force to be the main army, and on the evening of 21 April Marshal Lannes' men routed its rearguard in the suburbs of Landshut, north of the river, then crossed a burning bridge to storm the city. When Marshal Masséna's IV Corps approached along the right bank of the Isar, the Austrians abandoned their defence of Landshut and retreated further south. In the meantime twenty-three miles north Marshal Davout's III Corps was facing the main Austrian army.

Langensalza *(Austro–Prussian War)*, 1866

When war broke out between Prussia and Austria in 1866, Hanover and several other German states supported Austria. The bulk of the Prussian forces was sent into Bohemia to deal with the Austrians, but another army under General von Falkenstein marched into Saxony to deal with their supporters. At Langensalza, nineteen miles north-west of Erfurt, von Falkenstein's advance guard was repulsed by a Hanoverian army led by George V on 27 June with the loss of 2,000 casualties. Von Falkenstein then brought up the remainder of his 50,000 men, and two days later the Hanoverians surrendered, having lost 1,400 men. As Hanover was absorbed into the new German Empire, this was the last battle fought by independent Hanoverian forces.

Langport *(English Civil War)*, 1645

Following the Parliamentarian victory at Naseby, Sir Thomas Fairfax led a strong force into Royalist territory in south-west England. In defence of Bridgwater, Lord Goring brought Fairfax to battle at Langport, ten miles to the south-east, on 10 July 1645, but the Parliamentarian cavalry proved decisive. Some 300 Royalists were killed, nearly 1,500 taken prisoner, and the Parliamentarians were able to press on to storm Bristol. Langport has been described as 'perhaps the most glorious achievement of the New Model Army', because a cavalry force of 700 with minimal infantry and artillery support routed an estimated 7,000 Royalists. Goring left England after this battle and settled in Spain.

Langside *(Scottish Rebellion against Mary Stuart)*, 1568

After her escape from imprisonment at Lochleven, Mary, Queen of Scots, rallied an army of 6,000 under the Earl of Argyll to her cause. On 13 May 1568 this force met one of a similar size under the Regent, the Earl of Moray, at Langside, a southern suburb of Glasgow. A decisive cavalry charge killed 300 of Mary's troops, and the rest scattered in confusion. Mary fled to Cumberland, where she was imprisoned by Queen Elizabeth of England.

Lansdown *(English Civil War)*, 1643

After his victory in Cornwall at Stratton in May 1643, leaving troops to besiege Plymouth and Exeter, Sir Ralph Hopton marched his Royalist army into Somerset, where Sir William Waller held Bath with a strong garrison. Before attacking Waller, Hopton occupied much of the surrounding area, and he skirted Bath to the east before finally approaching it from the north. On 5 July the Royalists encountered Waller's entrenched position on Lansdown Hill and after a bitter struggle carried the day. The Royalists had suffered heavy casualties, however; next day an ammunition explosion seriously injured Hopton, and they retired towards Devizes, which they reached on 9 July, pursued by Waller. Failure to take Bath would have an adverse long-term effect on Charles I's cause in the south-west.

Laon *(Napoleonic Wars)*, 1814

With fewer than 47,000 men Napoleon faced an allied force of 85,000 under Field-Marshal Blücher advancing on the French capital, at Laon, seventy-seven miles north-east of Paris, in March 1814. On 9 March allied troops attacked Marshal Marmont's VI Corps, and south of Laon other French troops also came under attack; but during that day Napoleon held his ground. Next day Blücher did not press his attack vigorously, and the French were able to retreat having lost a total of 6,000 casualties to the allied 4,000. However the road to Paris, and Napoleon's ultimate defeat, now lay open.

Largs *(Norse Invasion of Scotland)*, 1263

When part of a large Norse invasion fleet was driven ashore during a storm near Largs, on the south-west coast of Scotland twenty miles south-west of modern Glasgow, Haakon IV landed men from the rest of the fleet to protect those who had been shipwrecked. On 2 October 1263, however, those ashore were attacked by Scots, who inflicted such heavy losses on them that the entire invasion project was abandoned.

La Rochelle *(Huguenot Uprising)*, 1627–8

Following disturbances in western France, in August 1627 the Duke of Angoulême cut off landward supplies to the Huguenot stronghold of La Rochelle on the Bay of Biscay. Three months later Cardinal Richelieu arrived to take charge of the siege against stubborn defenders, who were encouraged by promises of assistance from England. Three attempts to bring aid by sea failed and, with the assassination of the Duke of Buckingham in Portsmouth, realistic hopes of relief faded. Once Richelieu had constructed a mole across the entrance to the harbour and blocked access to the open sea, the fate of La Rochelle was effectively sealed. On 28 October 1628, therefore, the garrison surrendered. The fall of La Rochelle fatally weakened Huguenot resistance to a united Catholic France; and within a year the last of the hundred fortified towns allowed to the Huguenots under the Edict of Nantes (1598) had fallen.

La Rothière *(Napoleonic Wars)*, 1814

Three days after losing the village of La Rothière in north-east France, Field-Marshal Blücher with 53,000 men counter-attacked on 1 February 1814. With a little over 40,000 men Napoleon was aware of further allied forces under Prince von Schwarzenberg in the area and, although the Young Guard did once retake the village after it had fallen to the enemy, towards evening the French retreated from the field. In this action both sides lost about 6,000 casualties, but the advantage lay with Blücher, whose advance on Paris had not been halted.

Las Navas de Tolosa *(Spanish–Moslem Wars)*, 1212

Temporarily suspending rivalry amongst themselves, Christian rulers of the several Spanish kingdoms amassed an army which, led by Alfonso VIII of Castile, marched south to deal with a gigantic host of over 500,000 Moors under Mohammed ben Yacoub. Mohammed fell back south of the Sierra Morena, but Alfonso's men penetrated an unguarded defile to debouch onto the plain north of Jaen. On 16 July 1212 in this area, known as Las Navas de Tolosa, Alfonso attacked the Moors, and throughout the day a confusion of charges and counter-charges flowed back and forth across the plain. Eventually a massive Moorish charge was checked and the bulk of Mohammed's army fled. Possibly as many as 150,000 of the Moors were slain, and incursions into Christian territory of the Iberian peninsula were stopped. After their victory, however, the Christian monarchs once more began to quarrel amongst themselves.

Lauffeld *(War of the Austrian Succession)*, 1747

In June 1747 Austrian and British forces under Count von Daun and the Duke of Cumberland isolated 30,000 French troops at Lauffeld, just west of Maastricht. Marshal Saxe, however, brought up a strong relief force and committed the allies to battle on 2 July. Throughout the day Lauffeld constantly changed hands, but at length only a brave cavalry charge led by Sir John Ligonier enabled the allied army to retire in some order. Both sides suffered over 5,000 casualties, and Saxe's victory allowed the French to besiege Bergen-op-Zoom thirteen days later.

Laupen *(Swiss–Burgundian Wars)*, 1339

Seeking to relieve Laupen, ten miles south-west of Bern, which was being besieged by 15,000 Burgundians, 5,000 Swiss from the forest cantons under Rudolph von Erlach took up position on a slope above the besiegers. On 21 June 1339 the Burgundians sent cavalry to drive them away but found the Swiss halberds and pikes a formidable barrier. Meanwhile the Burgundian infantry had similarly failed to make progress, and the Swiss mounted a counter-attack to rout the enemy. Laupen was thus saved.

Le Cateau *(First World War)*, 1914

Following the battle of Mons on 23 August 1914, the British Expeditionary Force (BEF) under Sir John French retreated south-westwards. At Le Cateau, eighteen miles north of Saint-Quentin, on 26 August General von Kluck's German First Army encountered the British II Corps. Cut off from I Corps by the Oise river, General Smith-Dorrien made a stand, and for almost the entire day his three and a half divisions resisted the German First

Army. During the night II Corps managed to withdraw towards Saint-Quentin. It had lost 8,077 men and thirty-six guns at Le Cateau but had delayed von Kluck long enough for the rest of the BEF to retire to comparative safety.

Lechfeld *(Wars of the German States)*, 955

Twenty years after being repulsed by the Holy Roman Emperor, Henry I, in 955 Magyars from Hungary again began to raid into southern and eastern Germany. Henry I's son and successor, Otto the Great, gathered a large army from duchies under his control to repel them. Twelve miles south of Augsburg, at Lechfeld in Bavaria, in a savage encounter Otto routed the invaders, who fell back through modern Austria across the Lech river. This victory helped to enhance the reputation of Otto, and the Magyar menace further receded when they were Christianized in 970.

Legnano *(War of the Lombard League)*, 1176

During his struggle to subdue northern Italy, Frederick Barbarossa was confronted at Legnano, fifteen miles north-west of Milan, by an army organized by the Lombard League and supported by the Pope. On 29 May 1176 Italian infantry successfully resisted the German knights and, after a defeat which marked the first major triumph of infantry over feudal cavalry, Frederick Barbarossa fled Italy in disguise.

Leipzig *(Napoleonic Wars)*, 1813

Having withdrawn west of the Elbe river after failing to take Berlin, by 15 October 1813 Napoleon had 122,000 men in the area of Leipzig to resist three allied columns totalling over 200,000 men then converging on the city. On 16 October Prince von Schwarzenberg sent 78,000 Russian troops against Napoleon's southern defences, while 54,000 Prussians led by General Blücher attacked Marshal Marmont's VI Corps in the north. On neither front did the French yield. Both sides were reinforced so that by 17 October the allies numbered almost 300,000 and the French some 150,000.

During 18 October, the third day of the battle, the French were driven back into Leipzig, and during that night Napoleon withdrew across the Elster. When the bridge across the river was prematurely blown up, 20,000 French troops were trapped in Leipzig, which then fell to the allies. The so-called 'Battle of the Nations' cost Napoleon 38,000 casualties and 15,000 prisoners, in addition to another 15,000 wounded from previous actions who had to be left behind. The allies suffered over 50,000 casualties. Napoleon retired south-westwards but, despite this defeat, he refused to make peace on the basis of retaining France's natural frontiers of the Rhine, Alps and Pyrenees.

Le Mans *(Franco–Prussian War)*, 1871

Several non-regular armies raised from civilians took the field against the Prussians after the French defeat at Sedan. One of these, possibly over 100,000 led by General Chanzy, was attacked by 50,000 Prussians under Prince Frederick Charles at Le Mans, 117 miles south-west of Paris, on 10 January 1871. In three days the French were utterly routed, losing 10,000 casualties, 20,000 prisoners and seventeen guns, to Prussian casualties of under 3,500, proving that such piecemeal efforts by inexperienced troops could not save France from ultimate defeat.

Leningrad *(Second World War)*, 1941–4

When Operation Barbarossa was launched on 22 June 1941, the northern spearhead aimed at Leningrad and, with Finland also declaring war on the Soviet Union, the city came under fire on 4 September as ground units threatened it from north and south. The population of Leningrad, and troops who had retreated into the city, then endured lengthy and extreme privation, for, although the Germans established a siege, they were never able to capture the city. Eventually on 15 January 1944 four Russian relief armies attacked on a 120-mile front, and after five days the Germans abandoned the siege. Possibly as many as one million perished within the city during the siege, but its stubborn and much-publicized resistance boosted Allied morale while drawing north valuable German supplies of men and equipment.

Lens *(Thirty Years War)*, 1648

Whilst peace negotiations were in progress, with 15,000 men Archduke Leopold, brother of the Holy Roman Emperor, marched into north-east France. At Lens, eleven miles north of Arras, he was faced by a slightly inferior French army under the Great Condé. Condé deceived the Archduke into believing that the French were retreating, then doubled back on 2 August 1648 to attack Leopold's column on the march. The Habsburg army lost all its artillery and baggage; 4,000 men became casualties and 6,000 prisoners. This was the last battle of the Thirty Years War, and the Treaty of Westphalia was concluded two months later.

Leuctra *(Wars of the Greek City-States)*, 371 BC

When talks to end hostilities broke down due to Theban obstinacy, in July 371 BC 10,000 Spartans under Cleombrotus marched into Boeotia and, ten miles short of the capital, at Leuctra, met 6,000 Thebans led by Epaminondas. The Thebans concentrated the bulk of their force on the left and, sweeping aside the opposing Spartan right flank, rolled up the entire enemy line. Cleombrotus and 2,000 of his men perished; the Spartans were forced to withdraw from Boeotia, and their dream of hegemony over Greece vanished.

Leuthen *(Seven Years War)*, 1757

Marching south-eastwards towards Breslau (Wroclaw) from Liegnitz (Legnica) with 43,000 men, on 5 December 1757 Frederick the Great faced 72,000 Austrians led by Prince Charles of Lorraine and Count von Daun in entrenched positions near the village of Leuthen, north-west of Breslau. Using wooded hills to conceal his movements, Frederick first attacked the Austrian right, then, preceded by an artillery bombardment, launched a massive assault in oblique order on their left. In vain the Austrians attempted to change the axis of their line, and a decisive cavalry charge cleared them from the village. Austrian casualties totalled 6,000, but a further 20,000 men became prisoners, whilst Prussia suffered 5,000 casualties. This victory allowed Frederick to advance and take Breslau thirteen days later.

Leyden *(Revolt of the Netherlands)*, 1574

On 26 May 1574 General Valdez began an investment of the rebel city of Leyden, eight miles north-east of The Hague, with 8,000 Spanish troops and within a few days had erected sixty-two fortifications around its perimeter. In order to save Leyden, William the Silent ordered dykes to be cut south of it on 3 August. Fighting off the Spanish inland fleet, the Dutch Sea Beggars then used shallow-draft vessels to carry supplies to the starving citizens. At length, despite having received troop reinforcements, on 3 October Valdez raised the siege, which had cost him almost 10,000 casualties and the citizens 8,000. The military reputation of William the Silent was thus enhanced and resistance to Spanish rule strengthened.

Liège *(First World War)*, 1914

When German troops invaded Belgium on 4 August 1914, General von Emmich's Army of the Meuse penetrated the defensive system of twelve forts around Liège in the south-east on the left bank of the Meuse river and took the city three days later. In the meantime eleven of the forts under General Leman held out, and on 12 August the Germans brought up 420mm siege guns to pound them into submission. Five days later the last of the forts surrendered, but their resistance had allowed the British and French armies eleven days to deploy in readiness for the German advance on Paris.

Liegnitz I *(Mongol Conquests)*, 1241

Having shattered the Poles at Cracow in March 1241, a Mongol army under Kaidu, grandson of Genghis Khan, pressed westwards and encountered another Christian force near Liegnitz (Legnica) on 9 April. This large assembly of Teutonic knights, German infantry and remnants of the defeated Polish army led by the Duke of Silesia lacked cohesion and organization. Attacked by Mongol archers, then charged by Kaidu's cavalry, the allied force disintegrated with heavy loss, including the death of Silesia. With its right flank now secure, the Mongol army crossed the Carpathian Mountains to join up with the main body in Hungary.

Liegnitz II *(Seven Years War)*, 1760

Alarmed by the defeat of Prussian troops at Landeshut, Frederick the Great marched his 30,000 men into Silesia to reach Liegnitz, forty miles west of Breslau (Wroclaw), on 15 August 1760. Here he was almost surrounded by 90,000 Austrian and Russian troops and the same night began to withdraw towards Parchwitz. In the darkness Frederick's men encountered an Austrian force under Baron von Laudon, which was marching to complete encirclement of the Prussians. The Austrians were routed, losing 10,000 men in casualties and prisoners and eighty-two guns, and Frederick was able to continue his retreat. When defeat seemed probable, once more Frederick's military genius had been underlined.

Ligny *(Napoleon's Hundred Days)*, 1815

Seeking to gain control of the Low Countries, Napoleon crossed the border of modern Belgium on 14 June 1815 and seized Charleroi. Whilst Marshal Ney advanced towards Quatre Bras on the road to Brussels, with 77,000 men and 218 guns two days later Napoleon struck at Ligny, ten miles north-west of Namur, defended by Field-Marshal Blücher's 84,000 Prussians with 224 guns. As darkness fell, the French finally ejected the Prussians from their positions, and Blücher withdrew north-eastwards, having lost 28,000 men, including prisoners and deserters, to French losses of 11,500. Napoleon believed the Prussians to be utterly beaten, which was to prove a costly misjudgement, for Blücher's intervention late on the day of Waterloo would be decisive.

Lille *(War of the Spanish Succession)*, 1708

Lille, in north-eastern France, with its French garrison of 15,000 men commanded by the Duke of Boufflers, was besieged by an allied force under Prince Eugène on 12 April 1708, despite the Duke of Marlborough's wish simply to mask it. Relief attempts by the Duke of Vendôme and the Duke of Berwick failed and, when Marlborough successfully defended his new line of communications to Ostend, Lille was virtually doomed to surrender. The city held out, however, until 25 October, and the citadel garrison until

8 December. During the siege Eugène suffered 3,600 casualties and the French about 7,000, but Lille would return to French control before the end of the war.

Lilybaeum *(First Punic War)*, 250–241 BC

Following determined Roman advances the Carthaginian hold on Sicily was confined to the west coast, where the fortress of Lilybaeum on the westernmost point of the island with its 10,000 garrison was besieged by land and sea in 250 BC. The outer walls were penetrated by legionaries, but they could not carry the inner ramparts. Nor could the Romans at sea prevent the superior Carthaginian navy from getting supplies through to the defenders. The naval defeat inflicted on the Romans at Drepanum in 249 BC gave the Carthaginians virtual command of the sea, and the fortress held out until a Roman naval triumph off the Aegates Islands caused Carthage to sue for peace in 241 BC.

Limerick *(Irish Rebellion against William III)*, 1691

After defeats on the Boyne river and at Aughrim, the last stronghold held by Jacobites was Limerick, at the mouth of the Shannon river in the west of Ireland, which was besieged in the summer of 1691 by General Ginkel. The defenders led by the Earl of Lucan resisted until 3 October, when they surrendered. Under the terms of the Pacification of Limerick, with other Irish supporters of James II they were required to take an oath of allegiance to William and Mary or leave the country.

Lincoln I *(English Anarchy)*, 1141

During the struggle between Stephen of Blois and Matilda (Maud) for the English throne, Stephen laid siege to Lincoln castle. Supporters of Matilda crossed the Trent river, defeated the besiegers on 2 February 1141 and took Stephen prisoner. Later, while he was imprisoned in Bristol, Matilda was proclaimed Queen of England at Winchester.

Lincoln II *(First Barons' War)*, 1217

As one group of barons rebelling against Henry III campaigned against Dover, another laid siege to Lincoln in 1217. A royalist force led by the Earl of Pembroke broke through the siege lines to enter the city on 20 May 1217, and throughout that day confused fighting occurred in the streets. About half the rebel knights surrendered and only three were killed (including the Comte de Perche by Pembroke personally), but many of the baronial retainers were cut down. This encounter, sometimes called 'the Fair of Lincoln', together with a royal naval victory off Dover, persuaded many barons to give up the revolt.

Linköping *(Swedish–Polish Wars)*, 1598

When Sigismund III of Poland also inherited the Swedish crown, he attempted to establish Catholicism in Sweden. This provoked a rebellion led by his uncle Charles, and in 1598 the rebels clashed with forces loyal to Sigismund at Linköping, 110 miles south-west of Stockholm. Sigismund was defeated and deposed by Charles, who became Charles IX in 1604.

Lippe *(Germanic Wars of the Roman Empire)*, 11 BC

Aiming to subdue Germanic tribes, which were threatening the eastern part of Gaul, Drusus led a Roman army across the Rhine in 11 BC. Finding little opposition, the Romans marched back along the Lippe river which flows into the Rhine, where they were surrounded by a vast body of Germans. So confident of victory were the tribesmen that they were already sharing out their expected spoils when Drusus attacked their lines, broke the encirclement and put them to flight. After constructing a fort at Aliso (possibly modern Haltern), Drusus recrossed the Rhine into Gaul.

Lobositz *(Seven Years War)*, 1756

When the Prussians occupied Dresden on 2 September 1756, 18,000 Saxons fell back eleven miles south-east to Pirna on the Elbe river. With 30,000 Austrians Count von Browne hurried from Bohemia to aid the Saxons but was attacked by Frederick the Great with an equal number of Prussians at Lobositz, thirty-five miles north-west of Prague, on 1 October. Thick fog and rough ground reduced the battle to a series of skirmishes. The Austrians were eventually beaten back at the cost of 3,000 casualties to each side. This victory led to the surrender of Pirna and the impressment of the Saxon garrison and their eighty guns into Prussian service.

Lodi Bridge *(French Revolutionary Wars)*, 1796

Pursuing the retreating Austrian army of Baron de Beaulieu north-eastwards towards Milan, Napoleon took Lodi, fifteen miles south-east of the city, on 10 May only to discover the bridge over the Adda commanded by the Austrian rearguard. Deploying artillery to bombard the enemy defences across the river and despatching cavalry over a ford to embarrass them from the rear, late that day Napoleon sent Generals Masséna and Berthier with 6,000 men to storm the bridge. In crossing it the French suffered 400 casualties, but in the action on 10 May both sides reputedly lost 2,000. For Napoleon the way to Milan was now open.

Lodz *(First World War)*, 1914

Anticipating a Russian advance into Silesia, General von Hindenburg reinforced German forces in the Posen-Thorn area and on 11 November 1914 launched them south-eastwards towards Warsaw under General von Mackensen. In four days the Germans moved forward fifty miles, causing the Russians to halt their attack on Silesia, which had been started on 14 November. Before Lodz (seventy miles south-west of Warsaw) on 19 November von Mackensen was checked, and seven days later he had to extricate his force from imminent encirclement. However, by forcing the Russians to withdraw men for the defence of Lodz, von Mackensen had prevented the invasion of Silesia and, moreover, on 6 December the Russians abandoned Lodz so that their line could be straightened.

Loja *(Spanish–Moslem Wars)*, 1486

The Spanish offensive to reduce the Moorish kingdom of Granada began successfully with the capture of the stronghold of Alhama, but in 1482 Ferdinand of Castile and Aragon was beaten back from Loja, twenty miles west of Granada. Four years later he returned to besiege the place with a strong force, and after a bitter struggle his troops stormed the walls, to put Ferdinand within striking distance of the Moorish capital, twenty-one miles away.

Lonato *(French Revolutionary Wars)*, 1796

After pushing the Austrian army of Baron de Beaulieu beyond the Adige river, Napoleon despatched a force to besiege Mantua. He was then faced with another Austrian army of 50,000 under Count von Würmser, which debouched from the Alps. Leaving only a minimum number of troops before Mantua, Napoleon concentrated 43,000 at Lonato near the southern end of Lake Garda. Noting that the right flank of von Würmser's force, moving down the western side of Lake Garda, was threatening his lines of communication with Milan, Napoleon attacked it on 3 August 1796. The exposed Austrian force, commanded by General von Quosdanovich, was defeated before von Würmser could come to its aid, and the threat to Napoleon's lines of communication was removed.

Londonderry *(Irish Rebellion against William III)*, 1689

Defended by a garrison of 7,000 under the command of Major Baker, 30,000 Protestants were besieged in Londonderry on 19 April 1689 by Catholic forces under James II. Stubbornly the city held out for 105 days until, on 30 July, Colonel Kirke broke through the boom across the Foyle river with a naval expedition and brought provisions to the starving citizens. James II then raised the siege, having suffered 5,000 casualties. Countless Protestant refugees had perished and almost 3,000 of the garrison, including Baker.

Loos *(First World War)*, 1915

In support of General Joffre's offensive in Champagne, on 25 September 1915 French forces attacked in the area of Vimy Ridge, whilst further north the British First Army commanded by Sir Douglas Haig (despite his own reservations about the action) attacked Loos, ten miles north of Arras. Making use of gas, the British had early success, but in the face of German counter-attacks the assault petered out on 8 October with little overall gain at a cost of 60,000 British casualties. This heavy loss brought British casualties in 1915 to over 300,000 and shortly afterwards Haig succeeded Sir John French as Commander-in-Chief of the British armies.

Lose-Coat Field *(Wars of the Roses)*, 1470

Determined to reassert personal power, Edward IV took the field against Lancastrian rebel forces and routed them on 12 March 1470 at Empingham in Rutland, with such vigour that they fled, shedding their coats to gain more speed. Thus the battle became known as that of 'Lose-Coat Field'. The captured rebel leader, Sir Robert Welles, before his execution implicated the Duke of Clarence and the Earl of Warwick in the rebellion, but they escaped to the Continent before they could be apprehended.

Lostwithiel *(English Civil War)*, 1644

Despite losing control of the north of England after his defeat at Marston Moor in July 1644, Charles I moved to suppress the activities of the Earl of Essex against Royalist strongholds in the west of England. Gaining control of the dominating feature of Beacon Hill, 16,000 Royalists surrounded Essex and his men near Lostwithiel, thirty miles west of Plymouth, on 2 September. Although most of the enemy cavalry escaped, the bulk of the infantry and artillery were captured. After all arms and ammunition had been surrendered, the defeated Parliamentarian troops were released, but they later rejoined Essex and fought with him at Newbury a month later.

Loudon Hill *(Anglo–Scottish Wars)*, 1307

Early in 1307 Robert Bruce rallied support in Scotland for a renewal of the struggle against England. On 10 May his force was attacked at Loudon Hill, near the coast of modern Ayrshire, by an English army under the Earl of Pembroke. The English cavalry suffered heavy loss when it charged the Scottish spearmen, and Pembroke was obliged to concede a victory, which vastly enhanced Bruce's reputation, especially when the new English king, Edward II, withdrew his troops south of the border for seven years.

Lugdunum *(Civil Wars of the Roman Empire)*, 197

While Septimius Severus was consolidating his position in the east and in Rome, Clodius Albinus crossed from Britain to Gaul and gathered 50,000 men in support of his claim to the imperial throne. To deal with this threat Severus raised a similar number of troops and crossed the Alps from Italy. North of Lugdunum (Lyons) the two forces clashed in 197, when the Pannonian legions of Severus triumphed. Albinus was captured and beheaded.

Luleburgaz *(First Balkan War)*, 1912

Determined to recover from Turkey territory nominally granted to her but never acquired by the Treaty of San Stefano (1878), Bulgarian forces triumphed at Kirk-Klissa (Kirklarei), thirty-five miles east of Adrianople (Edirne), on 25 October 1912, and advanced south-eastwards. On 28 October they attacked Turkish positions at Luleburgaz, eighty miles north-west of Constantinople, and after three days of fighting the Turks fell back to a fortified line at Catalca, which protected the capital. Unable to make progress further, the Bulgarians agreed to an armistice on 3 December, and in May 1913 at the subsequent peace treaty Bulgaria gained Thrace and a stretch of the Aegean coast.

Lutter *(Thirty Years War)*, 1626

Learning of the defeat of Count von Mansfeld and the detachment of 8,000 men by General von Waldstein (Wallenstein) to join the Comte de Tilly's Catholic army, Christian IV of Denmark decided to retire towards Wolfenbüttel in Brunswick. Tilly, now with a force of 26,000, took up pursuit and came up with the Danes at Lutter, twenty miles from Wolfenbüttel. Here Christian turned to face his pursuer, deploying 15,000 men and twenty cannon across the line of his retreat. Despite stubborn resistance by the infantry and personal bravery by the King, the Danes were forced to give ground through sheer weight of numbers. Christian fled north-wards towards the North Sea coast, leaving 6,000 casualties, 2,500 prisoners and all his artillery on the field at Lutter. Thus the first Danish attempt to invade the Holy Roman Empire in support of the Protestants failed.

Lützen I *(Thirty Years War)*, 1632

When General von Waldstein (Wallenstein) marched his army of 19,000 men north-eastwards from Nuremberg towards Saxony, hoping to compel the Elector to join him, he was pursued by Gustavus Adolphus with a Swedish force of 16,000 men. At Lützen, fifteen miles south-west of Leipzig, Wallenstein deployed his army with its thirty guns to oppose Gustavus, knowing that a further 10,000 men under Count zu Pappenheim were hurrying south from Halle. On the morning of 16 November 1632, in misty conditions, Gustavus attacked the Catholic left, commanded by Count Holk, while Bernard of Saxe-Weimar attacked the right, which was anchored on the village of Lützen and commanded by Wallenstein in person. Zu Pappenheim arrived just as Gustavus seemed on the point of breaking through, but in the bitter fighting both he and Gustavus were mortally wounded. Despite the loss of their leaders, the Swedes fought fiercely, and Wallenstein was obliged to retreat under cover of darkness, leaving all his artillery and 6,000 casualties on the field. In imposing his first major defeat on Wallenstein, the Swedes suffered over 5,000 casualties (including 1,500 dead). Possibly the death of Gustavus indirectly led soon afterwards to that of Frederick V of the Palatinate, the 'Winter King' of Bohemia, who could no longer see victory for the Protestant cause.

Lützen II *(Napoleonic Wars)*, 1813

On the day that the French V Corps took Leipzig (2 May 1813), an army of 73,000 Russians and Prussians, under Prince Wittgenstein and General Blücher and watched by the King of Prussia and Tsar of Russia, attacked French positions south-east of Lützen. Perceiving the danger of this attack, Napoleon concentrated 100,000 men in the area of five villages, which frequently changed hands during the day. The allies made no positive progress, and during the night the two sovereigns ordered a retreat, which through lack of cavalry the French were unable to prevent. Casualties on both sides were high: the allies suffered 20,000, Napoleon slightly more. This defeat convinced Prussia that Germany would be liberated only once Austrian help had been secured.

Luzzara *(War of the Spanish Succession)*, 1702

During the summer of 1702 Marshal Vendôme deployed some 35,000 men in positions around Luzzara in Tuscany, fifteen miles south of Mantua, where on 15 August they were attacked by an Austrian force of some 25,000 under Prince Eugène. The French were driven from their trenches after a fierce struggle, with the loss of 4,000 casualties to Austrian losses of under 3,000. This victory brought no real advantage for Eugène, and he soon left Italy to join the Duke of Marlborough in central Europe.

Lys River *(First World War)*, 1918

Having failed to break through on the Somme in March 1918, General Ludendorff launched another attack along the Lys river in Flanders the following month. Preceded by a thirty-three-hour bombardment, on 9 April General Quast's Sixth Army drove westwards from Armentières south of the river against General Horne's British First Army. A Portuguese division in the British centre gave way, and Horne was forced to retreat five miles. Next day the German Fourth Army attacked the British Second north of Armentières, forcing it also to give way. On 11 April the two German armies linked up for a concerted drive towards the Channel coast. British reinforcements managed to slow the pace of this advance, on 21 April French assistance arrived, and eight days later the attack finally petered out. The Germans had gained some tactical advantage by securing an average gain of ten miles along the length of their assault. However, they now held an awkward salient south of Ypres and had suffered 350,000 casualties to Allied losses, almost entirely British, of 305,000 men.

Maastricht I *(Revolt of the Netherlands)*, 1579

Besieged by 20,000 Spanish soldiers under the Duke of Parma on 12 March 1579, the 2,000 garrison and armed citizens in the Dutch frontier town of Maastricht fought strongly and flooded the surrounding area. Two unsuccessful assaults were made in April, and Parma was forced to ring the town with a series of strongpoints, before at length carrying the defences of Maastricht after a four-month siege. This success cost Parma nearly 5,000 casualties, and in fury the Spaniards massacred almost 8,000 of the inhabitants.

Maastricht II *(Dutch War of Louis XIV)*, 1673

After Louis XIV had invaded the Netherlands in 1672, a French force laid siege to Maastricht on 16 June 1673. Using methods devised by the Marquis de Vauban, the besiegers carried the town in only thirteen days, for the maze of parallels and approaches rendered its defences ineffective.

Madrid *(Spanish Civil War)*, 1936–9

By 6 November 1936, the day that the Republican Prime Minister left the city for Valencia, strong Nationalist forces under General Mola supported by German and Italian aircraft were in position to assault Madrid. The defence of the capital was in the hands of General Miaja with a mixture of urban militia, the IX International Brigade and an assortment of other poorly armed volunteers supported by a limited number of Soviet aircraft and tanks. At dawn on 7 November 20,000 Nationalists under General Varela attacked, but not until 16 November did they cross the Manzanares river. A week later most of the University City was under Nationalist control, although both sides were now so exhausted that a stalemate developed on the ground. Complete investment of Madrid had not been achieved, though heavy bombing was carried out by Nationalist aircraft. Frequently costly attacks were made by the Nationalists in the opening months of 1937 to increase pressure on Republicans in Madrid, but then little positive action occurred for almost two years. Eventually the fall of Barcelona in January 1939 ended realistic hopes of a Republican victory in the war, and by now an estimated 400 people a week were dying of starvation in Madrid. Serious disagreement between forces within the city led to fighting amongst the defenders, and peace talks with General-issimo Franco broke down. On 26 March 1939 Franco therefore launched a major offensive, the Republican defence collapsed and on 31 March Nationalist troops marched into the Spanish capital. The Spanish Civil War had thus ended: the casualties on both sides during the battle for Madrid numbered tens of thousands.

Magdeburg *(Thirty Years War)*, 1631

In March 1631 Magdeburg, seventy miles south-west of Berlin, with its population of 30,000 and defended by a small Protestant garrison under Dietrich von Falkenberg, was besieged by a Cath-olic force commanded by Count zu Pappenheim. In April the Comte de Tilly took over personal direction of the 22,000 be-siegers, and on 18 May, alarmed at the approach of Gustavus Adolphus with another Protestant force, he attempted to storm the city. For two days the defenders resisted, but finally on 20 May zu Pappenheim's men penetrated the defences. During the ensuing three days the attackers proceeded to loot, kill and burn until the entire city was in flames and over 20,000 of the inhabitants had perished. This sack of Magdeburg brought widespread revulsion, caused Saxony and the Netherlands to support the Protestant cause and deprived Tilly of a useful supply base in northern Germany.

Magenta *(Italian Wars of Independence)*, 1859

In support of the Piedmontese in their struggle against Austrian domination of Italy, early in 1859 some 50,000 French troops under the Comte de MacMahon crossed the Ticino river into Lombardy. At Magenta, fourteen miles west of Milan, on 4 June they met the Austrian army of slightly superior numbers comman-ded by Count von Clam-Gallas. After confused and bitter fighting in which each side suffered about 5,000 casualties, the Austrians were defeated. Later, for this victory, MacMahon was created Duke of Magenta. This campaign, however, was characterized by inept generalship, with the Austrians failing to attack the French army as it marched northwards across their front, and both sides eschewing the strategic use of railways in preference for more traditional, leisurely campaigning.

Maida *(Napoleonic Wars)*, 1806

In 1806 the new King of Naples, Joseph Bonaparte, sent a French force of 6,500 men under Comte Reynier into Calabria (the southernmost region of Italy) to deal with a British expedition of 5,000 men, led by General Stuart, which sought to restore Ferdinand IV to the throne. On 6 July the British attacked the French at Maida, twelve miles south-west of Catanzaro and effectively guarding northern access to the toe of the peninsula, after a fierce bayonet charge breaking their ranks. Stuart's victory brought little permanent benefit, for French reinforcements caused him to re-embark in September.

Málaga I *(Spanish–Moslem Wars)*, 1487

On 17 April 1487 Ferdinand of Castile and Aragon laid siege to the important Moorish seaport of Málaga, sixty miles south-west of Granada, with some 50,000 men. For four months the garrison resisted until at length forced to surrender on 18 August, whereupon most of the inhabitants were sold into slavery. Ferdinand had now cleared the area west of Granada, preparatory to an assault on the Moorish capital.

Málaga II *(Spanish Civil War)*, 1937

Three Nationalist columns began to converge on Málaga (northeast of Gibraltar) on 17 January 1937 and on 3 February reached the outskirts of the city, defended by 40,000 ill-equipped militiamen under Colonel Villalba. The Republicans held out for only three days, and survivors fled up the coast harassed by Nationalist tanks and aircraft, leaving Generalissimo Franco in control of southern Spain.

Malborghetto *(French Revolutionary Wars)*, 1797

With northern Italy virtually under his control Napoleon marched 43,000 French troops across the Alps to carry the war into the heartland of Austria. Archduke Charles Louis, brother of the Holy Roman Emperor, deployed 33,000 men in the passes to check this advance. On 23 March 1797 General Masséna routed Austrian defenders at Malborghetto in the Carnic Alps, ninety miles north-east of Venice, causing the Archduke to fall back and agree to a preliminary peace on 18 April.

Maldon *(Danish Invasions of England)*, 991

During the reign of Ethelred II (the Unready) Danish invaders again ravaged the English coasts. In August 991 one group threatened Maldon in Essex, demanding tribute from the town. Led by Byrhtnoth, the citizens resisted, and most of them (including Byrhtnoth) were slain, allowing the victorious Danes to plunder the area at will and underlining Ethelred's military weakness.

Maloyaroslavets *(Napoleonic Wars)*, 1812

Evacuating Moscow on 19 October 1812, Napoleon marched south-west towards Kaluga, preceded by 15,000 men under his step-son, Eugène de Beauharnais. With 20,000 men and eighty-four guns, General Docturov moved to intercept this body, believing it to be a foraging party. Discovering that it was in fact the advance guard of the Grand Army, he made a stand at Maloyaroslavets, on the Luzha river seventy-five miles south-west of the Russian capital. Throughout 24 October, with reinforcements arriving for both forces, the battle swayed back and forth in the village. At length the Russians retired, with each side having suffered over 5,000 casualties. Napoleon now decided to change the line of his general withdrawal to that via Smolensk. Hence the action at Maloyaroslavets had important strategic repercussions.

Malplaquet *(War of the Spanish Succession)*, 1709

In an effort to relieve Mons, which was being besieged by 100,000 British, Dutch, German and Austrian troops under the Duke of

Marlborough and Prince Eugène, the Duke of Villars concentrated 90,000 French soldiers just north of the village of Malplaquet, fifteen miles east of Valenciennes. Here the French prepared
a strong defensive position, protected by palisades and entrenchments, which was attacked by the allies on 11 September 1709.
Marlborough assaulted both wings of the enemy and, although the
Dutch were held on the left, Eugène gradually edged forward
through thick forest on the right. After seven hours of heavy
fighting 30,000 allied cavalry attacked the centre, and the French
were driven back. This was the bloodiest battle of the war, with the
allies suffering 24,000 casualties and the French half that number.
It was also to be Marlborough's last, for he was dismissed from
command in 1711.

Mannerheim Line *(Russo–Finnish Wars)*, 1939–40

Following its declaration of war on Finland on 30 November
1939, the Soviet Union attacked both in the north, where Petsamo
was captured, and the south, where Soviet forces were held by the
Mannerheim Line. This construction of fortifications from the
Gulf of Finland to the inland lakes east of Helsinki was finally
assaulted by twenty-seven divisions under Marshal Timoshenko
on 11 February 1940. Ten days later the Russians had punched an
eight-mile gap in the line, and Finland was obliged to come to
terms with the victors. Russian casualties were reputedly 200,000
to some 68,000 Finns.

Mantinea *(Wars of the Greek City-States)*, 362 BC

In an effort to conclude fighting in the Peloponnesus, Epaminondas took command of the Theban and Boeotian troops and in 363
BC met a combined force of Athenians and Spartans at Mantinea,
which lay in a plain of south-east Arcadia, north of Tegea. Using an
oblique order attack, Epaminondas struck the enemy right with
his left wing and did not commit his own right until positive
progress had been made. The enemy forces were then routed but
Epaminondas fell during the pursuit, and Thebes was unable to
exercise the domination which this victory offered. The various
city-states therefore continued to quarrel among themselves.

Mantua *(French Revolutionary Wars)*, 1796–7

Crossing the Mincio river on 30 May 1796, Napoleon forced the Austrians to divide their strength, and 13,000 men with 500 cannon under General d'Irles concentrated in Mantua. On 4 June General Sérurier began an investment with 9,000 men, who were reinforced with heavy cannon early in July after the citadel in Milan had been successfully stormed. The advance of a strong Austrian force under Count von Würmser caused Napoleon temporarily to raise the siege on 31 July, but after von Würmser had been driven back, it was resumed on 24 August, although the garrison had by now been reinforced to 15,000 men. On 13 September it was further strengthened when von Würmser himself and 12,000 more troops entered the city. However, Austrian attempts to break out were repulsed and eventually, when all hope of relief had faded with the defeat of Austrian forces at Rivoli Veronese, five miles east of Lake Garda, von Würmser surrendered on 2 February 1797. During the siege some 18,000 Austrians and 7,000 French troops had died, mainly through disease. General peace negotiations were opened soon afterwards.

Marathon *(Greco–Persian Wars)*, 490 BC

Seeking to extend control over Greece, a Persian expedition of 15,000 men under Artaphrenes the Younger and Datis landed near Marathon, twenty-four miles north-east of Athens. On 12 September 490 BC the invaders were attacked by 10,000 Athenians and 1,000 Plataeans under Militiades. The Greeks were extended across the two-mile-wide plain of Marathon, with infantry in the centre and cavalry on the wings. The initial advance of the Greek centre was beaten back, but as it retreated the wings, which had been strengthened, wheeled inwards to envelop the Persians. In confusion the invaders fell back to their ships with the loss of some 6,400 to 192 Greek dead. This surprising reverse closed the campaign, and a decade elapsed before Xerxes mounted another invasion.

Marchfeld *(Bohemian Wars)*, 1278

Ottokar II, the Great, of Bohemia, then a powerful central European state, refused to recognize the Habsburg Rudolph I as Holy

Roman Emperor. After lengthy quarrelling the armies of the two rulers met on the plain of Marchfeld, north-east of Vienna, on 26 August 1278. The Bohemians were routed, Ottakar was killed and the dead ruler's son, Wenceslas II, succeeded only under Habsburg patronage. The Habsburgs were thereafter to stand supreme in the Danube Valley for over six hundred years.

Marengo *(French Revolutionary Wars)*, 1800

The French offensive in spring 1800 forced the Austrian commander, Baron von Melas, to concentrate 31,000 men at Alessandria. On 13 June Napoleon reached Marengo, two and a half miles short to Alessandria, with 23,000 French troops, who were attacked next morning by the Austrians. Caught by surprise, the French fought strongly but in mid afternoon were obliged to give way, retreating almost four miles, to San Giuliano. At this point, believing himself victorious, von Melas personally returned to Alessandria. However, the arrival of General Desaix with 6,000 fresh cavalry from the south-east allowed Napoleon to counter-attack, and by nightfall apparent defeat had been turned into triumph. Desaix was killed; French casualties totalled 5,835 and Austrian 9,402. On 15 June von Melas agreed to a truce and the withdrawal of his troops east of the Mincio and north of the Po rivers. This narrow victory received wild acclaim in France and greatly enhanced Napoleon's political and military reputation.

Margus *(Civil Wars of the Roman Empire)*, 285

In 285 a decisive clash occurred between the armies of two claimants to the imperial throne at Margus on the Morava river in Moesia (modern east Yugoslavia). The troops supporting Carinus, commander of Roman legions in the west, initially drove back those of Diocletian, who had been proclaimed Emperor by his own men. Long campaigns in Persia and the effect of the march to Moesia had weakened Diocletian's troops, but at a crucial point in the battle Carinus was assassinated by one of his own officers, and Diocletian won the day. A line of undisputed emperors then followed until the division of the Empire in 395.

Marignano *(French Wars in Italy)*, 1515

To deal with a hostile alliance of Pope, Holy Roman Emperor, Italian states and Swiss cantons, Francis I sent a French army of 30,000 men over the Alps in 1515. At Marignano, ten miles south-east of Milan, the French encountered some 25,000 Swiss on 15 September. The French artillery and cavalry took a heavy toll of advancing enemy infantry, but at nightfall the battle was as yet unresolved. Next day, reinforced by Venetian troops, the French finally forced the Swiss from the field. By then the French had suffered almost 10,000 casualties, the Swiss 13,000. Francis I recovered Milan, however, and both the Holy Roman Emperor and the Pope agreed to peace.

Marne I *(First World War)*, 1914

The failure of troops to hold the German advance along the French frontier during the first week of August 1914 opened the way for five German armies to penetrate between Verdun and Amiens, causing the French to fall back. On 30 August the French Sixth Army, on the left (north) of the Allied line, stood thirty miles from Paris. On its immediate right the British Expeditionary Force retreated across the Marne river on 3 September, and further south, to its right, the French Fifth and Third armies also fell back. Meanwhile on 31 August the First Army of General von Kluck on the extreme right (north) of German advance wheeled south-east to pass east of Paris. This was not a violation of the famous Schlieffen Plan, which did not specfically provide for a move-ment west of Paris, but the manœuvre did provide the French with an excellent opportunity to counter-attack. Reaching the Marne on 3 September, von Kluck crossed it a day behind the BEF but in his eagerness to advance had drawn ahead of the German Second Army on his left. In vain he was ordered to echelon back behind the Second Army, and the French seized the chance to attack the flank of his army as it passed east of Paris. On the morning of 6 September General Galliéni, military governor of Paris, and General Maunoury, commander of the French Sixth Army, laun-ched an assault on the flank of von Kluck's army. The French Fifth Army and the BEF shortly afterwards attacked the German Second and Third armies to prevent aid being sent to von Kluck.

French reserves transferred from the Moselle front were also rushed out from Paris in 600 taxi-cabs to join the fight against von Kluck. When the French Ninth Army attacked the junction of the German Second and Third Armies, fighting became general along a 100-mile front. For three days the struggle continued, with the security of Paris and, in reality, the whole of France at stake. At length the Germans began to retreat to the line of the Aisne on 9 September. Each side had roughly a million troops involved in the Battle of the Marne, and five per cent of these became casualties. Victory for the Allies meant that Paris had been saved and that there would now be no swift end to the war.

Marne II *(First World War)*, 1918

Following the limited success of German offensives earlier in the year and notably on the Aisne in June, on 15 July 1918 General Ludendorff attacked from both sides of Reims with forces which were to converge and meet at the Marne east of Paris. On the left (east) the German First and Third Armies made little progress before being checked by the French First Army of General Gouraud. But on the right, west of Reims, General von Boehn's Seventh Army penetrated between Château-Thierry and Epernay, reached the Marne and actually established a bridgehead beyond the river, before being checked on 17 July by the French Ninth Army with assistance from American, British and Italian units. Next day General Foch launched an Allied counter-offensive, which drove the Germans out of the territory gained since 15 July, and the final German offensive of the war had failed.

Marsaglia *(War of the Grand Alliance)*, 1693

Routed by the French at Staffarda in 1690, three years later the Duke of Savoy organized an English, Spanish and Austrian force to restore his fortunes. On 4 October 1693 this allied army clashed with Marshal de Catinat's French troops at Marsaglia (east of the Po) and were quickly driven back across the river with the loss of 6,000 men. This defeat, however, did not cause Savoy immediately to forsake the Grand Alliance, although she would make a separate peace with France three years later.

Mars-la-Tour *(Franco–Prussian War)*, 1870

Withdrawing westwards across the Moselle after their defeat at Colombey east of Metz on 14 August, 80,000 French troops under Marshal Bazaine found their way barred at Mars-la-Tour and Vionville by the German III and X Corps under General von Alvensleben. Bazaine failed to press home his attacks on 16 August with sufficient vigour and, having suffered some 15,000 casualties, accepted that he was unable to break through and began to retire eastwards once more towards Metz.

Marston Moor *(English Civil War)*, 1644

After Prince Rupert had relieved York early in June, the Parliamentarian besiegers retired seven miles west to Marston Moor. Here together with Scottish supporters under Lord Leven their total force numbered 20,000 infantry and 5,000 cavalry. Prince Rupert, reinforced by troops under the Earl of Newcastle and Lord Goring, commanded 11,000 infantry and 7,000 cavalry but nevertheless attacked the Parliamentarians on 2 July 1644. Towards evening he began to disengage his men, aiming to renew the conflict next day, when the enemy put in a telling cavalry charge led by Oliver Cromwell and the Earl of Manchester. The Royalists were swept from the field with the loss of 4,000 casualties and Charles I had effectively lost the north of England, for the cities of York and Newcastle were to surrender within four months.

Masurian Lakes I *(First World War)*, 1914

Once the Russian Second Army had been defeated at Tannenberg in East Prussia during August 1914, the German Eighth Army of General von Hindenburg turned to deal with the First Army of General Rennenkampf, which was deployed north of the Masurian Lakes. Reinforced by two corps from the western front and taking advantage of Russian failure to cover the Lützen gap in the lake system, through which General von François's German I Corps was able to debouch, Hindenburg attacked on 5 September. With his left flank seriously threatened, Rennenkampf ordered a retreat on 9 September and next day put in a counter-attack to enable his exhausted troops to escape encirclement. Nevertheless, East Prussia was clear of Russian invaders by 13 September for the loss of 10,000 casualties against an estimated 120,000 from Rennenkampf's army. For his mismanagement of the whole offensive against East Prussia, the commander of the Russian North-Western Front, General Jilinsky, was dismissed. Yet withdrawal of two corps from the Western Front did weaken the German armies at a critical point in that theatre.

Masurian Lakes II *(First World War)*, 1915

As part of a plan to force Russia out of the war, on 7 February 1915 the German Eighth Army struck eastwards in heavy snow against the southern flank of the Russian Tenth Army of General Sievers, positioned north of the Masurian Lakes. As the surprised Russians fell back, they were attacked the following day from the north by the newly formed German Tenth Army of General von Eichhorn. Stubborn resistance by the Russian XX Corps allowed the bulk of the other three corps to escape, but fighting ceased on 21 February. Some 200,000 Russians had become casualties or prisoners and, although German casualties in battle were comparatively light, many troops suffered severely from exposure in the bitter conditions. This defeat seriously undermined the plan of Grand Duke Nicholas to drive into Silesia with his northern and southern flanks secure.

Maxen *(Seven Years War)*, 1759

Aiming to isolate 42,000 Austrian troops under Count von Daun in Saxony, General von Finck with a Prussian army of 12,000 sought to outflank the enemy in November 1759. To forestall this attempt to cut his lines of communication, von Daun retired from Dresden ten miles south to Maxen, where he surrounded von Finck's army. After vainly attempting to break out of encirclement for two days, von Finck surrendered on 20 November, but von Daun failed to capitalize on his advantage and went into winter quarters. Nevertheless, his success at Maxen completed a miserable year for Prussian armies and left Frederick the Great politically insecure. For his failure, von Finck was later court-martialled and imprisoned.

Megalopolis *(Macedonian Conquests)*, 331 BC

Whilst Alexander the Great was in Persia, Agis III of Sparta gained support from Achaea, Elis and Arcadia in a rebellion against Macedonian domination in the Peloponnesus. Megalopolis, the Arcadian capital, refused to join the rebels, who then besieged it in 331 BC. Macedonian forces under Antipater marched to its relief, routed the rebels and killed Agis. Resistance to the power of Macedonia by the Greek city-states now ceased until the death of Alexander eight years later.

Mentana *(Italian Wars of Independence)*, 1867

After French troops were withdrawn from Rome in 1866, knowing the weakness of the papal garrison and impatient to capture the city, the Italian patriot Giuseppe Garibaldi amassed 10,000 supporters and prepared to attack. Aware of the political consequences of such an action, he was not encouraged by Victor Emmanuel II. With Rome in danger, in October 1867 Napoleon III of France despatched a small force to aid its defence, which together with papal troops brought the garrison up to 5,000. When Garibaldi at length made his attack on 3 November 1867, his more numerous force was routed at Mentana, ten miles north-east of Rome, at a cost of 1,100 casualties and 1,000 prisoners. The defenders suffered 182 casualties, and their success was due mainly to the bravery of the papal zouaves and the efficiency of the French *chassepôt* rifles. Garibaldi was captured and sent to the island of Caprera, off northern Sardinia. As a result of this battle, the incorporation of Rome into the new Italian state was postponed for a further three years.

Mergentheim *(Thirty Years War)*, 1645

In 1645 the Vicomte de Turenne with a French force marched to Mergentheim, twenty miles south of Würzburg on the Tauber river, by way of Heilbronn and Rothenburg. Here the army demanded rest and, while it was in a state of partial disorganization, a combined Bavarian and Austrian force under Baron von Mercy and General von Werth struck the French camp at dawn on 2 May. The surprised French lost most of their artillery and all their baggage, and Turenne was obliged to fall back on the Rhine with only one third of the force with which he had advanced. Reinforced there by the Great Condé, he planned a new but more cautious drive to the Danube.

Mesolongion *(Greek War of Independence)*, 1821–6

When the Greeks began actively to press for separation from Turkey and before an independent state was formally proclaimed the next year, in 1821 11,000 Turks laid seige to Mesolongion (Missolonghi) on the north side of the Gulf of Patras, guarding the entrance to the Gulf of Corinth. The small Greek garrison successfully resisted this and several further attempts to take the town and, although by early 1823 Turkish forces had subdued much of the rebellion in Greece, Mesolongion continued to hold out. It became such a symbol of resistance to oppression that a number of volunteers from other countries joined its defenders: in 1824 Lord Byron died of malaria in its defence. A more serious investment began on 27 April 1825 and ultimately, after the Turks had been reinforced by troops from Egypt, it led to the town's surrender on 23 April 1826. This reverse for the rebels persuaded France, Britain and Russia to intervene in the conflict to secure peace.

Messina *(First Punic War)*, 264 BC

Early in the third century BC, the port of Messina in north-east Sicily was seized by mercenaries from Campania, known as Mamertines, acting on behalf of Syracuse. Shortly afterwards, in 270 BC, the Carthaginians attacked and took Messina, but six years later a Roman army came to the Mamertines' assistance by expelling the Carthaginians from the city. The Syracusans, by now also hostile to the mercenaries who had taken control of it, and afraid of Rome, then launched an attack on Messina. They were beaten off by the Roman garrison, sued for peace and became allies of Rome against Carthage. Messina was declared a free city under Roman protection.

Messines *(First World War)*, 1917

Partly in order to gain time for General Pétain, who was busy restoring French morale after the mutinous events of the previous weeks, Sir Douglas Haig determined to clear the Germans off the dominant Messines Ridge, from which they could command the Ypres salient. On 7 June 1917 nineteen mines sapped under the German lines were exploded at dawn, following a ten-day artillery bombardment, and in the confusion the British Second Army seized the remains of the German positions. Although the British Fifth and French First armies moved up to exploit the gap, the Allied advance was halted on 14 June. The Germans had been ousted from their dominant positions, but success was of only limited tactical value.

Metaurus River *(Second Punic War)*, 207 BC

Ten years after invading Italy at the head of a strong Carthaginian army, Hannibal ordered his brother Hasdrubal to join him from Spain with as many men as he could muster. Eluding Roman attempts to stop him in the summer of 208 BC, Hasdrubal wintered in France and crossed the Alps in the following spring. Reinforced by Gallic allies, he advanced down the Adriatic coast of the Italian peninsula and sent a message asking his brother to meet him south of the Metaurus river (near modern Ancona). This message was intercepted by the Romans, who had already despatched Marcus Livius Salinator with a force to deal with Hasdrubal in the north, while Gaius Claudius Nero marched south to ensure that Hannibal remained in Lucania. On learning of Hasdrubal's message, Nero withdrew 7,000 men from the force opposing Hannibal and made a six-day march to join the northern army. Worried by the possibility of a Roman attack, Hasdrubal withdrew to the Metaurus river and was actually preparing to recross when the Romans caught him still south of it. Finding his advance checked by the Carthaginian left, Nero boldly marched his men behind the Roman line to reappear on the enemy right. This surprise manœuvre was decisive. Ten thousand Carthaginians were killed in the rout, including Hasdrubal, against 2,000 Romans, and Nero was able to march his battle-weary men back south before Hannibal knew either that they had gone or that his brother had been defeated. Reputedly his first intimation of the reverse was when his brother's head was propelled into the Carthaginian camp. This victory, due almost entirely to Nero's initiative, ensured that Hannibal would never dominate Italy.

Methven *(Anglo–Scottish Wars)*, 1306

After the execution of Sir William Wallace, Robert Bruce assumed leadership of the Scottish campaign for freedom from English control. Enraged that Bruce had been crowned King of Scotland at Scone, in 1306 Edward I sent an English army north to deal with the rebels. At Methven, seven miles north-west of Perth, on 19 June the Scots were utterly beaten and Bruce fled to an island off the Irish coast. Here, according to legend, encouraged by the persistence of a spider building its web, he determined to return to continue the fight.

Metz *(Franco–Prussian War)*, 1870

Marshal Bazaine withdrew his troops into the fortress of Metz on the Moselle river following his defeat at Gravelotte on 18 August 1870. The city was then besieged by Prussian troops under Prince Frederick Charles. Several French attempts to break out through the siege lines failed, and the defeat of French forces at Sedan on 2 September had ended hope of rapid relief. Although Paris still held out, on 27 October Bazaine surrendered Metz with its garrison of almost 180,000 men, including three marshals and 6,000 officers, with all their equipment. After the war Bazaine was court-martialled and sentenced to twenty years' imprisonment. Had he fought on in Metz, many Prussian troops would not have been free to combat the non-regular forces raised by Léon Gambetta outside Paris.

Meuse–Argonne *(First World War)*, 1918

In a combined effort to break through the Hindenburg Line, in mid September 1918 Marshal Foch planned four virtually simultaneous assaults. In the north the Belgians would attack from the area of Ypres, further south the British around Cambrai, then the French and at the extreme south of the line the Americans; the latter two attacks were to be in the Meuse–Argonne area. On 26 September the French Fourth and American First Armies went forward but in difficult hilly terrain found resistance stiff. Not until 31 October was the Argonne forest cleared, which marked a ten-mile advance by the Americans, and by this date the French had reached the Aisne river after a twenty-mile advance. In the meantime attacks further north had also been successful and the Germans were in general retreat on the whole front.

Milazzo (*Italian Wars of Independence*), 1860

The Thousand Redshirts of Giuseppe Garibaldi, augmented by local volunteers, had driven the Neapolitans out of north-west Sicily by the summer of 1860. Marching eastwards, they reached the port of Milazzo, seventeen miles west of Messina, where Colonel del Bosco had Neapolitan troops in entrenched positions. Garibaldi attacked on 20 July 1860 and succeeded in carrying the entrenchments as the royal troops fell back to Messina. A month later Garibaldi would cross from that town to the Italian mainland.

Minden I (*Germanic Wars of the Roman Empire*), AD 16

Intending to avenge the massacre of the legions of Varus, Emperor Tiberius sent eight Roman legions under his nephew Germanicus Caesar into Germany. Marching north along the Ems river, Germanicus Caesar crossed the Weser at Minden and east of the river encountered a large coalition of Germanic tribes led by Arminius, the conqueror of Varus. On this occasion the legions triumphed on the battlefield. Arminius was wounded and, after fighting off determined attacks on his columns as they withdrew, Germanicus Caesar returned safely to the south. But neither he nor Arminius would fight another major battle, for within five years both were dead.

Minden II (*Seven Years War*), 1759

After the French victory at Bergen in April 1759, the Marquis de Contades advanced north on Hanover with 60,000 men. To bar his way the Duke of Brunswick deployed 45,000 Hanoverian, British and Prussian troops to hold Minden on the Weser river, thirty-five miles south-west of Hanover. On 1 August the two forces came into conflict, and Brunswick detached 10,000 men to threaten the enemy rear. Through a mistaken order the British and Hanoverian infantry advanced on the French cavalry, and this surprise tactic caused the line to break. Only the failure of Lord George Sackville to charge with the cavalry prevented a major victory, an error for which he was later court-martialled. Contades was able to withdraw from the field in an orderly manner, but he had lost 7,000 men in casualties and prisoners plus forty-three guns. For a total 3,000 casualties, half in the ranks of the six British regiments present, Hanover had been saved.

Minsk *(Second World War)*, 1941

In pursuit of the objectives of Operation Barbarossa, the centre of the three-pronged German attack on the Soviet Union advanced rapidly north of the Pripet Marshes towards Minsk, 200 miles inside the frontier. On 27 June 1941 two panzer groups linked up east of the city, so trapping a vast number of Soviet soldiers. Although in the six days' fighting which followed many Russians did break out, when resistance in the pocket ended on 2 July 300,000 had become casualties or prisoners.

Moesia *(Dacian Wars of the Roman Empire)*, AD 89

During the reign of Emperor Domitian the tribes of Dacia, in the area of modern Romania north of the Danube river, united under the leadership of Decebalus, crossed the Danube and invaded the Roman province of Moesia. In AD 87 Cornelius Fuscus was killed at the head of Roman legions attempting to subdue the Dacians. Two years later a Roman army led by Calpurnius Julianus crossed the Danube and defeated the Dacians. Moesia was thus brought fully under Roman control once more, but when Decebalus formed an alliance with Germanic tribes, Domitian negotiated a peace with him, which brought bitter opposition in Rome.

Mogilev *(Napoleonic Wars)*, 1812

As French forces crossed the Niemen river in June 1812 and began to advance on Moscow, Russian troops fell back without risking a major battle. When the right wing of the French advance reached Minsk, it threatened to isolate the Russian Second Army of Prince Bagration. On 23 July, therefore, with 48,000 men Bagration struck north to attack Marshal Davout's III Corps of 25,000 men, who held Mogilev on the Dnieper river. Despite his numerical advantage, Bagration failed to dislodge the French, who incurred 1,000 casualties to the Russian 4,000. However, Bagration then undertook a long counter-march to cross the river below Mogilev and escape serious loss, which would at length adversely affect the French advance in the battles ahead.

Mohacs I *(Ottoman Wars)*, 1526

With Belgrade already under his control, Suleiman the Magnificent gathered a Turkish army of 100,000 and started to advance northwards, causing Louis II of Hungary to assemble an army of 20,000 reinforced by 10,000 Poles and concentrate them at Mohacs on the Danube river, 130 miles east of Agram (Zagreb). On 29 August Louis II attacked the Turks, when they appeared, but his disorganized troops suffered heavy loss. The following day Suleiman counter-attacked with devastating effect and drove the Christians from the field. The allied force lost 10,000 killed, including Louis II and seven bishops, and the Turks went on to take Budapest. With Hungary in his hands, Suleiman now posed a direct threat to Austria and central Europe, and Magyar independence was lost for over a century.

Mohacs II *(Ottoman Wars)*, 1687

Following the Turkish failure to take Vienna in 1683, the Sultan's troops fell back into southern Hungary, harassed by different Christian rulers. Close to the site of Suleiman the Magnificent's victory at Mohacs 160 years before, on 12 August 1687 they were attacked by a strong force under the Duke of Lorraine. Thoroughly defeated, the Turks fled across the Danube, and shortly afterwards discontented elements forced the deposition of Mohammed IV in favour of Suleiman II. The prolonged threat to central Europe had at last been removed and Hungary cleared of the Turks.

Mohi *(Mongol Conquests)*, 1241

Whilst a northern column cleared Poland, which might have menaced their right flank, the main Mongol body under Subotai crossed the Carpathian Mountains into Hungary. To protect his kingdom, Bela IV assembled an army reputed to number 100,000, which caused the Mongols to retire cautiously behind the Sajo river, a tributary of the Tisza. Eagerly pursuing his foe, Bela advanced to Mohi, west of the Sajo, but during the night of 10–11 April 1241 two Mongol detachments crossed the river and attacked the Hungarian flanks at dawn, while Subotai's main force launched missiles over the river. As the Hungarians faltered, the main Mongol body forded the Sajo, and by noon Bela's men had been routed, possibly with as many as 70,000 casualties. This was the summit of the Mongols' achievement west of the Carpathians, for they now separated into raiding bands and soon afterwards returned eastwards to elect a new chief khan on the death of Genghis's son Ogotai.

Mollwitz *(War of the Austrian Succession)*, 1741

Taking advantage of the international political confusion, following Maria Theresa's accession to the Austrian Empire, in December 1740 Frederick the Great advanced into Silesia with 30,000 Prussian troops in support of his claim to the Austrian province. Early in 1741 Count von Neipperg moved to challenge him with 20,000 Austrians. On a snow-covered field at Mollwitz, thirty-five miles south-east of Breslau (Wroclaw), on 10 April 1741 the two armies clashed. The Prussians had sixty cannon to their enemy's eighteen, but the Austrians held an advantage in cavalry, and these quickly drove in the Prussian right. The steady Prussian infantry, making use of oblique order tactics, repulsed persistent enemy charges and then moved forward to outflank the Austrian left. Von Neipperg was forced to retire, leaving about 5,000 casualties and prisoners behind; the Prussians lost some 2,500. This defeat exposed Austrian military weakness and prompted France, Bavaria and Saxony to declare war on the new Empress in pursuit of their separate territorial ambitions. Henceforth, the conflict would no longer be confined to Silesia.

Mondovi *(French Revolutionary Wars)*, 1796

Although he had consolidated the French position in northern Italy by his victory on 15 April 1796 at Dego, east of the Bormida valley and thirty miles west of Genoa, Napoleon still found himself between an Austrian army under Baron de Beaulieu in the east and Sardinian troops led by Victor Amadeus III in the west. Deciding to deal with the Sardinians first, Napoleon turned west and attacked them on 21 April with 36,000 men before the town of Mondovi, ten miles east of Cuneo. The Sardinian force was driven into and beyond the town. Two days later, with his force reduced to half its original 25,000 and the capital of Turin threatened, Victor Amadeus III surrendered his army and came to terms with the victor, leaving Napoleon free to concentrate on the Austrians.

Mons I *(Dutch War of Louis XIV)*, 1678

Although peace terms had been agreed on 10 August 1678, William of Orange believed himself betrayed and four days later attacked French troops near Mons. Caught by surprise, nevertheless the French were rallied by the Duke of Luxembourg and inflicted heavy loss on the Dutch, who were repulsed. This action saw the opening of the military career of Luxembourg, and despite the Dutch attack the Peace of Nymwegen (Nijmegen) was signed the following year to end seven years of war.

Mons II *(First World War)*, 1914

As the Germans swept through Belgium in accordance with the Schlieffen Plan, on the extreme left of the Allied line the British Expeditionary Force of four divisions (70,000 men and 300 guns) took up position at Mons, thirty-five miles beyond Charleroi. On 23 August it was attacked by the German First Army of 160,000 men and 600 guns. Though hopelessly outnumbered, for nine hours the British held their ground, suffering 4,244 casualties before retreating in good order. Even this short delay in the German advance allowed units in the rear to reform, but the price was a heavy one for the British regular army to pay.

Mons Badonicus *(Rise of England)*, *c.*500

Once the Romans had withdrawn from Britain early in the fifth century, English tribes from the continent of Europe invaded. According to legend, King Arthur rallied opposition to the invaders and fought a series of battles against them, the greatest of which was Mon Badonicus about 500, in which the English advance in southern Britain was halted for fifty years. The location of this battle is obscure, though there is evidence to suggest that it was on the Wiltshire Downs.

Mons-en-Pévèle *(Franco–Flemish Wars)*, 1304

Determined to avenge his defeat at Courtrai two years earlier, in 1304 Philip the Fair despatched another French army into Flanders. On 18 August it met a Flemish force at Mons-en-Pévèle, but this time the Flemings did not enjoy good defensive cover. Despite brave fighting by their infantry the French cavalry broke through the Flemish line and used sword and lance effectively to cut down those who fled. Some 6,000 Flemings fell, French pride was restored, and at the ensuing peace Philip gained a number of French-speaking towns in the north-east of his country.

Mons Graupius *(Roman Conquest of Britain)*, AD 84

During the reign of Emperor Domitian, Caledonian tribes in the Highlands of Scotland swept into Lowland areas and prompted Gnaeus Julius Agricola, Roman governor of Britain, to lead an expedition to subdue them. At Mons Graupius in the Highlands the legions encountered 30,000 Caledonians led by Calgacus and utterly routed them, killing one-third. At a cost of 360 Roman lives the immediate trouble had been quelled, but Agricola could not afford to garrison northern Scotland, which never knew permanent Roman occupation. A corruption of the name of this battle later gave rise to 'Grampian' and hence 'Grampian Mountains'.

Montebello *(Napoleonic Wars)*, 1800

Not knowing that General Masséna had evacuated Genoa the previous day, on 5 June 1800 General Lannes, in command of the

French advance guard, pressed on over the Lombardy Plain and across the Po river. Fifteen miles south of Pavia, at Montebello, he encountered General Ott with 17,000 Austrians and thirty-five guns marching north after the fall of Genoa. Heavily outnumbered, Lannes fell back until General Victor came up with 6,000 reinforcements. Taking the offensive, the French then drove off the Austrians, who suffered 4,000 casualties to the French 500. Victor's arrival possibly saved Lannes from a heavy reverse and so preserved valuable troops for Napoleon's campaigns later that year.

Montenotte *(French Revolutionary Wars)*, 1796

When Napoleon took over his first major command in Italy on 27 March 1796, his 40,000 men and sixty guns were faced by 30,000 Austrians under Baron de Beaulieu in the east and 25,000 Sardinians in the west, together having 150 guns. Determined to prevent a junction of these two bodies, on 12 April Napoleon launched General La Haye with 9,000 men against the Austrian right of 6,000 under Count von Argenteau occupying the heights of Montenotte, fifteen miles north-west of Savona on the Gulf of Genoa. As La Haye carried out a frontal attack, General Masséna worked his way round the enemy right, and by dawn on 13 April von Argenteau had only 700 men directly under his command, having suffered 2,500 casualties and had the rest of his force dispersed. This victory, Napoleon's first in high command, cut communications between the two enemy forces and left him free to concentrate on the Sardinian army, as originally planned.

Montereau *(Napoleonic Wars)*, 1814

After checking the allied advance on Paris in the Marne valley, Napoleon hurried south to defeat Prince von Schwarzenberg's army at Mormant on 17 February 1814, prompting von Schwarzenberg to retire and to leave a rearguard to defend the village of Montereau at the junction of the Seine and Yonne rivers. On 18 February French cavalry under General Gérard, supported by field artillery, captured the village, causing 5,000 allied casualties and capturing fifteen guns. This relieved immediate pressure south-east of Paris, but it proved only a minor setback to the allied advance. Nevertheless, once more the determination of Napoleon to fight bitterly for his capital was demonstrated.

Montfaucon *(Franco–Norman Wars)*, 886

Norman invaders made frequent incursions into French territory to the south, and in 885 one such foray led them to the walls of Paris. Unable to take the city, they began to besiege it. Charles the Fat refused to take the field against the invaders, but Eudes (Odo), Count of Paris, raised a force to challenge them at Montfaucon, fifteen miles north-west of Verdun. Here in 886 the invaders were routed with heavy loss, and Paris was saved. For his failure to defend the kingdom, Charles the Fat was deposed the following year.

Montiel *(Castilian Civil Wars)*, 1369

When Edward the Black Prince and his English troops, who had secured Pedro I, 'the Cruel', on the throne of Castile and Leon, withdrew across the Pyrenees after disagreement with the Castilians, rebellion broke out against Pedro. Aided by French soldiers under Bertrand du Guesclin, Henry of Trastamara took the field against royal troops at Montiel (seventy miles south-east of Ciudad Real) in 1369. Pedro I was killed and his army utterly defeated. Trastamara was proclaimed king, and Guesclin returned to harass the English in Aquitaine, safe in the knowledge that he possessed a firm ally south of the Pyrenees.

Montijo *(Spanish–Portuguese Wars)*, 1644

After sixty years of Spanish domination the Portuguese declared themselves independent in 1640, but the new king, John IV, soon found himself the target of numerous Spanish plots. In 1644 a Portuguese army led by General d'Albuquerque crossed the border and defeated the Spanish at Montijo, eighteen miles north-east of Badajoz. Although this secured peace for the remainder of John's reign, his successors faced more Spanish threats, and not until 1668 did Spain formally accept Portuguese independence.

Montlhéry *(Franco–Burgundian War)*, 1465

Long-standing enmity between Burgundy and France erupted into open conflict, and in 1465 Charles the Bold, Duke of Burgundy, joined an anti-French league with the Dukes of Alençon, Berry, Bourbon and Lorraine, whose army faced that of Louis XI at Montlhéry, fifteen miles south of Paris in July. The French were defeated, and Louis was obliged to sign the Treaty of Conflans. By diplomatic manœuvres, however, Louis XI was soon able to expose the fragility of the alliance and cause it to disintegrate.

Mookerheide *(Revolt of the Netherlands)*, 1574

With a force of some 8,000 patriots, Prince Louis and Prince Henry of Nassau, brothers of William the Silent, were holding Mookerheide on the Meuse river, when on 14 April 1574 they were attacked by 5,000 Spaniards. The poorly armed Dutch were routed with possibly 4,000 casualties and the certain death of both brothers.

Morat *(Swiss–Burgundian Wars)*, 1476

Despite defeat at Grandson in March, Charles the Bold of Burgundy marched some 20,000 mercenaries into Switzerland to lay siege to Morat on the eastern shore of Lake Morat. The Burgundian force failed to detect the arrival of a superior Swiss army, which struck its left flank decisively on 22 June 1476. The besiegers were quickly driven from their positions, many were caught on the plain in a determined pursuit, and others were trapped on the shores of the lake. Swiss chroniclers claim that 8,000 of the enemy were killed to some 500 Swiss. Certainly Charles the Bold was compelled to withdraw into Lorraine, and Swiss morale rose perceptibly.

Morgarten *(Austro–Swiss Wars)*, 1315

In the dispute between rival claimants to the Holy Roman Emperor, the Swiss cantons supported Louis IV of Bavaria against the Habsburg Frederick the Handsome, and thus Frederick's brother, Archduke Leopold, advanced into Switzerland with 15,000 men. On 15 November 1315 1,500 Swiss infantry ambushed the Austrian column in the narrow pass of Morgarten, at the southern end of Lake Ageri. Rolling boulders and tree trunks down the steep slopes, the Swiss caused utter confusion in the enemy ranks; then they advanced to cut down the Austrians as they fled. This battle not only established the reputation of the Swiss infantry but demonstrated the wisdom of fighting on ground of one's own choosing.

Mortimer's Cross *(Wars of the Roses)*, 1461

Following their victory at Wakefield in December 1460, Lancastrians planned to march on London and free Henry VI from Yorkist control. A second Lancastrian force under the Earls of Pembroke and Wiltshire marched from Wales, aiming to join the advance. On 2 February 1461 this second body met a Yorkist army under Edward, Duke of York (the future Edward IV), at Mortimer's Cross, in Herefordshire, and was completely defeated. Many of the defeated, including Owen Tudor, grandfather of the future Henry VII, were beheaded, and Edward then marched eastwards to join the Earl of Warwick, who was preparing to block the main Lancastrian advance in London.

Mortlack *(Danish Invasion of Scotland)*, 1010

Danish raids on the east coast of Scotland threatened to result in permanent occupation, and in 1010 Malcolm II called out every available man to repel the incursion of Danes under Sweyn I 'Forkbeard'. At Mortlack (forty miles north-west of Aberdeen) in a desperate battle the Scots overcame the invaders and forced them to flee to their ships. In later years a monument was raised at Dufftown to this decisive victory, for defeat would inevitably have led to a permanent Danish foothold in Scotland.

Moscow *(Second World War)*, 1941

Having been halted near Smolensk whilst the capture of Kiev in the south was completed, sixty divisions of Army Group Centre commanded by Field-Marshal von Bock resumed the German advance on Moscow on 2 October 1941 in a bid to cover the last 200 miles before winter closed in. On the right General Guderian's

Second Panzer Group moved forward through Orel towards Tula, 100 miles south of Moscow. In the centre Vyazma fell and, as the Third and Fourth Panzer Groups swung north to take Kalinin above Moscow on 15 October, the Ninth Army pushed forward to within forty miles of the capital. Heavy rain and dogged Russian resistance slowed progress early in November, and on 20 November a sudden drop in temperature froze the quagmires overnight, four days after the Germans had launched a major assault. Tula in the south was surrounded but did not fall; units of the Fourth Army penetrated the suburbs to come within sight of the Kremlin, but determined defence by soldiers and civilians pushed them back after two days. By 5 December the German attack had ground to a halt, and next day, using huge pincers from the flanks, General Zhukov counter-attacked with winter-trained troops from Siberia. One hundred new Russian divisions came into the line to recapture Kaluga, Kalinin, Vyazma and Rzhev. By 15 January 1942 the Russians had advanced some 100 miles west of Moscow, and the Germans had lost their first major battle of the Second World War on land.

Mount Tifata *(Civil Wars of the Roman Republic)*, 83 BC

Following successful conclusion of the First Mithridatic War, Lucius Cornelius Sulla landed at Brundisium (Brindisi), on the south-eastern coast of Italy, in the spring of 83 BC. He was not welcomed triumphantly, and an army under Caius Norbanus took position to bar his advance on Rome. Advancing northwards cautiously, Sulla encountered the hostile force at Mount Tifata, east of Capua and forty miles north-east of Naples. Sulla's veterans were completely successful, wintered in Capua and resumed their march successfully to take Rome the following year.

Mount Vesuvius *(Third Servile War)*, 75–71 BC

For the third time in its history the Roman Empire faced an uprising of the slaves which it controlled when in 73 BC the Thracian slave Spartacus gained control of the area of Mount Vesuvius, ten miles south-east of Naples. Thousands of fugitive slaves then turned this into an armed sanctuary, which two separate assaults by Marcus Licinius Crassus could not capture. At length in 71 BC Pompey successfully overran the rebels, killed Spartacus and executed other leaders.

Mühlberg *(War of the Schmalkaldic League)*, 1547

In his drive to reunite the Holy Roman Empire and re-establish Catholicism during the period of the Reformation, Charles V encountered opposition from the Schmalkaldic League of Protestant princes. The League was weakened by internal disagreements, and Charles was able to subdue princes in southern Germany, then turn north to deal with the Elector of Saxony and Philip of Hesse. Crossing the Elbe, a force of 13,000 Imperial and papal troops attacked the combined army of the two rulers at Mühlberg, thirty-five miles east of Leipzig, on 24 April 1547. The Protestants were defeated and the two leaders taken prisoner. Although both men were forced to make concessions to the Emperor, the Reformation could not be quelled at this late stage, and full Catholic control over northern Germany would never be re-established.

Mühldorf *(War of the Imperial Succession)*, 1322

After nine years of dispute, armies of the two claimants to the Holy Roman Empire met at Mühldorf, on the Inn river forty-five miles east of Munich. Louis of Bavaria triumphed and the Habsburg Frederick the Handsome was imprisoned until three years later he became joint Emperor with Louis, as Frederick III.

Münchengrätz *(Austro–Prussian War)*, 1866

Shortly after the outbreak of war, as the Prussian First Army of Prince Frederick Charles and the Army of the Elbe commanded by General von Bittenfeld (together totalling 140,000 men) advanced through the mountain passes of Bohemia, they encountered an Austrian advance corps under Count von Clam-Gallas. At Münchengrätz (Mnichovo Hradiste, forty miles north-east of Prague) on 28 June the Austrians were driven back for the loss of 300 casualties and 1,000 prisoners, and, after a second skirmish, they withdrew to the area between Sadowa and Königgrätz, where the decisive battle of the short war would soon be fought.

Munda *(Wars of the First Triumvirate)*, 45 BC

In 45 BC Julius Caesar could claim mastery of the west except for Spain, where Gnaeus and Sextus, sons of the late Pompey, were fomenting rebellion. Julius Caesar marched a reinforcement army to join Roman legions already in the peninsula and brought the enemy to battle at Munda, in the south, on 17 March. Through skilful manœuvring Julius Caesar compensated for his deficiency in numbers, and the supporters of Pompey were routed with the loss of some 20,000 in casualties and prisoners. Sextus escaped, but Gnaeus was captured and executed. For the loss of 1,000 casualties in this, his last, battle Julius Caesar had ended resistance in Spain.

Muret *(Albigensian Crusade)*, 1213

In response to a call from the Pope to deal with the Albigenses, heretics in the south, Simon de Montfort took charge of Catholic crusaders from the north of France. In a savage battle at Muret (ten miles south of Toulouse) in September 1213, the Albigenses, led by Raimond VI, Count of Toulouse, were defeated and the way was opened for French domination of the south-west, as Pedro II of Aragon, who supported the Albigenses, fell in the battle and Castilian interest north of the Pyrenees now faded.

Mursa *(Civil Wars of the Roman Empire)*, 351

While Constantius II was campaigning in Persia, his brother Constans, ruler of the Western Roman Empire, was deposed by Flavius Popilius Magnentius. Hurrying back from his campaign, with 40,000 men Constantius met Magnentius with a force of 50,000 at Mursa (at the junction of the Drave and Danube rivers) on 28 September 351. Magnentius suffered 12,000 casualties, Constantius almost 15,000, but Magnentius was forced to withdraw from the field, and two years later he committed suicide, which allowed reunification of the Empire under Constantius.

Mutina *(Civil Wars of the Roman Republic)*, 43 BC

The assassination of Julius Caesar on 15 March 44 BC resulted in a struggle for power between Romans. In the course of this Mark

Antony laid siege to Mutina (Modena), 200 miles north of Rome, with four legions in an attempt to overcome opposition from Decimus Brutus. On 14 April 43 BC the besiegers were attacked by three armies under Octavian, Aulus Hirtius and Vibius Pansa, but Antony's men held their ground, killing Pansa. A week later a second attempt to relieve Mutina was successful, although Hirtius fell in this action, and Antony fled into Gaul to form an alliance with Lepidus. In November they were joined by Octavian and officially formed the Second Triumvirate.

Mytilene *(Great Peloponnesian War)*, 427 BC

Relying on Spartan assistance, the island of Lesbos rebelled against Athenian control in 428 BC. Before the Spartans could act, however, Paches reached Lesbos, landed 1,000 hoplites and began an Athenian siege of the city of Mytilene. A desultory attempt at relief was made by Alcidas, but in May 427 BC Mytilene surrendered. All males were condemned to death, though only the leaders of the revolt were executed.

Myton *(Anglo–Scottish Wars)*, 1319

A year after Robert Bruce captured Berwick-on-Tweed, the last English stronghold in Scotland, Edward II laid siege to the fortress. In an effort to divert the attention of the besiegers, Sir James Douglas led a Scottish column south into Yorkshire, where the Archbishop of York hastily assembled a defensive force. On 20 September 1319 the two bodies clashed at Myton, near the Swale river, where the Scots triumphed. As the Archbishop's men included a number of priests and monks, the Scots dubbed this battle 'the chapter of Myton'. The defeat prompted Edward II to raise the siege of Berwick through fear of Scottish activity south of the border.

Näfels *(Austro–Swiss Wars)*, 1388

Invading Switzerland for the third time in the fourteenth century, the Austrians penetrated into Glarus canton. In a battle very much like that at Morgarten in 1315, less than 1,000 Swiss ambushed 6,000 Austrians at Näfels, south of Lake Wallen, on 9 April 1388.

After disorganizing the invaders by rolling boulders down on them, the Swiss infantry attacked and put the enemy to flight. This victory discouraged the Austrians from further major incursions, and six years later they agreed that the cantons should become part of the Holy Roman Empire, taking them a step closer to complete independence.

Naissus *(Gothic Invasions of the Roman Empire)*, 269

In 268 a horde of 300,000 Goths swarmed into Asia Minor and the Balkans, threatening the security of the Roman Empire. The following year Emperor Claudius II marched into the area of modern Yugoslavia at the head of a strong Roman force and met a large body of Goths at Naissus (Nis), eighty-five miles north-west of Sofia. The legions were hard pressed until 5,000 men, whom Claudius had concealed in the mountains in the enemy rear, attacked. In the confusion the Goths were routed, with the loss of some 50,000 casualties, and for his success Claudius was named 'Gothicus'.

Nájera *(Hundred Years War)*, 1367

When Pedro I, 'the Cruel', of Castile and Leon, was challenged by his brother, assisted by French troops under Bertrand du Guesclin, as Prince of Aquitaine Edward the Black Prince went to his aid. At Nájera (Naverrete), fifty miles east of the Castilian capital of Burgos, on 3 April 1367 the rebel force was defeated. But the Black Prince soon quarrelled with Pedro I, and the intervention brought no real advantage to the English.

Namur I *(War of the Grand Alliance)*, 1695

A key point at the junction of the Sambre and Meuse rivers, the city of Namur was taken by the French after a thirty-six-day siege in 1692. Three years later, encouraged by the death of the Duke of Luxembourg and his replacement as commander of the French forces by the less able Duke of Villeroi, William III decided to recapture the city. With the aid of Baron von Coehoorn, the Dutch engineer who had fortified Namur, he attacked in July and finally brought about its surrender on 1 September. The cost of such an operation may be gauged by the fact that the French defenders had only half the 18,000 casualties suffered by the besieging forces.

Namur II *(First World War)*, 1914

In the German advance during the opening weeks of the First World War, General Karl von Bülow's Second Army reached Namur, forty miles south-east of Brussels, on 20 August 1914. Taking his main force across the Sambre above the city, von Bülow detached troops to invest this last stronghold barring the way into France. Garrisoned by 37,000 Belgians, defended by a circle of strong forts and further protected by minefields, trenches and wire fences, Namur appeared impregnable. But it was no proof against 100,000 Germans supported by the 420 mm and 305 mm siege weapons which had reduced Liège. In conjunction with 400 other heavy guns, the siege cannon fired two-ton shells into the fortifications, and on 25 August the inevitable surrender occurred.

Nancy *(Swiss–Burgundian Wars)*, 1477

Driven from Switzerland in 1476, Charles the Bold, Duke of Burgundy, took up a strong defensive position at Nancy in Lorraine, seventy miles west of Strasbourg. Here he was attacked on 5 January 1477 by the Swiss, who successfully carried the Burgundian position by an outflanking movement. In the fighting Charles was killed, and this battle effectively ended the power of Burgundy, which was incorporated into France shortly afterwards.

Naroch Lake *(First World War)*, 1916

In response to appeals from France, the Russians launched an attack on German lines at Naroch Lake in White Russia, north of the Pripet Marshes. On 18 March 1916 the Tenth Army attacked and initially made progress. But the deficiencies of the Russian artillery, well-directed German counter-attacks and a change of weather, which turned the terrain into marsh, meant that the advance petered out on 26 March, having cost 100,000 Russian casualties to no positive avail. German forces had not been drawn away from the Western Front, and the Russians had lost invaluable troops.

Narva *(Great Northern War)*, 1700

In 1700 40,000 Russian troops under Prince Dolgoruky were besieging the Swedish-held city of Narva in modern Estonia. On 30 November Charles XII landed 8,000 troops nearby and attacked the Russian entrenchments during a snowstorm. Although some Russians showed determination, the smaller Swedish force raised the siege in three hours for the loss of under 1,000 casualties to 10,000 Russians. This decisive reverse had an important effect on the Russian army, which was thoroughly reorganized by the Tsar, Peter I.

Naseby *(English Civil War)*, 1645

In the spring of 1645 Charles I marched north from Oxford, seeking to recover prestige lost following his defeat at Marston Moor the previous year. After taking Leicester, his 9,000 men advanced through Market Harborough and took up a strong defensive position on a ridge one mile north of the village of Naseby in Northamptonshire, where they were challenged by Sir Thomas Fairfax and 13,000 Parliamentarians on 14 June. Early exchanges were indecisive until Prince Rupert, mistaking a tactical withdrawal for retreat, led the Royalist cavalry against the enemy left and, gaining rapid success, foolishly pressed his pursuit at a time when the remainder of the Royalist line was under attack. The Royalist left and centre then broke, and Charles' force lost its artillery, baggage and almost 5,000 casualties. This defeat ensured that the Royalist cause would not eventually triumph.

Nechtanesmere *(Northumbrian Invasion of Scotland)*, 685

Under Ecgfrith Northumbrian forces advanced into Scotland until on 20 May 685 they met a Pict army at Nechtanesmere, near modern Forfar. Ecgfrith was killed and Northumbrian expansion halted at the Firth of Forth.

Neerwinden I *(War of the Grand Alliance)*, 1693

Under the direct command of William III an allied army took up a strong defensive position, with its flanks protected by streams, at the village of Neerwinden, north-west of Liège. Here it was attacked on 29 July 1693 by the Duke of Luxembourg with some 40,000 French troops. When the French launched a fierce assault on the centre of the line, William reinforced the threatened area from the wings, giving Luxembourg the opportunity to commit his reserves against the weakened flanks. Due to the personal bravery of William, the allies managed to execute a successful retreat, although many men were drowned in the Landen and Geete rivers. William lost 18,000 casualties and 104 guns, the French suffered less than 10,000 casualties. This was Luxembourg's last major battle before his death.

Neerwinden II *(French Revolutionary Wars)*, 1793

Following the execution of Louis XVI in January 1793, the French faced a hostile alliance of the main European countries. Nevertheless, General Dumouriez launched an offensive into the Low Countries and at Neerwinden, twenty-two miles north-west of Liège, encountered an Austrian army nominally under the command of the Prince of Saxe-Coburg. On 18 March Dumouriez was severely beaten; the Austrians recaptured Brussels and drove the French out of the Austrian Netherlands. After this defeat Dumouriez changed to the allied side.

Nemecky Brod *(Hussite Wars)*, 1422

After his defeat at Kutna Hora, the Holy Roman Emperor Sigismund withdrew south-eastwards pursued by 10,000 Hussites under Jan Žižka. 23,000 Imperial troops were caught and attacked at Nemecky Brod on 10 January 1422 and put to flight with an estimated 10,000 casualties. The victorious Hussites soon quarrelled between themselves over doctrinal differences, and Žižka died in 1424; nevertheless, resistance to the Catholic Empire continued and at length in 1436 a measure of religious autonomy was secured for Hussite Bohemia.

Neuve-Chapelle *(First World War)*, 1915

Faced by French criticism of British inactivity and a demand that his forces should resume full responsibility for the Ypres salient, the British commander-in-chief Sir John French determined to launch a narrow-front attack on Neuve-Chapelle, fifteen miles south-west of Lille. Thus on 10 March 1915, preceded by a short but massive artillery bombardment, the British First Army advanced towards the village, which was quickly taken. Extension of the original front, inadequate artillery support for the new areas and a delay in bringing up reserves allowed the Germans to reorganize. By 13 March 16,000 further German troops had been brought up, and the attack soon ground to a halt with very little territorial advantage gained. British casualties numbered 13,000, and this failure contributed to a public outcry in the United Kingdom about the shortage of shells on the Western Front.

Neuwied *(French Revolutionary Wars)*, 1797

Whilst one Austrian army was engaged in Italy in 1797, commanded by General Werneck, another was stationed in the Rhineland. On 18 April a large French force under General Hoche attacked Werneck's army at Neuwied, seven miles north-west of Coblenz. Driven from the field, the Austrians fell back across the Lahn river, losing several thousand casualties and most of their artillery. On the same day the Austrians concluded a truce with Napoleon at Leoben.

Neville's Cross *(Anglo–Scottish Wars)*, 1346

Taking advantage of the absence of Edward III, who was on the Continent fighting in the Hundred Years War, David II of Scotland led a force into northern England. Challenged by levies under Barons Percy and Neville, the Scots took up a defensive position at Neville's Cross in Durham. They were attacked by the English on 17 October 1346 and overwhelmed, after first being disorganized by archers and spearmen. David II was captured and held for ransom, but this reverse did not end Scottish resistance.

Newburn *(First Bishops' War)*, 1640

During the so-called Bishops' War, due to Scottish rejection of Anglican episcopacy, a Scottish force under Alexander Leslie crossed the Tweed into Northumberland. At Newburn on the

Tyne near Newcastle on 28 August 1640, Leslie encountered an inferior royal force led by Viscount Conway. The raw English levies were thoroughly disorganized by a heavy bombardment from the Scottish artillery and abandoned their positions, having suffered few casualties. Subsequently Newcastle was evacuated and Charles I came to terms with the Scots.

Newbury I *(English Civil War)*, 1643

At Newbury in Berkshire, fifty-three miles west of London, 14,000 Parliamentarian troops under the Earl of Essex intercepted a similar number of Royalists led by Charles I, who were marching on the capital from the west of England. On 20 September 1643 the two armies fought an indecisive battle, in which the Royalist cavalry and Parliamentarian infantry distinguished themselves. During the night, however, Charles retired from the field, leaving his enemy in secure possession of London.

Newbury II *(English Civil War)*, 1644

Once more, in 1644, Charles I marched on London from the west with 9,000 men and was again checked at Newbury. Here on 27 October he failed to pass a Parliamentarian force twice the size of his own under the Earls of Essex and Manchester. As on the first occasion the year before, the Royalists retired from the field during the night, but this battle gave impetus to a reorganization of the Parliamentarian forces under Sir Thomas Fairfax and Oliver Cromwell rather than Essex and Manchester.

New Carthage *(Second Punic War)*, 209 BC

In 210 BC Publius Cornelius Scipio (later Scipio Africanus) took a Roman force to the Carthaginian colony of Spain to avenge the death of his father and uncle at the hands of Hannibal's two brothers, Hasdrubal and Mago. The following year the young commander led his men down the east coast to surprise the enemy stronghold of New Carthage (Cartagena), which was successfully stormed in seven hours. This was the first important victory for young Scipio.

Nicopolis *(Ottoman Wars)*, 1396

Alarmed by the growing Ottoman menace in south-eastern Europe, Sigismund of Hungary gathered a force of some 50,000 men on the Danube in the spring of 1396, reinforced by 2,000 French led by the Duke of Nevers. Advancing down the Danube from Buda, this body laid siege to Nicopolis (Nikopol), in Bulgaria, on the southern bank of the Danube twenty miles north-east of Plevna in September 1396. Bajazet I hurried from his own siege of Constantinople, reaching the plain of Nicopolis four miles south of the city on 25 September. Without waiting for support, French cavalry charged the Ottoman ranks, broke through initially, then encountered determined defence from the Janissaries. Once the French had been scattered, the Turks fell upon the Hungarians, killing a large number and capturing some 10,000. Only a few of the Christian nobles including Nevers were spared for ransom; the rest of the prisoners were executed. Meanwhile Sigismund had escaped in a galley via the Danube into the Black Sea, and the crusade against Turkey had ended in ignominy.

Nieuwpoort *(Revolt of the Netherlands)*, 1600

In late June 1600 Maurice of Nassau deployed some 11,000 men among the sand dunes of Nieuwpoort, ten miles south-west of Ostend, where on 2 July he clashed with a Spanish army of similar size under Archduke Albert of Austria. The Dutch adapted to the broken ground more quickly and through their greater mobility gradually broke the enemy line. Although the Spaniards suffered heavy loss, the battle was indecisive, and next year Maurice could not prevent an investment of Ostend.

Nola *(Second Punic War)*, 215 BC

Hannibal's overwhelming victory at Cannae in 216 BC did not cause the Roman Empire to disintegrate, and he was forced to pay attention to his sea communications with Carthage. From his headquarters at Capua, he therefore set out the following year to capture the port of Naples. Sixteen miles north-east of it, at Nola, he encountered a strong Roman defensive position commanded by Marcus Claudius Marcellus. Hannibal's troops were repulsed from the village and, lacking siege equipment, were obliged to retire. Marcellus had thus inflicted the first defeat on Hannibal in Italy.

Nördlingen I *(Thirty Years War)*, 1634

Early in September 1634 a combined force of 33,000 Imperial and Spanish troops under Archduke Ferdinand (later Ferdinand III) laid siege to Nördlingen, forty miles north-west of Augsburg, as a Protestant army of 25,000 commanded by the Duke of Saxe-Weimar and Field-Marshal Horn advanced to the relief of its Swedish garrison. Ferdinand's men deployed south of the town to meet the Protestants, and during the night of 5–6 September Horn moved his troops towards a dominant hill on the Catholic left. At dawn Horn seized the hill, but a counter-attack recaptured this vital position during the morning, and repeated Swedish assaults were then repulsed. At midday Horn decided to abandon this objective and marched his weary survivors across the rear of Saxe-Weimar's troops, who had been dealing with the main Catholic force. Noting this manœuvre, Ferdinand launched a fierce frontal attack on Saxe-Weimar's line, broke through and attacked the flank of Horn's column. The Protestants were then annihilated: 17,000 were reported dead and 4,000, including Horn, captured. This was a severe blow to the Protestant cause and left the Habsburgs dominant in central Europe, which prompted the French to invervene in support of Sweden in 1635. Thus the events at Nördlingen led to an open clash between the two powerful Catholic dynasties and the end of remaining vestiges of religious purpose in the war.

Nördlingen II *(Thirty Years War)*, 1645

When 15,000 French troops under the Great Condé invaded Bavaria in 1645, the Imperial army of 12,000 led by Baron von Mercy took up position at Allerheim, south-east of Nördlingen, to bar their way to the Danube. On 3 August the French attacked the Imperial position, and after very heavy fighting, in which von Mercy was killed and the defenders suffered over 5,000 casualties, the village was taken. As the Imperial force retreated to the

Danube, the French, who had lost about 4,000 casualties, were too exhausted to pursue, and when Condé fell sick, they retired to Philippsburg on the Rhine. Although peace did not come for another three years, this was the last major encounter of the war.

Normandy *(Second World War)*, 1944

A fifty-mile stretch of the Normandy coast from the base of the Cotentin peninsula eastwards was chosen for Operation Overlord, the Allied invasion of Europe in 1944. Guarding this section of the Atlantic Wall defences was the German Seventh Army, part of Field-Marshal Rommel's Army Group B, though the overall German commander, Field-Marshal von Rundstedt, had a total of thirty-six infantry and six panzer divisions in the northern coastal areas of France. Transported by 4,000 ships and covered by 4,900 fighter aircraft and 5,800 bombers, Allied troops landed on Utah, Omaha, Gold, Juno and Sword beaches at dawn on 6 June, preceded by paratroops dropped during the night to secure vital bridges on the flanks to enable ease of break-out from the beach-heads and prevent German reinforcements menacing the beaches. The three eastern beaches were secured on the first day by the British Second Army, and American forces on Utah rapidly advanced inland. The American 1st Division on Omaha, however, only held on precariously. The landings had been achieved for the loss of 11,000 casualties, including 2,500 dead, on the first day; consolidation of the beachheads then took place. On the right American troops reached the western coast of Cotentin peninsula on 18 June after severe hand-to-hand struggles, finally to take the port of Cherbourg nine days later. Elsewhere German reinforcements caused considerable problems, and in the eleven-day offensive aimed at the town of St-Lô the Americans suffered 11,000 casualties. Not until 20 July did the British Second Army on the Allied left capture Caen and, although four days later the invaders were poised for a major break-out, at this point only one fifth of the designated area had been taken from the Germans, for whom Field-Marshal von Kluge had replaced Rundstedt in command. The first forty-eight days of the fighting in France had cost the Allies an estimated 122,000 casualties and the Germans 117,000. But the beachheads had been secured and German resources, required to cope with the Russian advance in the east,

Allied advance through Italy and the strategic bombing campaign against the homeland, could ill afford such losses.

Northampton *(Wars of the Roses)*, 1460

When the Earl of Warwick landed at Sandwich in June 1460, after returning from his brief exile on the Continent following his defeat at Empingham in March, he prepared for a decisive challenge to Henry VI, who gathered his Lancastrian forces at Northampton, sixty miles north-west of London. Warwick attacked on 10 July before the King had completed his defensive preparations. In the opening assault Sir Edmund Grey betrayed the King and allowed Yorkists to penetrate the line of entrenchments, and the Duke of Buckingham and the majority of Lancastrian nobles perished in the rout which followed. Henry VI was taken prisoner and made to submit to Yorkist control, although his wife, Queen Margaret, soon began to organize another army to fight for his cause.

Novara I *(French Wars in Italy)*, 1513

In 1513 the French faced a re-formed League of Cambrai determined to expel them from northern Italy. As a result on 6 June 13,000 Swiss attacked the camp of the 10,000 French under Louis de la Trémouille, who were defending Novara, twenty-eight miles west of Milan. The defenders were caught by surprise, and through a day of bitter fighting Swiss pikemen gradually gained the ascendancy. Both sides lost about 5,000 men, and many German mercenaries, fighting for the French, surrendered only to be executed by the victors. This reverse forced Louis XII to withdraw his army into France.

Novara II *(Italian Wars of Independence)*, 1849

Seven months after it had been agreed, Charles Albert of Sardinia renounced the armistice with Austria on 12 March 1849. The veteran Austrian commander in Lombardy, Field-Marshal Radetsky, promptly seized Mortara and with 45,000 men prepared to deal with a slightly larger force of Piedmontese at Novara. On 23 March, for the second time in eight months, the Piedmontese were overwhelmed by more disciplined Austrians and driven from the field in disorder. This defeat led to the abdication of Charles Albert and ultimately a peace treaty by which the Austrians received a large indemnity.

Novgorod *(Rise of Russia)*, 862

In the late eighth century Scandanavian vikings, known as Varangians or Rus, began to push south from the Baltic towards the Black Sea. Overrunning Slavonic settlements in their path, in 862 they reached the centre of Novgorod in north-west Russia, 300 miles from Moscow. Led by Rurik, they stormed it, and he founded a line of princes which ruled there for some 700 years.

Novi Ligure *(French Revolutionary Wars)*, 1799

A number of defeats at the hands of Russian and Austrian armies had forced the French to abandon northern Italy in the summer of 1799, with the exception of a bridgehead at Genoa. General Joubert was despatched to ensure that the city did not fall and deployed 35,000 French troops in the Ligurian hills to block the enemy advance. The Russian commander, Count Suvorov, sent a superior Russian and Austrian army against the French entrenchments at Novi Ligure, between Genoa and Alessandria, on 15 August. After sixteen hours, for the loss of some 8,000 casualties and prisoners, allied troops successfully stormed the fortified heights, and General Moreau gathered the scattered remnants of the French army to escape north-eastwards. The French lost 11,000 in casualties and prisoners, including Joubert and four of his divisional commanders killed. This was the last of the battles which in four months had ejected the French from all the territory conquered by Napoleon three years previously.

Numantia *(Lusitanian War)*, 143–133 BC

Occasional revolts occurred against Roman administrators who had assumed control of the Iberian peninsula after the defeat of the Carthaginians. In 143 BC one such revolt, led by Viriathus, became known as the Lusitanian War and was centred on the fortified city of Numantia, in the centre of the Iberian peninsula west of Saragossa. Twice in 141 BC Roman attempts to storm the city were repulsed, tentative peace proposals were rejected and, although Viriathus was assassinated in 140 BC, the revolt continued to flourish. Two successive Roman commanders were defeated by sorties of the garrison and replaced in command. At length, in 133 BC Scipio Aemilianus, grandson of Scipio Africanus, attained command of these besiegers. Fifteen months later the city fell, and for his success Scipio assumed the name 'Numantinus'.

Oberhollabrunn *(Napoleonic Wars)*, 1805

After his capture of Vienna on 13 November 1805, Napoleon turned north with a French army of 110,000 men in an attempt to cut off General Kutuzov's 40,000 Russians in Lower Austria. At Oberhollabrunn, twenty-five miles north of Vienna, on 16 November the French encountered 7,000 Russians deployed by Prince Bagration to halt their advance. Throughout that day two French corps under Marshals Lannes and Soult plus the cavalry of Marshal Murat attempted to clear the way. But, despite losing half his men and being compelled to retire during the night, Bagration delayed Napoleon's advance long enough for Kutuzov to withdraw safely to the east and regroup.

Olmütz *(Seven Years War)*, 1758

After retaking Schweidnitz and thus clearing Silesia of enemy forces, at the opening of the third year of the war Frederick the Great marched into Moravia and laid siege to Olmütz (Olomouc) on the March river, 120 miles south-west of Cracow, in May 1758 with 40,000 men. He had insufficient troops to invest the town completely, so the Austrian commander, Count von Daun, was able both to keep the garrison supplied and to harass the Prussian lines of communication, which proved particularly vulnerable. In June the Austrians cut off 4,000 waggons bringing up supplies of ammunition, so that on 1 July after seven weeks Frederick was forced to raise the siege. As he withdrew into Bohemia, his baggage train of some 5,000 waggons required a strong military escort, which weakened his main army. Frederick's failure at Olmütz demonstrated the danger of fighting at a distance from magazines and the vulnerability of ponderous supply trains protected by insufficient troops.

Oltenita *(Crimean War)*, 1853

Following Russian occupation of the provinces of Moldavia and Wallachia in July, three months later the Turkish Empire declared war and sent Omar Pasha with an army over the Danube. At Oltenita, at the junction of the Arges and Danube rivers, with a superior force Omar Pasha defeated a body of Russian troops on 4 November 1853. This provided an important boost to Turkish morale, being the first major victory over the Russians in nearly a hundred years.

Oporto *(Peninsular War)*, 1809

Once the remnants of Sir John Moore's force had been evacuated from Corunna in January 1809, few British troops were left in Portugal, and the French under Marshal Soult advanced to take Oporto, 170 miles north-east of Lisbon in March. The following month, however, Sir Arthur Wellesley took command of the British forces and with 30,000 men marched north from the Portuguese capital. Crossing the Douro river at night, he surprised Soult at Oporto on 12 May and recaptured the city with minor loss. The French suffered considerably more casualties than Wellesley in the battle and subsequent retreat into the mountains, and the British were now encouraged to invade Spain for the second time.

Orleans *(Hundred Years War)*, 1428–9

With most of France north of the Loire river in English hands, on 23 October 1428 with 5,000 men the Earl of Salisbury laid siege to Orleans, on the north bank of the Loire, sixty-five miles south of Paris, still loyal to the Dauphin. With strongpoints on the south bank and the island of Tourelles in the river under his control, Salisbury established an arc of six stockaded posts round the town on the north bank of the river and proceeded to bombard Orleans at leisure. Although Salisbury was killed and replaced in command by the Duke of Suffolk, the French showed little sign of raising the siege until Joan of Arc set out with a force from Blois, thirty-two miles to the south-west, on 25 April 1429. Persuading other French commanders to attack English positions south of the river and on Tourelles, she succeeded in driving off the English and raising the siege on 8 May. For on that day, demoralized by the failure of their fellows to the south, the English burnt their stockaded posts north of the river, and the siege of Orleans came to an end. This success proved an immense morale-booster to the French, established Joan of Arc's military reputation and effectively put her on the road to martyrdom at the stake in Rouen two years later.

Ostend *(Revolt of the Netherlands)*, 1601–4

Defeated in Nieuwpoort in 1600, the following year Archduke Albert of Austria marched north to Ostend and, unable to take it on 5 July 1601, began a regular siege. Although Maurice of Nassau found it impossible to relieve the city, the garrison held out stubbornly. Not until 14 September 1604 did Spaniards, under the Marquis of Spinola, finally fight their way in, and by this time scarcely a house remained undamaged. The besiegers suffered heavy loss, but their ultimate success reinforced Spanish hold over the southern provinces of the Netherlands.

Otterburn *(Anglo–Scottish Wars)*, 1388

Aided by a force of French troops, in 1388 the Earl of Douglas crossed into northern England with a Scottish army. Sir Henry Percy (Hotspur) gathered some 9,000 men in Northumberland to oppose them but on 15 August rashly attacked the inferior Franco–Scottish body in camp at Otterburn, between Newcastle and Jedburgh. Although Douglas was killed, the Scottish spearmen drove back the English and inflicted 2,000 casualties upon them. Percy was captured and later ransomed. After this victory, celebrated in the ballads *Otterburn* and *Chevy Chase*, the Scots were free to ravage at will in the border area until the turn of the century.

Oudenarde *(War of the Spanish Succession)*, 1708

With Bruges and Ghent in French hands, the Duke of Vendôme marched towards Oudenarde, thirty-two miles west of Brussels. This manœuvre caused the Duke of Marlborough and Prince Eugène to hurry westwards from Brussels at the head of 80,000 English, Dutch and Imperial troops. After marching fifty miles in sixty-five hours, the allies crossed the Scheldt river below Oude-narde on 11 July 1707 and caught Vendôme's 100,000 men by surprise. Sending Prince Eugène against the French left, Marlborough himself held the enemy in the centre and sent Field-Marshal Overkirk (Ouwerkerk) and a Dutch force to outflank the French right. By sundown the two allied wings had almost enveloped half the enemy force, and the French withdrew from the field, having suffered 6,000 casualties and lost 7,000 prisoners. At a cost of 3,000 casualties the Battle of Oudenarde had regained for the allies the strategic initiative in Flanders.

Ourique *(Rise of Portugal)*, 1139

As a reward for his efforts against the Moors, Henry of Burgundy was created Count of Portugal by Alfonso VI of Castile and Leon in 1094. After Henry's death his son, Alfonso Henriques, launched a campaign against the infidel and in 1139 attacked the Moorish fortress of Ourique, thirty miles south-west of Bela, in the south-west of modern Portugal. The young Count won an outstanding victory and proclaimed himself Alfonso I, king of an independent Portugal. Four years later this position was recognized by Castile and the Pope.

Pandosia *(Macedonian Conquests)*, 331 BC

Greek inhabitants of the southern city of Tarentum (Taranto), known as Italiotes, had long been at war with the state of Lucania to the west when Alexander of Epirus, uncle of Alexander the Great, brought a force across the Ionian Sea to their aid. After initial success, Alexander clashed with the Lucanian army at Pandosia in 331 BC. During the battle he was assassinated, reputedly by an exiled Lucanian, and the Italiotes were driven back into Tarentum, with their hopes of expansion dashed.

Panormus *(First Punic War)*, 251 BC

Three years after the Romans seized Panormus (Palermo), on the north-west coast of Sicily, the Carthaginian capital in Sicily, Hasdrubal (son of Hanno) took steps to recover it. As the Carthaginians approached, Lucius Caecilius Metellus attacked with light troops, which retired into the city when challenged strongly. The elephants which pursued them plunged into a deep ditch around Panormus, and many were killed, as Metellus led his legionaries out of the city to strike the Carthaginian flank. Hasdrubal was forced to retreat with the loss of all his elephants.

Paris I *(Napoleonic Wars)*, 1814

While Napoleon was striking east of Paris, four allied columns under Prince von Schwarzenberg converged on the capital, causing Marshal Marmont to fall back into the city with a few thousand regulars to join with 20,000 regulars and National Guardsmen already there. At dawn on 30 March 1814 three allied columns attacked French positions at Vincennes, Belleville and Montmartre, whilst the fourth attempted to outflank the Montmartre lines. The defenders fought hard under Marmont and Marshal Mortier, but in the early hours of 1 April, with the Montmartre lines turned and 4,000 casualties incurred, the city fell. The allies suffered 8,000 casualties, but Napoleon was persuaded that further resistance was hopeless. Five days later he therefore abdicated in favour of his son.

Paris II *(Franco–Prussian War)*, 1870–71

With Napoleon III overwhelmed at Sedan and with Metz under siege, 146,000 Prussians commanded by Count von Moltke surrounded Paris on 20 September 1870. Inside were some 170,000 troops under General Trochu, but two attempts to break out were foiled, and on 27 December almost 200 Prussian guns began to bombard the city. In three weeks an estimated 12,000 shells were fired, claiming 365 casualties. With food supplies low and after suffering 28,450 military casualties, on 28 January 1871 Paris surrendered. Ten days earlier, in the Hall of Mirrors at Versailles, William I of Prussia had been proclaimed Emperor of Germany.

Paris III *(Commune Uprising)*, 1871

In favour of continuing the war against Prussia, the population of Paris and the National Guard opposed the National Assembly's decision to accept peace terms on 1 March 1871. When French troops sent to suppress the rebels actually fraternized with them, they were withdrawn to Versailles, where the government of the Third Republic sat, and Paris was left in rebel hands. On 28 March the Central Committee of the National Guard resigned and was replaced by an elected Commune. However, the French government were soon able to use released prisoners of war to challenge its control. On 21 May 130,000 troops under Marshal MacMahon fought their way into the city and for a week were met with fierce resistance from 30,000 National Guardsmen and armed citizens, who fought from behind barricades and numerous vantage-points. Eventually Paris was taken at a cost of 873 government troops dead, though over 20,000 Communards were either killed or executed during the fighting and another 10,000 were to be executed or imprisoned later. The damage to buildings in Paris was widespread.

Parma (*War of the Polish Succession*), 1734

In support of her ally Russia, Austria faced a coalition of Spain, France and Savoy in Italy, and on 29 June 1734 Count Mercy with 30,000 men found himself faced by a French force led by Marshal de Coigny at Parma, seventy-five miles south-east of Milan. Mercy was killed and the Austrians lost 6,000 casualties before retreating. Within a year they had been driven out of Milan and the Po valley by the French.

Passchendaele (*First World War*), 1917

Sir Douglas Haig launched a major offensive on 31 July 1917 from the Ypres salient to capture high ground in north-west Belgium from which the Germans had dominated the British lines for three years. Heavy rain and dogged German resistance made for slow progress, although the axis of advance was shifted south to Sir Herbert Plumer's Second Army. On 30 October the final assault on the ridge was carried out, and at length on 6 November two Canadian brigades stormed into Passchendaele village, less than seven miles from Ypres. The German guns had been silenced at a cost of 240,000 British casualties in the three-month battle, also known as Ypres III. These losses appalled the British War Cabinet, whose Prime Minister had never favoured another frontal assault of this nature. They may well have encouraged him actively to pursue an alternative source of military strength and establish the Royal Air Force.

Patay *(Hundred Years War)*, 1429

Retiring after raising the siege of Orleans, an English force under the Earl of Shrewsbury was attacked by the French at Patay, twenty miles to the north-west, on 18 June 1429. Surprised by a flank assault, the English were disorganized and Shrewsbury was taken prisoner, but Sir John Fastolf managed to withdraw the bulk of the troops. This battle, in which the English suffered almost 2,000 casualties, further enhanced the reputation of Joan of Arc and assisted the revival of French morale.

Pavia I *(Alemanni Invasions of the Roman Empire)*, 271

Having failed to stem the advance of the Alemanni into Italy at Placentia, Emperor Aurelian withdrew to reorganize his forces before challenging the invaders once more at Pavia (Ticinum). This time the legionaries defeated the enemy and drove them back across the Alps.

Pavia II *(Wars of the Western Roman Empire)*, 476

As a result of a military *coup* by his father, Orestes, Romulus Augustulus was proclaimed Emperor at Ravenna in 475, but he was almost immediately challenged by Odoacer, leader of the Heruli tribe. On 27 and 28 August 476 the rival forces met at Pavia, seventeen miles south of Milan. Orestes was killed and on 4 September his son was deposed. This battle effectively ended the Western Roman Empire, for Odoacer now determined to rule under suzerainty of the Eastern Emperor at Constantinople.

Pavia III *(Lombard Invasion of Italy)*, 569-72

Led by Alboin, in 568 Lombards crossed the Alps into northern Italy and the following year laid siege to Pavia. Unable to command assistance from the Emperor in Constantinople, the inhabitants held out for three years before imminent starvation forced them to yield. The Lombards then made Pavia the capital of their new kingdom in Italy.

Pavia IV(*Conquests of Charlemagne*), 773–4

Five years after becoming King of the Franks, Charlemagne crossed the Alps into Italy to assist the Pope against the Lombards. Having been outflanked by the Franks, Desiderius, the Lombard king, had taken refuge within the walls of Pavia, and Charlemagne lacked the necessary equipment to breach the city's defences. He therefore besieged Pavia in September 773, and ultimately in June 774 Desiderius surrendered it, agreeing personally to enter a monastery.

Pavia V *(French Wars in Italy)*, 1525

Once more crossing the Alps into Italy with a large French army, Francis I laid siege to Pavia in late 1524. In February 1525 the Marquis of Pescara advanced some 20,000 Imperial troops, mostly Spanish, to relieve the city. When the Spanish attacked the siege lines on 21 February, they were driven back by accurate artillery fire, and the French cavalry then counter-attacked. As the Spanish infantry held firm, Pescara deployed 1,500 arquebusiers on the French flank. These succeeded in disorganizing Swiss mercenaries in the ranks, and a second Spanish attack carried the day. Francis was captured, taken to Madrid and obliged to surrender all French claims to Italy.

Peipus Lake *(Rise of Russia)*, 1242

Two years after repulsing a Swedish force from the north, the city of Novgorod was threatened by Livonian knights from Riga in the west. In 1242, therefore, Alexander Nevski marched out to meet the attackers on the frozen waters of Lake Peipus. In a battle fought entirely on ice, the Russians were successful and the knights withdrew. This ensured the independence of Novgorod and enhanced the military reputation of Alexander, who four years later also gained control of Kiev.

Pen (Danish Invasions of England), 1016

With Ethelred II ('the Unready') reluctant to exert his power, his son Edmund 'Ironside' claimed the throne and rallied Saxon forces to resist Canute, son of the Danish king Sweyn I, who had landed in England to lay claim to the throne himself. In 1016 at Pen in modern Somerset Edmund defeated the invaders, although Canute refused to recognize him as Edmund II when he succeeded his father shortly afterwards.

Perusia (Wars of the Second Triumvirate), 41–40 BC

With Mark Antony in Egypt, his wife Fulvia and brother Lucius led a rebellion against Octavian, the only ruler of the Triumvirate in Rome. Although the revolt forced Octavian to flee from Rome, in 41 BC loyal forces under Marcus Vipsanius Agrippa besieged the rebels in Perusia, eighty-five miles north of Rome, and at length obliged them to surrender in March 40 BC.

Peterwardein (Ottoman Wars), 1716

When the Holy Roman Empire supported Venice in its war with the Ottomans, in 1716 Prince Eugène of Savoy took 40,000 troops, mostly veterans of the War of the Spanish Succession, into the Balkans. On 5 August he encountered 100,000 Turks at Peterwardein, on the Danube in modern Yugoslavia, forty miles northwest of Belgrade. The experienced Imperial troops crushed the enemy, causing 20,000 casualties and capturing 200 pieces of artillery, for the loss of 3,000 casualties. Eugène was then free to march on Belgrade, which he captured the following year.

Pharsalus I (Wars of the First Triumvirate), 48 BC

Retreating south-west after his defeat at Dyrrachium with 20,000 men, Julius Caesar was followed by Pompey with a force double that size. Not until Caesar had retreated 200 miles and both armies had received further reinforcements did Pompey risk battle. On the plain of Pharsalus in eastern Thessaly on 9 August 48 BC Pompey attacked by sending Titus Labienus to outflank Caesar's right wing. Ready for such a manœuvre, Caesar attacked this force with a reserve detachment and drove it back, following up with a general advance. Pompey's centre under Metellus Pius Scipio fell back, and soon Pompey's army was in flight, Pompey himself fleeing to Egypt by ship only to be murdered later. Some 6,000 surrendered. Caesar reported 230 dead, but his true losses may well have exceeded 1,000. This victory did not end the civil war, but it virtually ensured Caesar's ultimate triumph.

Pharsalus II *(Greco–Turkish Wars)*, 1897

During the dispute over control of Crete, Turkish troops advanced against the Greeks in Thessaly. On 6 May 1897 Edhem Pasha led three divisions against Greek positions before Pharsalus and drove them back at a cost of 230 casualties. In the ensuing peace treaty, signed on 20 September, Turkey was indemnified for these losses and Crete placed under international control.

Philiphaugh *(English Civil War)*, 1645

By the summer of 1645 the Marquis of Montrose had secured control of Scotland for Charles I. With the Royalist cause waning in England, David Leslie was now able to challenge his supremacy, and on 13 September with 4,000 Covenanters he attacked and overran the Royalist camp at Philiphaugh near Selkirk. Montrose escaped capture, but Royalist control over Scotland had been ended.

Philippi *(Wars of the Second Triumvirate)*, 42 BC

Challenged by republican leaders Marcus Junius Brutus and Gaius Cassius Longinus, Mark Antony and Octavian crossed the Adriatic Sea in the summer of 42 BC. At Philippi, in Macedonia, ten miles from the Aegean coast, overlooking the inland plain east of Mount Pangaeus, with twenty legions they met 100,000 men under the republican leaders on 27 October. Brutus attacked Octavian on the triumvirate left and drove his legions back into their camp, but Longinus on the other flank could make little headway against Antony. Towards the end of the day, believing that Brutus had been defeated, Longinus committed suicide. Antony was then able to reinforce Octavian, and in a second battle on 16 November the other republican leader was overcome; in turn he also committed suicide.

Philippopolis I *(Gothic Invasions of the Roman Empire)*, 251

As the Romans were preoccupied with problems within the Empire in the third century, in the east Goths swarmed south of the Danube into Moesia and Thrace to besiege Philippopolis (Plovdiv), eighty miles south-east of Sofia. In 251 Emperor Decius marched to its relief but was beaten back, whereupon the Goths stormed the city, sacked it and put the inhabitants to the sword. Later that year Decius became the first Roman emperor to be killed by barbarians, as he fought to recover lost territory from the Goths.

Philippopolis II *(Fourth Crusade)*, 1208

Three years after his brother Baldwin had been defeated by Kaloyan in a similar enterprise, Henry of Flanders, the Latin Emperor in Constantinople, attacked the Bulgars by moving up the Maritsa Valley from Adrianople to Philippopolis in 1208. Under the weak leadership of their new ruler, Boril, the Bulgars were ill-equipped to resist strongly and Henry triumphed. Boril was therefore forced to withdraw beyond the Balkan Mountains and later to come to terms with Henry.

Philippsburg *(War of the Polish Succession)*, 1734

While fighting was taking place in northern Italy, less important action also occurred on the upper Rhine. Here an Imperial garrison was besieged in Philippsburg, eighteen miles north of Karlsruhe and east of the river, by a French force commanded by the Duke of Berwick. Berwick himself was killed during the siege but, resisting all efforts by Prince Eugène to relieve the fortress, the French went on to storm the walls successfully. The fall of Philippsburg had little effect on the course of the war, although operations connected with its attempted relief did see Prince Eugène in the field for the last time before his death two years later.

Piave River *(First World War)*, 1918

In the summer of 1918 the Italian General Diaz commanded fifty-seven, including five Anglo–French, divisions south of the Piave river in northern Italy. On 15 June fifty-eight Austrian divisions, commanded on the left (east) by General Bojna and on the right by Count von Hötzendorf, attacked in an effort to force Italy out of the war. Von Hötzendorf made some gains on the first day but was then checked by the Italian Sixth and Fourth Armies and the Anglo–French divisions. Bojna, however, crossed the lower Piave with the Austrian Fifth and Sixth Armies and advanced three miles south of the river. Heavy rain swept away several of the bridges which the Austrians had constructed over the river for supplies, and Italian resistance stiffened. With no prospect of reinforcements and von Hötzendorf unable to progress on the right, during the night of 22–23 June Bojna withdrew across the Piave again, having suffered an estimated 150,000 losses in casualties and prisoners. This was the last major offensive launched by the Dual Monarchy, which would be further humiliated at Vittorio Veneto in October and disintegrate as a political force after the War.

Pilsen *(Thirty Years War)*, 1618

Acting on behalf of Frederick of the Palatinate in support of the Bohemian Protestants, Count von Mansfeld marched into Bohemia with a mercenary army of 20,000 men. On 1 November 1618, he attacked Pilsen, a Catholic stronghold fifty-two miles south-west of Prague, and after fifteen hours fighting captured the town. This victory checked Catholic plans for an offensive against Prague and, after wintering in Pilsen, von Mansfeld continued his operations in Bohemia the following spring.

Pinkie *(Anglo–Scottish Wars)*, 1547

When the Scots objected to an English plan to marry the infant Edward VI to Mary, Queen of Scots, after the death of Henry VIII in 1547 the Duke of Somerset marched an English army towards Edinburgh. At Pinkie, east of the city, Scottish troops under the Earl of Huntly attacked the English on 10 September. Although the Scots enjoyed initial success, they were eventually repulsed by the English cavalry, supported by fire from naval vessels off-shore. Somerset then went on to occupy Edinburgh, but the infant Queen Mary was sent to France in advance of the English army. So military conquest did not bring England the desired marriage nor political settlement, and in 1548 Mary married Francis, the French dauphin.

Pirot *(Serbo–Bulgarian War)*, 1885

Repulsed by Bulgarian forces at Slivnica on 19 November 1885, 40,000 Serbians under Milan I fell back across their own border to Pirot, forty-five miles north-west of Sofia, where they were quickly attacked by a slightly larger Bulgarian army led by Alexander I. On 26 November 1885 the Bulgarians stormed into the town, only to be ejected the following morning and recapture it once more later the same day. Eventually through Austrian diplomatic intervention fighting was halted on 28 November, with both sides having suffered some 2,000 casualties, and early in the new year peace was formally concluded between Bulgaria and Serbia.

Placentia *(Alemanni Invasions of the Roman Empire)*, 271

Threatened by the incursion of a large body of the Alemanni from Germany into northern Italy, Emperor Aurelian hurried north. Reaching Placentia on the Po river, forty miles south-east of Milan, his army was attacked by the invaders in 271 and managed to repulse them after a bitter struggle. This Roman victory, however, served to delay not halt the enemy, who soon resumed their advance southwards.

Plataea I *(Greco–Persian Wars)*, 479 BC

Withdrawing his force of some 120,000 Persians from Athens into Boeotia, in August 479 BC Mardonius encountered an army of 80,000 Greeks commanded by the Spartan Pausanias at Plataea, near the Asopos river. The Greek hoplites proved too powerful for the Persians, who after the death of Mardonius were virtually annihilated. Reputedly half the Persian force was slain in this decisive battle, which ended Persian hopes of subduing Greece.

Plataea II *(Great Peloponnesian War)*, 429–427 BC

Defended by only 400 Plataeans and eighty Athenians, Plataea was besieged by a force of Spartans under Archidamus II in 429 BC. Before the investment had become complete, all non-combatants, with the exception of a few needed for special tasks, were sent out of the city. As provisions became more scarce, half the garrison managed to break through the Spartan lines and escape. Eventually in 427 BC the surviving defenders were obliged to surrender. The Spartans thereupon tried them for treason and executed 200 Plataeans and twenty-five Athenians.

Plevna *(Russo–Turkish Wars)*, 1877

Crossing the Danube river, the Russians reached the outer defences of Plevna, twenty miles to the south and eighty miles north-east of Sofia, which was defended by some 30,000 Turks under Osman Pasha on 20 July 1877. Two assaults by General Krüdener were beaten back at a cost of 20,000 casualties to the Turkish 5,000. Although considerable sympathy was aroused in other countries for the gallant defenders, little practical help was forthcoming, and by the beginning of December 100,000 besiegers, now commanded by Prince Carol, future King of Romania, ringed the city. In desperation taking 9,000 sick and wounded with him in carts, Osman crossed the Vid river with 25,000 men to break out of the trap. Russian reinforcements brought up by Count Todleben drove the Turks back over the Vid into Plevna, with the escape attempt having cost 5,000 Turkish casualties including Osman, who had been severely wounded. After 143 days, therefore, Plevna was obliged to surrender, and the Russians were able to continue their advance into the Balkans, having suffered 38,000 casualties before its walls.

Plovdiv *(Russo–Turkish Wars)*, 1878

Pressing southwards rapidly after the fall of Plevna, Russian troops under General Gurko attacked Plovdiv (Philippopolis) on the Maritsa river, 100 miles north-west of Edirne (Adrianople), on 17 January 1878. In the face of determined resistance by the garrison under Suleiman Pasha, the Russians burst into the fortified town, suffering 1,300 casualties in the process to the Turkish

5,000 casualties and 2,000 prisoners. The Turks were now in full retreat towards Constantinople. With Russian forces threatening their capital, the Turks were obliged to sign the humiliating Treaty of San Stefano, which involved heavy loss of territory. But fears of Russian domination of the Balkans and the Straits soon rallied international support for Turkey and a more equitable settlement at the Congress of Berlin (1878).

Poitiers *(Hundred Years War)*, 1356

Returning to English-held Aquitaine from a successful sweep into the French kingdom, Edward the Black Prince with 7,000 men was forced to stand and face 16,000 pursuers under John II 'the Good', of France, seven miles south-east of Poitiers. On 17 September 1356 Prince Edward deployed his troops among hedgerows and vineyards to take advantage of the skill of his longbowmen. Pressing forward to attack, the French were disorganized by the English archers, counter-attacked by infantry armed with spears and axes, then struck in the flank by cavalry as they hesitated. The heavily mailed French cavalry suffered particularly severe losses, and John II and some 2,000 of his men were also taken prisoner. Prince Edward was able to continue his retreat to Bordeaux, from whence his royal captive was sent to England.

Pollentia *(Wars of the Western Roman Empire)*, 402

When Alaric invaded northern Italy with a horde of Visigoths and marched on Milan, in 402 Flavius Stilicho recalled Roman troops from Britain and along the Rhine. As the invaders penetrated southwards, Stilicho manœuvred for a decisive interception and at length attacked the enemy camp at Pollentia (Pollenza) near the Adriatic coast, twenty-five miles south-west of modern Ancona, on 6 April, whilst the Visigoths were celebrating Easter. Recovering from initial surprise, the defenders counter-attacked vigorously, but gradually the more disciplined legions gained ascendancy. The camp was overwhelmed, and several thousand Visigoths became casualties or prisoners, the latter including Alaric's wife. The imperial army now drove the invaders back into the Alps, though in fact only a temporary respite had been gained.

Polotsk *(Russo–Polish Wars)*, 1579

Under Ivan IV, 'the Terrible', the Russians cleared Tartars from land west of the Volga, then turned towards Poland and Lithuania. On the right bank of the Dvina river they seized Polotsk, which Stephen Bathory determined to recover when he succeeded to the Polish throne in 1575. Accordingly four years later he assembled an army which stormed and recaptured it. Three years after this, Polish control of Polotsk was confirmed in a treaty ending hostilities between the two countries.

Poltava *(Great Northern War)*, 1709

Marching south from Poland into the Ukraine in the hope of securing strong reinforcements of Cossacks, Charles XII of Sweden encountered bitter winter conditions. By spring 1709 his men had to use their powder to relish rotten food, for the Swedish supply train had been turned back by Russian attacks. The Cossacks produced only 2,000 men. Nevertheless, in May, with under 20,000 effectives and little artillery, Charles determined to besiege Poltava on the Vorskla river, eighty-five miles south-west of Kharkov. Once the Swedes were committed, Peter I of Russia gathered 60,000 men and deployed 50,000 of them west of the Vorskla river in entrenched positions. Charles dared not attack Poltava without first dealing with these men, for fear of a flank attack. On 8 July the Swedes therefore moved against these troops, Charles being carried into battle on a litter due to a foot wound sustained a few days previously. As the attackers faltered under Russian artillery fire, Peter counter-attacked. The Swedes were driven south of Poltava towards the Dnieper river and, with the exception of 1,500 men including Charles who escaped to Turkey, the entire force was killed or captured. This battle was one of the most decisive in history, for it proved the worth of Peter's reorganized army, erased the memory of the Russian humiliation at Narva nine years previously and finished Sweden as a formidable military power.

Prague I *(Hussite Wars)*, 1420

After the execution of John Hus for heresy in 1415, his followers in Prague provoked a rebellion against the Roman Catholics. In response to a call from the Pope, the Holy Roman Emperor Sigismund raised a large force and marched on the city. Led by Jan Žižka, one of the extreme Taborite faction of the Hussites, the rebels closed the city gates and entrenched themselves on the Hill of Witkov outside the walls. Obliged to take this position, defended by a mere 9,000 men, Sigismund attacked on 14 July 1420, was repulsed and forced to abandon immediate plans to occupy Prague. He would return to Bohemia with a larger force committed to crushing the Hussites the following year.

Prague II *(Thirty Years War)*, see **White Mountain**

Prague III *(Thirty Years War)*, 1648

While peace negotiations were under way in Westphalia to end the Thirty Years War, a Swedish army under Count von Königsmarck invested Prague and demanded its surrender. With virtually no Imperial troops to assist them, the inhabitants determined to resist, despite the fact that twice before in the war the city had capitulated without a fight. With no prospect of outside help, the citizens hung on grimly for three months until the signing of peace on 24 October 1648 ended the war and saved the city.

Prague IV *(War of the Austrian Succession)*, 1744

Having concluded an alliance with France and Bavaria, in 1744 Frederick the Great marched into Bohemia with 80,000 Prussian troops and on 2 September laid siege to Prague. For six days the Austrian garrison resisted before surrendering the city, then Frederick penetrated deeper into Bohemia. But when no aid came from France, and Bavaria offered only token assistance, he was forced to withdraw once more, abandon Prague and return to Silesia after suffering heavy losses.

Prague V *(Seven Years War)*, 1757

When Frederick the Great arrived before Prague on 5 May 1757 with 64,000 Prussian troops, he discovered that Prince Charles of Lorraine had deployed a slightly larger force of Austrians in defensive positions along the Moldau river. Declining to attack at once, Frederick crossed the Moldau during the night and assaulted the Austrian right flank the following morning, but due to faulty reconnaissance he was repulsed with heavy loss. Reforming his lines and protecting the left flank with General von Zieten's cavalry, Frederick attacked a second time and forced Prince Charles to retire into Prague with some 30,000 men. In the fighting the Austrians lost 14,000 men in casualties and prisoners (including Count von Browne, who was killed) and 16,000 others retreated to join Count von Daun. The Prussians, who also lost some 14,000 men in casualties, prisoners and missing (including Count von Schwerin), now laid siege to Prague. Defeated by an Austrian relief force at Kolin in June, Frederick was obliged to raise the siege, however, and once more withdraw from Bohemia.

Preston I *(English Civil War)*, 1648

In support of Charles I some 15,000 Scots under David Leslie marched south to join 4,000 Royalists under Sir Marmaduke Langdale. At Preston in Lancashire on 17 August 1648 this combined force was attacked by 8,500 Parliamentarians under Oliver Cromwell. Although the Royalists fought bravely, many Scots fled the field, and Cromwell was victorious after three days of conflict. This defeat ended the King's hopes of regaining control of England.

Preston II *(First Jacobite Rebellion)*, 1715

Although failing to link up with the main body of Scots, 4,000 Jacobites led by General Forster occupied Preston and were attacked by royal troops commanded by General Wills on 13 November 1715. Throughout that day the Jacobites defended stoutly, but the following morning they were forced to surrender. Many of the defenders had managed to escape through the royal lines during the night; thus only 1,468 prisoners were taken. During the battle Wills' force suffered some 200 casualties, the Jacobites reputedly a mere forty-two. This reverse, however, effectively finished the insurrection.

Prestonpans *(Second Jacobite Rebellion)*, 1745

When the Young Pretender, Prince Charles Edward, landed in Scotland, Lord George Murray rapidly collected 2,000 men in his support. Marching south, they were intercepted on the Firth of Forth five miles east of Edinburgh at Prestonpans on 21 September by a royal army of some 3,000 troops under Sir John Cope. Despite their inferiority in numbers, the Scots charged and Cope's infantry gave way rapidly. The royal troops lost almost 2,000 in casualties and prisoners, the Scots only 140. This easy victory encouraged Prince Charles Edward to cross the border into England with some 4,500 infantry and 400 cavalry, only for this ill-conceived venture to falter at Derby in December.

Przemysl *(First World War)*, 1914–15

A fortified city in south-eastern Poland garrisoned by Austrian troops, Przemysl, 130 miles south-east of Cracow (Krakow), was the only land fortress to suffer a prolonged siege in the First World War. Russian efforts to capture it between 24 September and 11 October 1914 failed, but the siege was renewed on 6 November 1914, and eventually Przemysl capitulated on 22 March 1915. Russian occupation was comparatively short-lived, however, for three months later they were driven from the city.

Pultusk I *(Great Northern War)*, 1703

With Cracow (Krakow) in his hands, Charles XII of Sweden wintered in Poland and the following spring marched north with 10,000 men. At Pultusk, thirty-two miles north of Warsaw, he encountered a Saxon force of similar size under Field-Marshal von Steinau and attacked on 21 April 1703. The Saxons put up very little resistance before taking to their heels, having lost 600 dead and about 1,000 captured. Charles now turned towards the fortress of Thorn.

Pultusk II *(Napoleonic Wars)*, 1806

Advancing eastwards after defeating the Prussians at Jena, Napoleon faced resistance from large Russian forces determined to protect the area of Poland under the Tsar's control. On 26 December 1806 with 20,000 men Marshal Lannes moved swiftly on Pultusk to find it defended by 37,000 Russian troops under General Bennigsen. Lannes's attempts to cut the Russian lines of communication failed but, as Bennigsen retreated during the night to Ostroleka, leaving Pultusk in French hands, Lannes claimed victory. The French claimed 5,000 Russian casualties and prisoners and only 1,500 casualties themselves, although the Russians estimated 8,000 French casualties. The engagement was, in reality, indecisive, partly because Bennigsen avoided a battle of attrition.

Pydna *(Third Macedonian War*, 168 BC

In 169 BC Lucius Aemilius Paulus led a Roman army into Macedonia to avenge the defeat of another Roman force two years earlier. On 22 June 168 BC, after considerable manœuvring, Perseus of Macedonia attacked the Romans at Pydna, on the western shore of the Gulf of Salonika. In the opening phase of the battle the Macedonian phalanx drove back the Romans, but rough ground caused it to become disorganized, allowing Paulus to counterattack, and the legionaries proceeded to annihilate the Macedonian phalanx. The Romans lost about 100 killed, the Macedonians 20,000 plus 10,000 prisoners. As a result of this battle the power of Perseus was undermined, and the following year he was dethroned and taken captive in Rome.

Pyrenees, The *(Peninsular War)*, 1813

Advancing north through Spain, British troops under Viscount Wellington laid siege to San Sebastian on the Bay of Biscay. In the summer of 1813 Marshal Soult attempted to relieve the garrison, and between 25 July and 2 August a number of actions took place, principally at Roncesvalles, Maya and Buenzas, which became known collectively as the Battle of the Pyrenees. In denying the French victory at the cost of some 7,500 casualties, the British protected their own troops before San Sebastian and in northern Spain.

Quatre Bras *(Napoleon's Hundred Days)*, 1815

To achieve control of Flanders, Napoleon planned to drive a wedge between the Duke of Wellington and Field-Marshal Blücher's Prussians further east. Thus while Napoleon successfully engaged Blücher at Ligny, on 16 June 1815 Marshal Ney led 25,000 troops on the French left towards Quatre Bras on the road to Brussels. Attacking in the afternoon, Ney drove the Anglo–Dutch advance guard of 36,000 men under the Prince of Orange back into Quatre Bras. When the French appeared on the point of victory, Sir Thomas Picton brought his division decisively into action, though inexplicably Ney made no use of I Corps on his right. Darkness halted fighting, with the French having suffered 4,300 casualties to the allied 4,700, and during the night Wellington pulled back his men in good order to positions around Waterloo.

Quiberon *(French Revolutionary Wars)*, 1795

After the execution of Louis XVI, several royalist uprisings took place in the department of La Vendée in south-west France, and on 27 June 1795 a British fleet landed 3,600 French *émigrés* on the Quiberon peninsula to join the dissidents. General Hoche took a Revolutionary army into the area, however, and during 16–21 July crushed the rebels, taking 6,000 prisoners. Many of the prisoners, including some 700 *émigrés*, were executed and less than 2,000 managed to escape to England. This action by Hoche ended any serious threat from La Vendée, and all resistance there was finally suppressed early in the following year.

Raab *(Napoleonic Wars)*, 1809

Encouraged by news of Napoleon's successes in southern Germany, his stepson Eugène de Beauharnais with 45,000 men attacked Archduke John's Austrian army of 40,000 in north-eastern Italy. Fearful for his lines of communication, Archduke John retired eastwards. At length he made a stand on 14 June 1809 at Raab, seventy miles south-east of Vienna, but having suffered 5,000 casualties to the French 3,000, he continued his withdrawal into Hungary that night. As he crossed the Danube and moved upstream, Beauharnais besieged Raab with 23,200 men and 100 cannon and took it on 25 June, which allowed him to link up with Napoleon near Vienna, where by the beginning of July 160,000 French troops had been concentrated.

Rain *(Thirty Years War)*, 1632

Following his triumph at Breitenfeld and consolidation of the Protestant position in northern Germany, Gustavus Adolphus wintered near Frankfurt, in March 1632 moving into Bavaria at the head of some 25,000 men. As the Comte de Tilly with 20,000 men fell back eastwards, Gustavus crossed the Danube and on 14 April reached the left (west) bank of the Lech river, opposite the village of Rain, twenty miles south-east of Ratisbon, then occupied by Tilly. Next day Gustavus opened an artillery bombardment under cover of which the Swedes forded the river and attacked the Catholic entrenchments. Subjected to severe pressure, the defenders gave way, leaving their artillery and baggage to the victorious Swedes, and their commander, Tilly, mortally wounded on the field. Gustavus marched on to take Augsburg, Munich and Nuremberg in rapid succession.

Ramillies *(War of the Spanish Succession)*, 1706

Marching eastwards across the Spanish Netherlands (modern Belgium) towards Liège, the Duke of Villeroi with some 50,000 French troops and fifty guns found a similar force of allied English, German, Dutch and Imperial troops with 120 guns under the Duke of Marlborough deployed near the village of Ramillies, twenty-five miles south-east of Brussels. Feigning an attack on the French left (north), Marlborough sent the bulk of his cavalry against the enemy right flank on 23 May 1706. Quickly penetrating the French line, the allied cavalry then wheeled right to roll up the French line, as the infantry moved forward in a frontal assault. Disorganized by these attacks, the French were driven from the field with the loss of 15,000 men in casualties and prisoners plus fifty guns. Allied losses were less than 5,000. As a result of this victory Brussels and Antwerp fell to Marlborough, and Villeroi was replaced in his command by the Duke of Vendôme.

Rathmines *(English Civil War),* 1649

Towards the end of July 1649 a Royalist force led by the Marquis of Ormonde camped before Dublin, which was held by a Parliamentarian garrison under Colonel Michael Jones. As Ormonde prepared to attack, Jones suddenly sallied forth on 2 August, scattered the Royalist advance troops and swept into their camp at Rathmines. The Parliamentarians captured Ormonde's artillery and 2,000 prisoners and caused an additional 4,000 casualties in the Royalist ranks, thus destroying the only field army which might have effectively resisted Cromwell when he landed with Parliamentarian reinforcements to subdue Ireland.

Ravenna I *(Gothic Conquest of Italy),* 491–3

When Theodoric the Great, King of the Ostrogoths, invaded Italy in 489, Odoacer of the Neruli was attempting to rule the lawless land from Ravenna. Twice Odoacer failed to halt. Theodoric's advance and eventually fell back into his capital. For almost three years he was besieged until, under the protection of a truce, the Ostrogoths were permitted to enter Ravenna, near the northern Adriatic coast forty miles south-east of Bologna. Once inside they treacherously turned on the garrison, executed Odoacer and took control of the peninsula. Half a century later they were in turn overthrown by Justinian, the Byzantine emperor.

Ravenna II *(Wars of the Byzantine Empire),* 729

In 726 Leo III, the Byzantine Emperor, decreed image-worship in the Church to be illegal, which brought him into conflict with the Pope. To enforce his decree, Leo despatched an army to Ravenna, where it encountered a force loyal to the Pope. The Byzantines were driven back to the coast and obliged to re-embark for Constantinople. This battle widened the breach between the Byzantine Empire and the Church.

Ravenna III *(Frankish Invasion of Italy),* 756

Under Aistulf the northern Italian kingdom of Lombardy seized Ravenna in 751, which greatly alarmed the Pope. Stephen II therefore asked the Frankish king, Pepin the Short, for assistance, and in 756 the Franks marched south over the Alps. The Lombards were chased out of Ravenna with little ceremony, and the conquered territory was given to the Pope by Pepin. Known as the 'Donation of Pepin', this became the foundation of a temporal Papal State.

Ravenna IV *(Franco–Spanish Wars)*, 1512

When the League of Cambrai broke up, Pope Julius II held Ravenna, which was promptly besieged by a French force under the Duke of Nemours. The Spanish King Ferdinand, also ruler of Naples, sent an army commanded by the Marquis of Pescara to relieve Ravenna, and on 11 April 1512 Pescara attacked the French siege lines. Under heavy fire from Spanish cannon and arquebuses mounted on wheels, the French infantry held firm, whilst Nemours deployed twenty-four cannon to enfilade the Spanish ranks. When these opened a bombardment, Pescara's men quickly became disorganized and a French infantry assault swept them from the field in confusion. Nemours himself fell in the battle, which only served to persuade the Holy Roman Empire and the Swiss cantons to join the anti-French coalition.

Ré, Ile de *(Anglo–French Wars)*, 1627

Seeking to aid the rebel Huguenot stronghold of La Rochelle, which was besieged by French troops under Cardinal Richelieu, in 1627 Charles I sent an English force led by the Duke of Buckingham to seize the Ile de Ré in the Bay of Biscay. The expedition landed in July but failed to take the citadel, which held out until French reinforcements arrived in October, forcing Buckingham hastily to raise the siege and retire. This fiasco cost the English several hundred lives, and two future attempts to assist La Rochelle proved equally abortive.

Reading *(Danish Invasions of England)*, 871

During 871 several battles occurred between the Danes and West Saxons under Ethelred I and his brother Alfred. Four days after winning a minor skirmish at Englefield, in an effort to win a decisive victory the brothers determined to attack the Danish camp at Reading, on the Thames forty miles west of London. In vain the West Saxons repeatedly and bravely charged the enemy entrenchments, but at length they were driven from the field with heavy loss, encouraging the Danes to advance westwards, where they would soon again defeat the West Saxons at Wilton.

Reims *(Napoleonic Wars)*, 1814

Following his defeat at Laon on 10 March 1814, Napoleon retired to Soissons on the Aisne river, fifty miles north-east of Paris, where he learnt that forty miles away Reims had fallen to the enemy. Swiftly marching less than 30,000 men in that direction and risking attack by Field-Marshal Blücher's vastly superior army, Napoleon routed General St-Priest's 13,000 Russians and Prussians. Reims was thus recaptured at a cost of less than 1,000 casualties to 6,000 incurred by the enemy. This was, however, Napoleon's last victory of the war, for he was now north-east of Paris and flanked by two superior Allied armies.

Reval *(Baltic Wars)*, 1219

Pressing eastwards in a quest for the German Baltic lands, in 1219 a Danish army under Waldemar II clashed with German troops at Reval (now Tallinn in modern Estonia). At a point when the Danes were under considerable pressure, according to different legends a red and white flag (the Dannebrog which later became the national banner) either miraculously came into Waldemar's possession or appeared in the sky. Rallied by this phenomenon, the Danes swept their opponents from the field and went on to conquer much of the south Baltic coastline.

Rheinfelden *(Thirty Years War)*, 1638

Early in 1638 the Protestant German army of the Duke of Saxe-Weimar invested Rheinfelden on the upper Rhine eight miles east of Basle. With Rheinfelden masked, Saxe-Weimar began passing his troops over to the right bank of the river on 2 March. About half were across when they were attacked by a Bavarian force under General von Werth. During the night Saxe-Weimar withdrew his men on both sides of the river upstream and then brought the remainder of his forward troops, who had escaped von Werth's men, back across the river. By the morning of 3 March, Saxe-Weimar had his entire force on the left bank of the Upper Rhine above Rheinfeld. Meanwhile, believing that his enemy had been beaten, von Werth had already crossed the river and was caught completely by surprise near Rheinfeld when Saxe-Weimar suddenly attacked. The Bavarians were routed and von Werth was captured, but Saxe-Weimar lost the veteran Huguenot commander the Duke of Rohan, who was mortally wounded, though he was now able to advance on the key fortress of Breisach.

Riade *(Wars of the German States)*, 933

Taking advantage of a negotiated truce with Magyar irregulars from the area of modern Hungary, the Holy Roman Emperor Henry I strengthened fortifications within the border of Saxony and Thuringia. With his defences secure, he broke the truce in 933 and attacked the enemy at Riade on the Saale river, just south of Merseberg. His heavy cavalry were too strong for the lightly armed Magyars, who were crushed. This, the first severe defeat inflicted on these irregular forces, brought a further twenty years' peace.

Rieti *(Italian Wars of Independence)*, 1821

Deposed by his subjects in the kingdom of Naples in 1820, Ferdinand IV called on the Austrian army in northern Italy for assistance. On 7 March 1821, therefore, 10,000 Neapolitan rebels under General Pepe found themselves confronting almost 80,000 Austrian regulars at Rieti, forty-two miles north-west of Rome. Until the main Austrian force was committed to the battle, the Neapolitans fought well, but then they were overwhelmed. Pepe was exiled and Ferdinand restored to his throne by the victorious Austrians, shortly afterwards becoming Ferdinand I, King of the Two Sicilies.

Riga I *(Swedish–Polish Wars)*, 1621

In pursuit of his claim to the Swedish throne, Sigismund III of Poland joined with the Holy Roman Emperor at the outbreak of the Thirty Years War in 1618. Although not fully involved in the war, in August 1621 Gustavus Adolphus of Sweden laid siege to Riga, on the south Baltic coast some 250 miles south-east of Stockholm, defended by a few hundred Poles. Despite its inferiority in numbers, the garrison resisted several assaults until Swedish artillery caused a breach in the walls on 11 September. Four days later the remnants of the defenders surrendered and the port was granted self-government under Swedish suzerainty.

Riga II *(First World War)*, 1917

After collapse of the Russian attack on Lemberg (Lvov), Field-Marshal von Hindenburg believed that one further German offensive would force Russia out of the war. Thus on 1 September 1917 General von Hutier's Eighth Army was launched across the Dvina river against Riga. Within two days resistance had been overcome and, with Petrograd (Leningrad) threatened, internal disorder culminating in the Bolshevik revolution on 7 November (the October Revolution according to the old calendar) determined that Russia would take no more aggressive action during the war.

Rimnik *(Russo–Turkish Wars)*, 1789

In alliance with Joseph II, Holy Roman Emperor and Emperor of Austria, Catherine II the Great, of Russia, attacked the Ottomans and, after defeating them at Focsani in August 1789, despatched a combined Austro–Russian force under Prince Frederick Josias of Saxe-Coburg and General Suvorov deep into Moldavia (part of modern Romania). At Rimnik on 22 September 25,000 allied troops encountered over 50,000 Turks and utterly defeated them, when according to legend very few escaped. In reward for his success Suvorov was made Count Rimniksky. The defeated Sultan died, apparently through shame at his enormous loss, before the close of the year.

Rio Barbate *(Moslem Conquest of Spain)*, 711

With the coastline of North Africa in their hands, Moorish troops crossed the Straits of Gibraltar into southern Spain in 711. With 15,000 men King Roderick, the Visigoth, attempted to stem the advance of 12,000 invaders, who were led by some 7,000 Arab and Berber cavalry. This cavalry proved decisive in a brief, bitter encounter at Wadi Bekka, on the Barbate river near Cape Trafalgar, on 19 July. Roderick perished and his troops were scattered, leaving the invaders to ride on and set up their capital at Córdoba. Before summer ended they also subdued the Visigoth capital of Toledo.

Rio Salado *(Spanish–Moslem Wars)*, 1340

In an effort to stem the Christian counter-offensive into the southern part of the Iberian peninsula, the Moors gathered reinforcements from Africa and advanced against the combined forces of Castile and Portugal. On the Rio Salado, near Tarifa, the Moors were decisively beaten on 30 October 1340, and thereafter they were confined to their previous conquests in the south. For his part in this battle Alfonso IV of Portugal became known as 'the Brave'.

Rivoli *(French Revolutionary Wars)*, 1797

In a fourth attempt to relieve the besieged fortress of Mantua, 28,000 Austrian troops under Baron Alvintzy advanced down the Adige valley and on 14 January 1797 attacked the heights of Rivoli, fourteen miles north of Verona. Here some 30,000 French troops and sixty cannon under Generals Joubert and Masséna were not fully deployed to resist them. The French gained an hour's respite by negotiating under a flag of truce, whilst taking up strong defensive positions. When the Austrians attack was renewed, their four divisions were routed, with the loss of 3,300 casualties and 7,000 prisoners. On the following day Joubert surrounded and captured a fifth Austrian division, which had become isolated in his rear, and for the loss of 2,500 casualties the French had ensured that no aid would reach Mantua. For his part in this battle Masséna was later created Duke of Rivoli.

Rocourt *(War of the Austrian Succession)*, 1746

Encouraged by Prussian withdrawal from the war, Prince Charles of Lorraine took an Austrian army into the Netherlands to pursue the fight against France. The anti-French coalition was weakened, however, by the withdrawal of British troops to deal with the Jacobite Rebellion at home, and Marshal Saxe took the opportunity to advance. At Rocourt, on the Meuse three miles north of Liège, on 11 October 1746 he met and defeated a combined Dutch and Austrian force under Prince Charles, which lost some 5,000 men in casualties, enabling Saxe to continue his advance.

Rocroi *(Thirty Years War)*, 1643

Crossing the border of the Spanish Netherlands (modern Belgium) into France in the spring of 1643, General de Melo laid siege to Rocroi west of the Meuse river, fifty-five miles north-east of Reims, with 26,000 Spanish troops, including 8,000 cavalry. This prompted the French commander Louis II de Bourbon, Prince of Condé (the Great Condé) to advance to its relief with 22,000 men, who clashed with the enemy drawn up south of the town on 19 May. Both forces had their cavalry deployed on the wings, and initially Condé made progress on the Spanish left. Soon however the Spanish cavalry also moved forward against the French left, and the situation was evenly balanced until Condé suddenly wheeled inwards. Cutting through the Spanish infantry, he boldly attacked and routed cavalry on the opposite wing, then annihilated the cream of the enemy infantry, which he had isolated by his bold cavalry attack. Never again was the Spanish infantry such a formidable force, and from this day may be traced the decline of Spanish military influence and power. Of 18,000 infantry in action, 7,000 Spaniards were captured and 8,000 killed. Condé admitted 4,000 casualties, and next day he entered Rocroi in triumph.

Rome I *(Wars of the Western Roman Empire)*, 410

With the Roman force weakened after the murder of Flavius Stilicho, Visigoths under Alaric poured into northern Italy. Twice bought off by the citizens of Rome, in 410 they again approached the city, from which Emperor Honorius had fled to Ravenna. Once more Alaric demanded a heavy ransom and, when negotiations broke down, he attacked the city. Possibly with the assistance of traitors within, the Visigoths entered Rome by the Salarian Gate in the north-east of the wall on 24 August 410 and proceeded to pillage and sack. The fall of Rome clearly demonstrated the weakness of the Western Roman Empire, and other barbarians were encouraged to attack it. Alaric, pressing on southwards, enjoyed little further personal success, for before the year was out he had died.

Rome II *(Wars of the Western Roman Empire)*, 455

Despite frequent barbarian invasions of the Empire, internal political quarrels led to considerable instability at Rome. Following the murder of Emperor Valentinian III, Petronius Maximus ascended the imperial throne, but his reign would be short. In the late spring of 455 the Vandal king Genseric arrived off the mouth of the Tiber with a large fleet from North Africa. Finding little opposition, he landed a large force and advanced on Rome, which he reached on 2 June. For the next fourteen days the capital was subjected to savage plundering. Maximus perished and the Western Roman Empire never recovered from this episode, although it would nominally continue as an independent entity for another twenty years.

Rome III *(Wars of the Byzantine Empire)*, 537–8

Following his reconquest of North Africa from the Vandals for the Byzantine Empire, late in 535 Belisarius landed in Sicily, captured the island, and crossed to the mainland with 8,000 men early the next year. Advancing northwards he seized Naples and succeeded in taking Rome on 10 December 536 with virtually no resistance from the Ostrogoth defenders. But the Gothic leader Vitiges reacted swiftly and in May 537 laid siege to Rome with 30,000 men. For over a year Belisarius was penned in the former capital of the Roman Empire until reinforcements arrived from Constantinople. As they approached, Belisarius emerged from the city and drove the besiegers northwards in early summer 538. Within two years virtually the whole peninsula had been recovered and Vitiges captured, so Belisarius returned to Constantinople in triumph.

Rome IV *(Wars of the Byzantine Empire)*, 546–7

The recapture of the bulk of the Italian peninsula from the barbarians in 538 by Belisarius did not bring permanent peace, for the Ostrogoths under Totila soon took the offensive once more. Sweeping southwards at first they by-passed Rome, but eventually they laid siege to the city with its garrison of 3,000 under Bassus in the autumn of 546. A relief force under Belisarius proved too weak to penetrate the besiegers' lines, and eventually Totila stormed the city on 17 December and sacked it. The following year Belisarius manœuvred Totila away from Rome and reoccupied it in February. In turn, however, he had to abandon the city to the barbarians when obliged to campaign in the north. Rome now experienced a prolonged period of uncivilized squalour.

Rome V *(Norman Seizure)*, 1084

In his dispute with the Pope the Holy Roman Emperor Henry IV marched on Rome and deposed Gregory VIII. Calling for assistance, Gregory employed the Norman mercenary Robert Guiscard to expel the Imperial troops. Guiscard gathered a motley collection of adventurers, who recaptured the city and restored Gregory but then began to pillage Rome. As a result the Pope was forced to seek temporary refuge from the excesses of his deliverers at Salerno, where he died the following year. Rome remained the centre of a struggle between the Empire and Papacy until the Concordat of Worms (1122).

Rome VI *(War of the League of Cognac)*, 1527

After the defeat of France at the Battle of Pavia, the Pope organized the League of Cognac, which proved powerless to prevent penetration of Habsburg forces under Charles V, King of Spain and Holy Roman Emperor, southwards along the Italian peninsula. Under the immediate command of the Duke of Bourbon the 30,000 Habsburg army stormed into Rome on 6 May 1527 and proceeded to pillage and sack the city. Some thousands (possibly as many as 8,000) of the inhabitants perished, and the Pope took refuge in the castle of Sant' Angelo, which he was shortly afterwards allowed to leave. By the Treaty of Barcelona

(1529), on regaining the Papal States including Rome and being promised military assistance against the Turks, the Pope now formally recognized Charles as Holy Roman Emperor.

Rome VII *(Italian Wars of Independence)*, 1849

In the course of hostilities between Sardinia and Austria, a republic of Rome was proclaimed on 9 February 1849 after the Pope had left the city. To restore papal rule, 6,000 French troops under General Oudinot landed at the port of Civitavecchia, thirty-nine miles north-west of Rome, on 24 April and attacked the city five days later. They were repulsed by republican defenders organized by Giuseppe Garibaldi with the loss of almost 1,000 men in casualties and prisoners. After receiving over 10,000 reinforcements, Oudinot attacked once more on 3 June and, having been repulsed a second time, settled down to conduct a tight siege and bombard the defenders with his artillery. By 30 June Garibaldi realized his hopeless position, came to terms with the French and two days later marched 5,000 survivors out of Rome. The short-lived Roman republic thus fell, and Garibaldi's force was to be attacked and dispersed by Austrian troops as it made its way northwards.

Roncesvalles *(Conquests of Charlemagne)*, 778

Tempted by disunity amongst the Moors in Spain, Charlemagne led a Frankish army into Pamplona, then down the Ebro river to besiege Saragossa. Learning that the Saxons were in revolt, however, he was forced to raise the siege and return over the Pyrenees. Although the bulk of his men crossed safely, the rearguard and baggage train were ambushed by Basques in the mountain pass of Roncesvalles, and not one Frank in these detachments escaped slaughter. Among those to die was the paladin Roland, which led to the epic of medieval literature *Chanson de Roland*.

Rossbach *(Seven Years War)*, 1757

In the summer of 1757, with hostile forces closing in from west, east and south, Frederick the Great of Prussia decided to strike westwards against 41,000 French and Austrian troops commanded by the Prince of Soubise. Reduced to some 21,000 effectives after several forced marches, Frederick occupied high ground north-east of the village of Rossbach, twenty-six miles south-west of Leipzig. On 5 November allied troops attempted to turn the Prussian left flank. Using a small force to screen his manœuvres, Frederick deployed his main body so that the cavalry under General von Seydlitz followed by seven battalions of infantry struck the enemy column in its flank, then swept down on the surprised infantry. In less than an hour Soubise was in flight and his army had been routed, the allied army suffering 7,500 losses in casualties and prisoners. At a cost of under 600 casualties Frederick had eliminated the threat from the west, although he remained in grave danger elsewhere, and had enhanced his own military reputation. In London his triumph was prematurely celebrated as the crowning victory of the Protestant cause.

Rouen I *(Anglo–French Wars)*, 1204

The English struggle with Philip Augustus of France for posses-sion of Normandy had proved indecisive during the reign of Richard I, but once John came to the English throne, the French began to gain the advantage. In March 1204 the main English bastion in Normandy, Château Gaillard, fell and the French pressed on to attack Rouen, on the Seine sixty-five miles north-west of Paris. On 24 June, after a short resistance, it was captured and the English were now rapidly ejected from all their territory north of the Loire.

Rouen II *(Hundred Years War)*, 1418–19

Having overrun most of Normandy in the three years after his victory at Agincourt, in the summer of 1418 Henry V laid siege to Rouen, chief city in northern France. In preparation for a long siege, the garrison commander, Guy de Boutillier, turned all non-combatants (estimated at 12,000) out of the city. But the English refused to allow them through the siege lines, and they were forced to endure a pitiful and dangerous existence in the area between the opposing armies for some months. After a cursory attempt at relief had failed, Rouen surrendered on 19 January 1419 and the English army moved on towards Paris.

Rouen III *(Hundred Years War)*, 1449

Gradually forcing the English out of France in the twenty years after their victory at Orleans, the French still could not capture Rouen. In 1449, however, encouraged by the presence of a strong body of French troops in the area, the inhabitants rebelled against the garrison, which was obliged to take refuge in the castle. On 29 October the Duke of Somerset finally surrendered there, and the city, which had served as the English administrative centre in northern France for thirty years, reverted to French control.

Roundway Down *(English Civil War)*, 1643

When Royalist troops under Sir Ralph Hopton retired into Devizes in Wiltshire on 9 July 1643, following their retreat from Bath, they were besieged by a Parliamentarian force commanded by Sir William Waller. Prince Maurice, younger brother of Prince Rupert, advanced with another Royalist body from Oxford to the relief of the town. On 13 July 1643 he attacked the besiegers on the heights of Roundway Down just outside Devizes. The Parliamentarians were swept from their positions by Prince Maurice's cavalry and simultaneously attacked in the rear by infantry coming out of Devizes. Put to flight, they lost over 1,000 men in casualties and prisoners (an estimated 600 were killed), and Prince Maurice went on to capture Bristol twelve days later.

Rudnik Ridges *(First World War)*, 1914

Launching a second invasion of Serbia on the night of 7–8 September 1914, a mere fortnight after failure of the first, the Austrian commander Field-Marshal Potiorek with his Fifth and Sixth Armies drove back the Serbian defenders. By 2 December they had occupied Belgrade, but their supply lines back through the mountains were now perilously stretched. Meanwhile General Putnik had deployed three Serbian armies along the Rudnik Ridges, south of Belgrade, and the day after the fall of the Serbian capital he launched a counter-offensive. Inspired by the appearance at the front of their seventy-year-old king, Peter I, the Serbs fought furiously, and after five days the Austrians began to retire. On 15 December Belgrade was reoccupied and, as the invaders fell back still further, it became apparent that once more their plans to overrun Serbia had failed. However, casualties had been heavy, with estimates of 100,000 killed on both sides since the beginning of the invasion attempt on 7–8 September.

Saalfeld *(Napoleonic Wars)*, 1806

Reacting swiftly to Prussian demands on 7 October 1806 that he withdraw west of the Rhine, Napoleon despatched columns north-east from Würzburg to threaten enemy columns which were already on the move. Unaware of the French manœuvres, Prince Louis Ferdinand crossed the Saalè river with 9,000 Prussian and Saxon troops. On 10 October he was attacked by 5,500 men of the French V Corps, led by Marshal Lannes in person, and driven back under the walls of Saalfeld, sixty-five miles south-west of Leipzig. In a desperate attempt to retrieve the situation, Prince Louis Ferdinand led a cavalry charge against Lannes's troops, but in vain. He was killed, and altogether the Prussians lost 1,400 men in casualties and prisoners and twenty guns. Lannes then forded the Saale to join Napoleon's main body in the action at Jena.

Sablat *(Thirty Years War)*, 1619

After capturing Pilsen for the Protestants in November 1618, Count von Mansfeld, the mercenary leader, wintered in the city. The following spring with 20,000 men he set out for the Catholic stronghold of Budweis, seventy-five miles south-east. Short of his destination, he was attacked by an army raised by Emperor Ferdinand II and under the command of the Comte de Bucquoy. Near the village of Sablat Mansfeld's main body came under fire on 10 June 1619, and at nightfall the Protestant column was forced to withdraw, having lost 1,500 in casualties and prisoners and its entire baggage train. This Catholic victory only reinforced Bohemian determination to resist Ferdinand II and support the Protestant, Frederick V of the Palatinate, as king.

Sacile *(Napoleonic Wars)*, 1809

When war once more broke out between France and Austria in 1809, both countries deployed their troops for action along the

Danube river, but the first battle took place in Italy. Here Eugène de Beauharnais, Napoleon's stepson, commanded an army of 37,000 men and was opposed by 40,000 Austrians under Archduke John. An inconclusive clash occurred between the two armies at Sacile in north-eastern Italy, near the head of the Adriatic Sea, on 16 April 1809. Feeble leadership was demonstrated by both commanders, and, when the Austrians moved to threaten the French line of retreat, Beauharnais promptly fell back behind the Piave river. Not until Napoleon advanced on Vienna later in the month was Archduke John obliged to retire into Hungary.

Sadowa *(Austro–Prussian War)*, 1866

In pursuit of the Prussian plan to concentrate three invading armies at Gitschin (Jicin) in north-eastern Bohemia, the First Army and the Army of the Elbe, together numbering 125,000 men, crossed the Bohemian Mountains. Unwilling to meet them in battle, the Austrian commander, Field-Marshal von Benedek, began to withdraw his force of 205,000 south-eastwards towards Königgrätz (Hradec Kralove) on the Upper Labe (Elbe) river. Before he could cross, however, the Prussian First Army of Prince Frederick Charles caught him at Sadowa, sixty-five miles east of Prague. The Prussians planned to hold von Benedek until the Second Army under the Crown Prince (Frederick William) could come up on the left (east) flank from Silesia. But a rash attack by the Prussian 7th Division on the morning of 3 July brought on a major battle. Taking advantage of their superior numbers, the Austrians counter-attacked vigorously, and Prussian troops were in some danger until the Second Army eventually arrived on the field early in the afternoon. With his 100,000 men the Crown Prince proceeded to carry the key to the Austrian position, a vital hill at Chlum, and when his cavalry attacks failed to recover the hill, von Benedek retired under the cover of artillery fire. In one of the most decisive victories in European history the Prussians had inflicted losses of 40,000 in casualties and prisoners on the Austrians for 9,000 of their own. Tactically one of the important reasons for success was Prussian use of a breech-loading rifle, which not only allowed the firer to reload from a prone position but gave a much faster rate of fire than the Austrian muzzle-loader.

St Albans I *(Wars of the Roses)*, 1455

Learning that Edward, Duke of York, with some 3,000 men was marching south towards London, Henry VI assembled 2,000 Lancastrian supporters and advanced to St Albans, twenty miles north-west of the capital. Whilst the Duke of York attacked St Albans on 22 May 1455 with his main force, the Earl of Warwick led a detachment of cavalry around the city to cut Lancastrian lines of communication. The royal force was thus heavily defeated with the loss of 300 dead, including several nobles. As a result of this, the opening conflict in the Wars of the Roses, the King came under Yorkist control.

St Albans II *(Wars of the Roses)*, 1461

Advancing south after its victory at Wakefield, the Lancastrian army reached St Albans, where a force under the Earl of Warwick aimed to delay its progress until Yorkist reinforcements could arrive. On 17 February 1461, however, the Lancastrians launched a surprise attack, captured the city and reputedly killed half the defending force. In the confusion the Earls of Warwick and Norfolk escaped, but they were obliged to leave behind Henry VI, their prisoner, to rejoin Queen Margaret, who was with the attackers. Had the King moved to London immediately, he might have regained undisputed control of the country; instead he took his army away to the north. This allowed Warwick to reorganize his scattered forces and encouraged Prince Edward of York to proclaim himself Edward IV on 4 March.

St-Denis *(French Wars of Religion)*, 1567

When strife once more broke out between Huguenot and Catholic factions in France, Charles IX despatched a Catholic army under the Duke of Montmorency seven miles north-east of Paris to St-Denis. Here it met an inferior Huguenot force under Louis I de Bourbon, the Prince of Condé, and Gaspard de Coligny. The royal cavalry carried the day, but Montmorency was killed in the action, which had no decisive effect on the conflict as a whole.

Saintes *(Anglo–French Wars)*, 1242

Believing that unrest in France would give him an opportunity to recover Angevin lands lost by his father, Henry III concluded an alliance with French rebels and landed with an English force on the Bay of Biscay in the summer of 1242. Virtually no assistance came from their French allies, and on 21 July the English were attacked thirty miles inland at Saintes by a French royal force, which had crossed the Charente river. The invaders were defeated and, although this was only a minor skirmish, it persuaded Henry to abandon the war against Louis IX and retire to Gascony, then under English control.

St-Mihiel *(First World War)*, 1918

Following limited Allied successes in the late summer of 1918, General Ludendorff decided to withdraw German troops from the St-Mihiel salient, twenty miles south-east of Verdun, on 11 September. Next day, before evacuation could effectively get under way, sixteen divisions of the American First Army under General Pershing, supported by French artillery and tanks, the French II Colonial Corps and air force units commanded by Colonel William Mitchell, attacked the salient from north and south. Within thirty-six hours it had been entirely eliminated, with 15,000 prisoners and 443 guns captured, at a cost of 7,000 American casualties. Failure to close the net swiftly allowed some 40,000 Germans to escape, and insufficient reserves could be brought up in time to mount an effective pursuit.

St-Quentin I *(Franco–Spanish Wars)*, 1557

When fighting once more broke out between France and Spain in 1557, the Comte d'Egmont led a combined Spanish and Flemish force into north-eastern France from the Spanish Netherlands. This caused the Duke of Montmorency to hurry towards St-Quentin on the Somme river, eighty miles north-east of Paris, with a relief army of 20,000 men, but he was trapped nearby in a narrow defile on 10 August. The French were utterly routed, with 14,000 becoming casualties or prisoners, including Gaspard de Coligny, who was held captive for three years.

St-Quentin II *(Franco–Prussian War)*, 1871

The last remaining French army in the field in 1871 comprised 40,000 men under General Faidherbe. At St-Quentin on 19 January it encountered 35,000 Prussians commanded by General von Goeben and was decisively beaten. The French suffered 12,000 losses in casualties and prisoners to the Prussian 2,400. Now all hope had gone of relieving Paris, which surrendered nine days later.

Salamanca *(Peninsular War)*, 1812

Once the fortresses of Ciudad Rodrigo and Badajoz had been taken, Viscount Wellington led 48,000 British, Portuguese and Spanish troops into northern Spain. At length on 22 July 1812 he brought Marshal Marmont's slightly superior French army to battle at Salamanca, 100 miles north-west of Madrid. Marmont believed that Wellington was retreating and gave the allied force an opportunity to attack his flank. During this successful assault Marmont was wounded, leaving Comte Clausel to extract the French from a dangerous situation. Wellington's troops suffered fewer than 6,000 casualties, but the French lost twice that number plus twelve guns. After this important victory Wellington marched on the Spanish capital and briefly occupied it, when Joseph Bonaparte and his government fled.

Salerno *(Second World War)*, 1943

Six days after the British Eighth Army landed on the Italian mainland in the south, on 9 September 1943 the Allied Fifth Army commanded by General Clark made an amphibious landing at Salerno, thirty miles south of Naples (Operation Avalanche). Landing on the right (south) of the Bay of Salerno, the American VI Corps quickly pushed fifteen miles inland, whilst on the left the British X Corps captured Battipaglia and the town of Salerno. But on 12 September the Germans mounted a fierce counter-offensive which drove the Allies back to within two miles of the coast in some places. Massive air support and reinforcement by the American 82nd Airborne and British 7th Armoured divisions stemmed the German advance, so that on the evening of 15 September Field-

Marshal Kesselring began to withdraw his forces from the vicinity of the beachhead. Next day units of the British Eighth Army arrived from the south, and the Salerno landings were no longer in danger.

Salonika *(Ottoman Wars)*, 1430

While the Ottoman Empire was weak after its heavy defeat in Asia Minor at Angora (Ankara) in 1402, Venice gained control of the Aegean port of Salonika as part of a defensive pact with the Byzantine Empire against the Turks. Under Murad II, however, Turkish strength revived and the Ottomans launched an attack on Salonika with its Venetian garrison of 1,500 men on 1 March 1430. Resistance proved of little use; Salonika swiftly fell to the attackers and was to remain in Turkish hands until 1912. Surviving defenders were either executed or sold into slavery, and the Ottomans now resumed their conquest of south-eastern Europe.

Sambre River *(Gallic Wars)*, 57 BC

Having wintered in Burgundy, Julius Caesar moved his Roman legions into north-western Gaul in 57 BC to deal with a hostile confederation of Gallic tribes. Quickly defeating the Suessiones and Bellovaci, he moved further north and camped close to the Sambre river. On the far side were the Nervii, still defiant. Caesar sent a force of cavalry across the river to scout the enemy position, but they were routed and the enemy then swarmed over the Sambre to attack the main Roman camp. In fierce fighting two legions on the right were surrounded and in danger of annihilation, when Caesar personally rode down the line urging his troops to greater effort. In the ensuing Roman counter-attack, the 50,000 tribesmen were cut to pieces, and possibly only 500 escaped. This victory allowed Caesar to deal with the Aduatuci, the remaining threat in the north-east.

Santander *(Spanish Civil War)*, 1937

Having captured Bilbao on 14 August 1937, General Davila with 106 Nationalist battalions began to drive westwards through the Cantabrian Mountains towards Santander on the Bay of Biscay.

The city was defended by 50,000 poorly equipped Republican troops under General Ulibarri and, when they were subjected to artillery bombardment and air attack, they fell back offering little resistance. On 23 August many of those involved surrendered, and two days later Davila entered Santander, as Ulibarri and other Republican leaders fled to France.

Sant' Angelo *(Imperial Invasions of Italy)*, 998

Learning that Crescentius the Younger had deposed Gregory V, the first German Pope, the Holy Roman Emperor Otto III marched an army into Italy. Attacking Crescentius' force, the Imperial troops confined them in a castle at Sant' Angelo on the Garigliano river near Cassino. When the castle was successfully stormed, Crescentius was captured and later executed, allowing Otto to restore Gregory to the papacy.

Santarem *(Portuguese Civil Wars)*, 1834

Two years after the infant Maria II succeeded to the Portuguese throne, in 1828 Dom Miguel, the regent and her uncle, usurped the throne, forcing the Queen into exile. Loyalist forces gradually gained the upper hand in the civil war which followed, however, and on 14 February 1834 brought the rebels to battle at Sanatarem, on the Tagus river forty-three miles from Lisbon. Under the Duke of Saldanha they decisively defeated Dom Miguel, who was forced to give up all claims to the Portuguese throne.

Saragossa I *(Spanish–Moslem Wars)*, 1118

Although there was little conflict between Christians and Moors in central and southern Spain in the late eleventh century, in the north-east Pedro I of Aragon and Navarre captured Huesca from the Moors and established his capital there. His successor, Alfonso I, carried the war further south and in 1118 stormed and captured Saragossa on the Ebro river, which became the Aragonese capital until the fifteenth century.

Saragossa II *(Peninsular War)*, 1808–9

When the citizens of Saragossa, 170 miles north-east of Madrid, rebelled against Joseph Bonaparte's appointment as King of Spain, the city was besieged by French troops under Marshal Lefebvre in June 1808. After less than two months the siege was raised, but it was re-established in December by Marshals Moncey and Mortier. The garrison was ably commanded by General de Palafox and the siege commemorated later in Lord Byron's *Childe Harold*, through the legendary efforts of the Maid of Saragossa, who took the place of her wounded lover on the battlements. On 22 January 1809 Marshal Lannes assumed command of the besiegers. Under his direction the French stormed into the city on 20 February and, after heavy fighting, forced Palafox to surrender.

Sasbach *(Dutch War of Louis XIV)*, 1675

After crossing the Rhine into Baden in the spring of 1675 with a French army, the Vicomte de Turenne manœuvred troops of the Holy Roman Empire under Count Montecuccoli into a desperate position at Sasbach, close to the French and Swiss borders and ten miles north-west of Freiburg. A French victory seemed certain, but Turenne was killed early in the battle and his subordinates proved unable to exploit the advantages of the situation. Although the French inflicted considerably more casualties on the enemy than they incurred themselves, they retired across the Rhine into Alsace. To replace Turenne Louis XIV recalled the Great Condé to command; however, by now the French had lost the initiative in the area.

Saxa Rubra *(Civil Wars of the Roman Empire)*, 312

Having defeated supporters of Valerius Maxentius in northern Italy, Constantine I marched on Rome to deal directly with his rival for the imperial throne. On Constantine's approach, Maxentius moved out of the capital to Saxa Rubra, nine miles north, and here on 27 October 312 Constantine is reported to have seen a flaming cross in the sky with the words '*In hoc signo vinces*' ('By this sign thou shalt conquer'). Next day the two armies clashed, and Constantine's cavalry soon scattered the enemy horse on both wings, leaving the unprotected infantry to be overwhelmed. Many of the vanquished, including Maxentius, were cut down fleeing across the Milyian Bridge (Pons Mulvius) or drowned in the Tiber river. The sight of the flaming cross and this subsequent victory reputedly led Constantine to accept Christianity.

Schwechat *(Hungarian Revolt against Austria)*, 1848

In the wave of revolutionary fervour which swept central Europe in 1848, the Hungarians rose against Austrian rule and marched on Vienna. Within the city sympathizers put up barricades, and Austrian regulars under the Prince Windischgrätz, who had previously suppressed an insurrection in Prague, moved against the advancing rebels. In the south-eastern suburb of Schwechat, the rebels proved no match for the Austrian regulars and were routed on 30 October. The following day von Windischgrätz bombarded Vienna into submission.

Sedan *(Franco–Prussian War)*, 1870

After Marshal Bazaine had withdrawn his troops into the fortress of Metz on 19 August 1870, Emperor Napoleon III took personal charge of the Comte de MacMahon's 130,000 men at Châlons-sur-Marne, determined to relieve the beleaguered army. As Napoleon's troops marched eastwards, they were pushed further north by the manœuvres of the newly formed Prussian Army of the Meuse. The two Prussian armies, encircling Sedan (on the Meuse fifty-five miles north-east of Reims) from north and south respectively, then met at Illy. In vain the French attempted to fight their way out of the trap on 1 September. On that day the French lost 17,000 casualties and 21,000 prisoners, and when General de Wimpffen surrendered Sedan the following day, another 83,000 became prisoners. Both MacMahon and the Emperor were captured in one of the most crushing defeats in French history. Metz could no longer expect relief, the Prussians were able to march on Paris virtually unhindered and, with the abdication of Napoleon III, the Second French Empire came to an end.

Sedgemoor *(Monmouth's Rebellion in England)*, 1685

On 11 June 1685 the Duke of Monmouth, natural son of Charles II, landed at Lyme Regis in Dorset, planning to lead a Protestant revolt against the accession of the Catholic James II to the throne. While he was collecting some 4,000 supporters, James II despatched the Earl of Feversham to the west of England with 2,500 royal troops to deal with the insurrection. When hopes of support from Scotland faded, Monmouth risked a night attack against the royal troops at Sedgemoor, near Bridgwater in Somerset, on 6 July. Recovering from initial surprise, Feversham's more experienced soldiers dealt with the attackers ruthlessly, particularly the cavalry under John Churchill (later Duke of Marlborough). Most of the rebel force was either captured or killed: Monmouth escaped only to be found and later beheaded, and in the so-called 'Bloody Assizes' Judge Jeffreys sentenced 1,000 of the prisoners to either transportation or death. Effectively, therefore, the Battle of Sedgemoor ended Monmouth's Rebellion.

Selby *(English Civil War)*, 1644

Threatened by a Scottish army from the north, the Earl of Newcastle sent Colonel John Bellais with 3,300 Royalist troops to deal with a Parliamentarian force under Sir Thomas Fairfax, which was approaching from the south. On 11 April 1644 at Selby, on the River Ouse twelve miles south of York, Bellais was routed by Fairfax, with the loss of over 1,000 men in casualties and prisoners and all his baggage and artillery. Newcastle was now obliged to withdraw into York, due to the twin threat from north and south.

Selinus *(Carthaginian Invasion of Sicily)*, 409 BC

Renewed civil war in Sicily allowed some 50,000 Carthaginian troops to land on the south-west coast and lay siege to Selinus. A Syracusan relief force under Diocles set out too late to aid the defenders, who were obliged to surrender after nine days. Selinus was sacked, the prisoners were taken into captivity, and the Carthaginians advanced to besiege Himera in the north.

Sellasia *(Wars of the Hellenistic Monarchies)*, 221 BC

When Cleomenes III of Sparta threatened to conquer the entire Peloponnesus, the Achaean League of northern cities appealed to Antigonus III of Macedonia for assistance. With the help of 10,000 Macedonians, the allied army defeated the Spartans at Sellasia, twelve miles north of Sparta, forcing Cleomenes to flee to Egypt. But the victory proved a mixed blessing, for Antigonus proceeded to extend his rule over most of the Peloponnesus.

Sempach *(Austro–Swiss Wars)*, 1386

Marching into Switzerland with 4,000 men divided into three columns, in an effort to resolve long-standing disputes, Leopold III, Duke of Austria, encountered 1,500 Swiss troops near the village of Sempach (seven miles north-west of Lucerne) on 9 July 1386. The leading column of 1,500 Austrians drove back the enemy vanguard, but the main body came up before the second column could effectively come into action, and it was dispersed by Swiss infantry. Discouraged by the fate of their fellows, men of the third Austrian column fled without coming into battle. Thus Leopold III and the majority of his knights, who had dismounted to fight on foot, were slaughtered. The power of Swiss pikemen and halberdiers had once more been sharply illustrated on the battlefield, but in the political affairs of the Holy Roman Empire the cantons still had scant impact.

Seneffe *(Dutch War of Louis XIV)*, 1674

Having successfully resisted French attempts to invade Holland, Prince William of Orange (later William III of England) marched south into the area of modern Belgium to support Spanish troops threatened by 50,000 French soldiers under the Great Condé. On 8 August 1674 the combined army of some 45,000 came into action in William's first and Condé's last major battle. Realizing the strength of Condé's dispositions, the allies began to retire but in so doing exposed their flank to attack. The French immediately took advantage of this opportunity and were only denied success when Prince William made a stand at Seneffe, six miles south-west of Nivelles. For seventeen hours the struggle continued until fighting petered out with neither side having gained a decisive advantage, although the French were obliged to retire eastwards once more. It was estimated that in all some 14,000 troops were killed on the battlefield.

Sentinum *(Third Samnite War)*, 295 BC

Crossing the Apennines with five legions, Quintus Fabius Maximus reached Sentinum (Sasso Ferrato) in northern Italy, thirty-five miles south-west of Ancona on the Adriatic coast. Here he encountered a hostile force, mainly comprising Samnites and Gauls. The war chariots of the Gauls made initial progress on the Roman left, but on the opposite wing the Samnites were driven back, thus allowing Maximus to attack the Gauls in the flank. This proved decisive, and for the loss of 8,200 men the Romans reputedly killed 25,000 of the enemy and captured 8,000 others. this defeat persuaded the Samnites to come to terms with Rome, although their allies continued to fight.

Sepeia *(Rise of Sparta)*, 494 BC

In 494 BC only the city-state of Argos remained to challenge Spartan supremacy in the Peloponnesus. In that year, however, Spartans under Cleomenes I surprised the main Argive force at Sepeia, reputedly whilst the men were dining. As a result of the overwhelming victory which they gained, the Spartans dominated the Peloponnesus, which ultimately led to conflict with Athens.

Sevastopol I *(Crimean War)*, 1854–5

Following their victory at the Alma river, the allied force of some 60,000 men marched south towards the Russian naval base of Sevastopol, situated on an inlet on the south-west coast of the Crimean peninsula. Instead of attacking from the north, it was decided to execute a flank march and occupy uplands south of the dockyard area of the city. To prevent entry of allied warships into the harbour, the Russians sank vessels across its entrance to the Black Sea, and on 28 September 1854 the allies decided to mount a regular siege. They had insufficient men for a complete investment, and, moreover, the Russians had marched 25,000 troops out of Sevastopol to act as a field army east of the city. The siege therefore took the form of lines only to the south of Sevastopol. From here batteries opened fire on 17 October, but by that time the defenders had considerably strengthened their fortifications under the guidance of General Todleben. Ravaged by disease and cold, the besiegers were forced to endure a painful winter on the uplands, and renewal of the bombardment in the following spring brought no greater success. On three occasions, at Balaclava, Inkerman and Tchernaya, the Russians threatened to dislodge the attackers' perilous hold, and an allied assault on the defences of Sevastopol on 18 June 1855 proved a costly failure. Eventually on 8 September French troops took the vital Malakoff siegework; that night the Russians blew up fortifications south of the harbour, retiring over a bridge of boats to the northern side. Here they remained for the duration of the war, and, in truth, the Allies only ever captured the southern part of the city. It had proved costly for defenders and besiegers, who had lost thousands of men through wounds and disease.

Sevastopol II *(Second World War)*, 1941–2

In October 1941 General von Manstein's German Eleventh Army invaded the Crimean peninsula and quickly overran all of it except Kerch and Sevastopol. Throughout the winter these military bases were held under loose siege until Kerch was attacked and taken in six days in May 1942. Von Manstein was then able to concentrate his entire strength against Sevastopol. On 3 June an all-out assault was launched, and the Soviet naval base was finally battered into surrender on 1 July after a 245-day siege. At the capitulation some 90,000 prisoners were taken.

Sevenoaks *(Cade's Rebellion in England)*, 1450

In early 1450 a revolt against taxation and other alleged government impositions, led by a certain Jack Cade, occurred in Kent. Henry VI sent an army to deal with the rebels, and at Sevenoaks, twenty miles south-east of London, the two forces met in battle on 18 June. The more numerous rebels, although lightly armed, overwhelmed the royal army, and Cade led his followers on to London. There they initially enjoyed support and some success but soon lost discipline, turned to pillaging, and the rebellion collapsed. Cade himself, who refused to lay down arms, was pursued into Kent and killed.

Sheriffmuir *(First Jacobite Rebellion)*, 1715

Declaring his support for the Old Pretender, the Earl of Mar raised a force of some 10,000 Highlanders in September 1715. No co-operation was achieved with other Jacobites in northern England, however, and Mar's men alone faced a royal force of 3,300 men under the Duke of Argyll at Sheriffmuir near Perth on 13 November. Although the action was indecisive, it effectively constituted a defeat for Mar, who needed a victory to gather more support. In fact, after the battle his supporters dispersed, and he was obliged to seek refuge in France the following February.

Shipka Pass *(Russo–Turkish Wars)*, 1877–8

During the time that Plevna was under siege, another Russian column of 7,000 men under General Radetski advanced into the Balkan Mountains to reach the Shipka Pass, sixty miles north-east of Plovdiv, on 21 August 1877. Here they were attacked by a larger Turkish force commanded by Suleiman Pasha. The Turks gained initial success until reinforcements allowed Radetski to recover lost ground and, when fighting died out on 26 August, both sides roughly held the positions that they had occupied five days previously. At this stage the Russians had suffered 4,000 casualties, the Turks possibly twice that number. Suleiman unsuccessfully attempted to clear the pass on 16 September, and no further major action occurred until the Russians took Plevna on 10 December. Russian forces at the Shipka Pass were then increased to 50,000; General Gurko assumed command and on 8 January 1878 launched a massive assault on the enemy entrenchments. Next day the defenders were overwhelmed, with the Turks having lost a further 4,000 casualties and 36,000 prisoners in this phase of the battle to Russian casualties of about 5,000. The invaders were free to press on southwards towards Constantinople.

Shkodër I *(Ottoman Wars)*, 1478

Still holding trading posts along the Greek and Albanian coasts, Venetians resisted the advance of the Ottoman Turks into south-eastern Europe. In 1478 the garrison of Shkodër (Scutari), a fortified town near the Adriatic coast of modern Albania, twice repulsed attempts to bombard it into submission, and eventually Mohammed II, 'the Conqueror', raised the siege and retired to Constantinople. The following year, when a peace treaty was concluded, the Ottoman Empire received Shkodër, and 500 survivors of the garrison were permitted to march out to safety.

Shkodër II *(First Balkan War)*, 1912–13

When the Balkan League of Greece, Serbia, Montenegro and Bulgaria declared war on Turkey in 1912, Montenegrin troops under Nicholas I besieged the Turkish town of Shkodër. Bulgaria and Serbia agreed to an armistice on 3 December, but Montenegro refused to come to terms. The siege therefore continued, and eventually on 22 April 1913 Shkodër was stormed, much to the annoyance of Montenegro's allies, who had assigned it to the newly created state of Albania. After mediation by Austria, Nicholas I yielded his conquest in accordance with allied wishes.

Shrewsbury I *(Roman Conquest of Britain)*, AD 50

In AD 50 Ostorius Scapula moved north to deal with opposition from Britons under Caractacus. The legions caught and defeated the rebels near Shrewsbury, close to the Welsh border, and Caractacus fled further north to seek refuge with the Brigantes. But this tribe surrendered him to the Romans, who later paraded him and his family through the streets of Rome in chains.

Shrewsbury II *(Percy's Rebellion in England)*, 1403

Four years after coming to the throne, Henry IV faced a rebellion from the Percy family of Northumberland in alliance with Owen Glendower. Hoping to overcome a small royal force under Henry (Hal), Prince of Wales, Sir Henry Percy (Hotspur) marched on Shrewsbury without waiting for his father, the Earl of Northumberland, to come to his aid and without co-ordinating his action with that of Glendower. Before the two forces could meet in battle, Henry IV brought troops to reinforce his son, and the combined royal army attacked Percy at Hateley Field, three miles north of Shrewsbury. Royal superiority in numbers offset the rebels' strong defensive position, and a charge led by Prince Hal had a decisive effect. Percy was mortally wounded, his uncle the Earl of Worcester captured and executed. The rebellion collapsed as a result of this royal triumph, but Northumberland, who took no part in the battle and was pardoned, waited for another opportunity to revolt.

Silistra *(Crimean War)*, 1854

Following their occupation of the principalities of Moldavia and Wallachia (modern Romania) the previous year, on 20 March 1854 Russian troops under Field-Marshal Paskevich crossed south of the Danube river to besiege the Turkish fortress of Silistra, seventy miles west of the Black Sea. Unofficially assisted by two British officers, who were on leave, the garrison resisted, although no important aid came from the Turkish government. At length Paskevich raised the siege, after losing 10,000 casualties, and retired over the Danube. Meanwhile, Britain and France had declared war on Russia in defence of Turkey, and their troops were already within fifty miles of Silistra, having landed at the Black Sea port of Varna. Three weeks after the Turks repelled Russian troops from Silistra, the allied governments decided to despatch their expeditionary forces to the Crimean peninsula.

Simancas *(Spanish—Moslem Wars)*, 934

Under Ramiro II of the Asturias, Leon and Castile, Christian states in the north-west of the Iberian peninsula began a long counter-offensive which would eventually clear the Moors from their conquests and drive them back across the Straits of Gibraltar into Africa. In 934 Ramiro II attacked Simancas, eight miles south-west of Valladolid, routed the Moors and gained the first important Christian victory south of the Pyrenees since the Battle of Covadonga in 718.

Sinsheim *(Dutch War of Louis XIV)*, 1674

Troops of the Holy Roman Empire and Spain were deployed to assist the Netherlands against France, and in 1674 the Vicomte de Turenne crossed the Rhine at Philippsburg to attack Imperial troops east of the river. At Sinsheim, twenty miles east of Philippsburg, Turenne met 10,000 of the enemy under the Duke of Lorraine on 16 June and with an equal number of French soldiers drove them from the field. He then laid waste the Palatinate to deny supplies to the enemy.

Slankamen *(Ottoman Wars)*, 1691

Reacting to Turkish conquests, including the occupation of Belgrade, under the Grand Vizier Mustafa Kuprili 20,000 troops of the Holy Roman Empire led by the Margrave of Baden-Baden advanced down the Danube to Slankamen, twenty miles northwest of Belgrade and close to the mouth of the Tisza river. On 19 August 1691 they encountered a Turkish force twice their size and routed it. Kuprili was killed, but the Empire was unable immediately to take advantage of Turkish disorganization, as it became involved in war with France in the west.

Slivnica *(Serbo–Bulgarian War)*, 1885

Seeking compensation for her annexation of Eastern Rumelia, 25,000 Serbian troops under Milan I invaded Bulgaria in November 1885. Initially they were opposed by only 10,000 troops under Stefan Stambolov near Slivnica, nineteen miles north-west of Sofia, but they made no appreciable progress on 17 November, the first day of the battle. During the night 5,000 Bulgarian reinforcements arrived, under Prince Alexander, who assumed command of the defenders, and next day the Bulgarians took the offensive. They were beaten back, and on 19 November, the third day of fighting, the Serbians launched another assault. When this was repulsed, Milan I retired over the border, having suffered 2,000 casualties. For the loss of almost 3,000 men, the new nation of Bulgaria had made the first defence of its territory.

Smolensk I *(Napoleonic Wars)*, 1812

Falling back before 175,000 men of the Grand Army as it advanced towards Moscow, the Russian Second Army of Prince Bagration effected a junction with the First Army commanded by General Barclay de Tolly to make a combined Russian force of almost 130,000 men. On 17 August 1812 leading units of Napoleon's force reached the outskirts of Smolensk, 210 miles west of Moscow, and soon 50,000 troops from both sides were in action. By the evening two suburbs were in French hands and, fearing that Napoleon might throw troops across the Dnieper river above the city and threaten communications with the Russian capital, Tolly set fire to Smolensk during the night and retired. The Russians suffered 10,000 casualties in this battle, the French slightly less.

Smolensk II *(Second World War)*, 1941

During the German advance on Moscow by Field-Marshal von Bock's Army Group Centre as part of Operation Barbarossa, forty-one divisions encircled Smolensk and thirty-four Soviet divisions in the area on 16 July 1941. Two days later the 10th Panzer Division fought its way into the city, but vigorous counter-attacks allowed many Soviet troops to escape the trap. Nevertheless, by the time that Smolensk fell on 6 August, an estimated 100,000 Soviet troops had become casualties or prisoners.

Sofia *(Wars of the Byzantine Empire)*, 981

Whilst the Byzantine Empire was preoccupied with internal problems, Tsar Samuel of Bulgaria extended his territory from the Black Sea to the Adriatic and south into the Peloponnesus. The Byzantine Emperor, Basil II, determined to deal with this growing menace in the north and marched into Bulgaria. Near Sofia, in 981, he was utterly defeated and forced to retire to Constantinople, so that for the next fifteen years the Bulgarians remained unchallenged by the Imperial troops.

Sohr *(War of the Austrian Succession)*, 1745

Insisting on Austrian recovery of Silesia before agreeing to peace, Maria Theresa sent an Austrian army of 30,000 men under Prince

Charles of Lorraine into north-east Bohemia to challenge 18,000 Prussians commanded by Frederick the Great. On 30 September 1745 the two armies met at Sohr (Soor), where an Austrian attack was defeated by steady defensive fire and the use of oblique line tactics. Frederick then counter-attacked to drive Prince Charles from the field with the loss of almost 6,000 casualties and twenty-two guns. The Prussians suffered only 3,500 casualties, but the Austrian defeat did not persuade Maria Theresa to abandon hopes of recovering Silesia, and the war continued.

Soissons (Rise of France), 486

Marching south from his capital at Tournai in 486, Clovis I, King of the Salian Franks, encountered an army led by Syagrius, the last Roman governor of Gaul. In a battle near Soissons, eighty-five miles away, on the banks of the Aisne river, Syagrius was killed, and Clovis gained control of Gaul between the Somme and Loire rivers, so firmly establishing the power of the Merovingian dynasty.

Solferino (Italian Wars of Independence), 1859

Following its defeat at Magenta on 4 June, the Austrian army retired eastwards across Lombardy and took up defensive positions five miles west of the Mincio river at Solferino. Almost 120,000 men with 450 guns were deployed on heights overlooking Solferino under the personal command of Emperor Franz Joseph. On 24 June 1859 they were attacked by a similar number of French and Piedmontese troops under the direction of Emperor Napoleon III and Victor Emmanuel II. After very heavy fighting allied troops led by the Comte de MacMahon captured high ground defended by General Scholick in the centre, whilst on the left Marshal Niel was successfully repulsing an Austrian advance. At nightfall, therefore, the Austrians withdrew across the Mincio, having suffered over 20,000 casualties, many of them to the French artillery. Allied losses were almost as great, and such was the slaughter that Napoleon III concluded a separate peace with Austria, whereby France received Lombardy. Shortly afterwards this was in turn ceded to Piedmont by France in return for Savoy and Nice. The Austrian defeat at Solferino and the subsequent territorial arrangements positively assisted the cause of Italian unification. Another side effect was encouragement towards formation of the International Red Cross due to the appalling conditions that wounded had to endure at this battle.

Solway Moss (*Anglo–Scottish Wars*), 1542

Reacting against English pressure to renounce their friendship with Catholic France, the Scots resorted to raiding across the border and in November 1542 poured 10,000 men into north-west England. On 24 November at Solway Moss in Cumberland they were attacked by an inferior English force, which took advantage of their poor organization to rout the invaders. News of this defeat is reputed to have hastened the death of James V, who was succeeded by his infant daughter Mary Stuart, Queen of Scots.

Somme I (*First World War*), 1916

Preceded by a massive artillery bombardment, which commenced on 24 June, the British Fourth, French Sixth and French Tenth Armies attacked German positions astride the Somme river between Arras and St-Quentin on 1 July 1916. Eighteen British divisions went forward on a fifteen-mile front in the north towards Bapaume, and sixteen French divisions further south against Peronne. The French Sixth Army did make some initial headway, but the British immediately encountered withering fire from prepared positions on low hills to their front. On the first day alone British casualties were almost 60,000 men, one-third of them killed, and it soon became evident that no major breakthrough could be effected. The British Fifth Army was brought up to reinforce the line between the British Fourth and French Sixth Armies, and on 15 September tanks were used for the first time in battle (though only eighteen were committed haphazardly), and the battle developed into a costly exercise in attrition. After ten weeks, on 18 November it petered out in miserable weather. The Allies had advanced about seven miles and captured 125 square miles of land, for which 650,000 Germans, 420,000 British and 195,000 French troops had become casualties. Thereafter British commentators have associated 'Somme' with indiscriminate slaughter.

Somme II *(First World War)*, 1918

Making use of troops transferred from the eastern front, now quiet after the capitulation of Russia, General Ludendorff launched an attack against the British Fifth and Third Armies on a fifty-mile front south of Arras. On 21 March 1918, preceded by a bombardment of 6,000 guns and a gas attack, the German Seventeenth, Second and Eighteenth Armies advanced and, although their seventy-one divisions moved forward only three miles in three days, as a result the British Fifth Army (General Gough) in the south withdrew behind the Somme to expose the flank of the Third Army (General Byng) further north. By evening of the fourth day, therefore, the Germans had extended their advance to fourteen miles, and a breakthrough between British and French troops in the area of Roye, thirty-five miles south-east of Amiens, seemed probable. But on 26 March Marshal Foch became co-ordinator of Allied forces on the Western Front (on 14 April, Commander-in-Chief). Although the Germans continued to advance and by 3 April were at Moreuil, twelve miles from Amiens, Allied reorganization, coupled with German problems in supply and communication, halted the offensive forty miles from its start line the next day. During fifteen days of fighting the Allies had lost almost 230,000 men (including 70,000 prisoners) and over 1,000 guns, and German casualties exceeded 200,000. Ludendorff's attempt to drive a wedge between the British and French thus failed.

Spicheren *(Franco–Prussian War)*, 1870

Shortly after the outbreak of war, the French advanced to capture Saarbrücken on 2 August 1870. They were soon forced to abandon it and fall back, as a Prussian army of 27,000 men commanded by General von Steinmetz invaded the Saar. At Spicheren (near Forbach, seven miles south-west of Saarbrücken) General Frossard sought to stem its advance with 24,000 French troops on 6 August 1870. Despite the bravery of individual French units, towards evening Frossard's men were driven from the field in confusion and fell back on Metz. The Prussians suffered 4,871 casualties, the French slightly less, and victory allowed the Prussians to move forward into eastern France.

Stadtlohn *(Thirty Years War)*, 1623

When Count von Mansfeld's mercenary troops failed to join him in Lower Saxony, Prince Christian of Brunswick began to withdraw his force of 16,000 Protestants west towards the Netherlands. Ten miles short of the border he was caught and forced to fight at the village of Stadtlohn in Westphalia, thirty-five miles west of Munster, by a superior Catholic force under the Comte de Tilly. Christian occupied high ground in front of a marsh, and after Catholic pressure had put cavalry on the wings to flight, his infantry were unable to make their escape through the soft terrain. Tilly's men overran the Protestant position, killing some 6,000 men, making another 4,000 prisoners and capturing all Christian's baggage and artillery. This débâcle ended Christian's reputation as a military commander, for that night he reached the Dutch border with only 2,000 of his men.

Stainmore *(Rise of England)*, 954

In an attempt to throw off English domination, Eric Bloodaxe, exiled King of Norway, attacked a Saxon army at Stainmore, near Edendale in Westmorland. The Norsemen were crushed, Bloodaxe was killed and the Viking kingdom of York came to an end.

Stalingrad *(Second World War)*, 1942–3

Originally the German summer offensive of 1942 planned the encirclement of Stalingrad, the communications and armament-producing centre on the Volga river, with Army Group B from the north and Army Group A from the south – a total of four armies. Hitler changed the plan, despatching Army Group A into the Caucasus in search of much-needed oil, whilst the Fourth Panzer and Sixth Armies dealt with Stalingrad. Once the advance got under way in June, progress was so swift that the Fourth Panzer Army was diverted to assist in the south, leaving General von Paulus' Sixth Army to take Stalingrad alone. Preceded by heavy bombing raids, German troops reached the Volga above and below the city and also pressed into the western suburbs. But the Russians doggedly refused to abandon Stalingrad and retire to the east bank of the Volga. Within the city General Chuikov's Sixty-Second Army fought for each building, and Hitler was forced to order General Hoth to take his Fourth Panzer Army towards Stalingrad once more, this time from the south. Secretly General Zhukov built up Russian forces on the flanks of the Sixth and Fourth Panzer Armies, which were guarded by allied Romanian and Italian units. On 19 November the Russians launched a massive counter-attack, and by 23 November the Sixth Army had been cut off in a pocket twenty-five miles long and twelve miles deep, which contained some 300,000 German and Allied troops. Hitler refused to allow von Paulus to fight his way out, and a relief attempt on 12 December (Operation Winter Storm) by Hoth failed; so did the Luftwaffe's airlift of supplies – mainly due to appalling weather conditions. Gradually the pocket was compressed and, having rejected a Russian call to surrender, it was heavily attacked on 10 January 1943. Short of medical supplies and food, the doomed men cut strips from the sides of the few living horses that remained to them, and human bones, acting as macabre signposts, pointed the way across frozen wastes. On 31 January von Paulus surrendered the southern part of the 'cauldron', which had been split by Russian action, and on 2 February all resistance ended. Ironically von Paulus was promoted Field-Marshal on the day that he surrendered, and he went into captivity with possibly 123,000 of his men, including twenty-four generals. Only 5,000 of these would ultimately return to Germany. By their success at Stalingrad the Russians raised the morale of the Allies and proved that the German Wehrmacht, until then apparently invincible, could be defeated. Both sides lost almost 200,000 men in casualties and prisoners during this battle.

Stallupönen, see **Gumbinnen**

Stamford Bridge *(Norse Invasion of England)*, 1066

Alarmed by news of the victory of Norse invaders at Fulford on 20 September 1066, Harold II marched rapidly north from London and five days later attacked the invaders at Stamford Bridge on the Derwent river, eight miles north-east of York. Having withstood the first English attack, the Norse were deceived by a feigned withdrawal, then surprised by a sudden wheel of the retreating English. By tactics similar to those used later by Normans to defeat him at Hastings, Harold II caused great panic in the Norse ranks. Many of the enemy were killed, including Harold Hardrada and Harold II's own half-brother Tostig, who had joined the Norse. The English triumph was complete, with few of the invaders escaping to their ships. This was the last Norse invasion of England, but shortly afterwards William and his Normans landed on the Sussex coast, and Harold II was obliged to hurry south once more to deal with them.

Standard, The *(Anglo–Scottish Wars)*, 1138

In the period of political confusion after the death of Henry I, when Matilda and Stephen both claimed the English throne, David I invaded Northumberland with a Scottish force. Rallied by the Archbishop of York, the English met and defeated the invaders at Cowton Moor, north of Northallerton, on 22 August 1138. The battle became known as that of 'The Standard', because the banners of saints including those of St Cuthbert of Durham and St Peter of York were carried by the English in a waggon onto the field of battle.

Steenkerke *(War of the Grand Alliance)*, 1692

After their capture of Namur in June 1692, French troops under the Duke of Luxembourg became a threat to Brussels, and William III of England took command of the Alliance armies. By the use of forced marches, he surprised the French in camp at Steenkerke (Steinkirk), fifteen miles south-west of Ostend, at dawn on 3 August. The allied vanguard of some 15,000 men quickly overran part of the French position, but Luxembourg coolly reorganized his men under fire, and their counter-attacks finally caused the tiring English infantry to give way. By noon William was forced to retire from the field, having suffered 8,000 casualties, although neither this reverse, nor one a year later at Neerwinden, proved particularly disastrous. The campaign in the Low Countries during this war was indecisive, underlined William III's caution as a military commander and resulted in no major frontier adjustments.

Stiklestad *(Scandanavian Wars)*, 1030

Although he had freed Norway from Danish and Swedish control, the Christian King Olaf II was forced into exile in 1028. Two years later, in an attempt to regain his throne, he landed with a loyal army north-east of Trondheim. But in a battle at Stiklestad nearby he was defeated and killed by pagan Norwegians supported by Danish troops. Olaf II later became a national hero and the country's patron saint on his canonization in 1164.

Stirling Bridge *(Anglo–Scottish Wars)*, 1297

After Edward I had proclaimed himself King of Scotland, enraged Scots under Sir William Wallace made destructive forays against English bases and villages north and south of the border. Preoccupied with war against France, Edward ordered the Earl of Surrey to deal with the rebels. Gathering a force of some 50,000 men, Surrey marched north and on 11 September 1297 began to negotiate the narrow Stirling Bridge over the Forth river, near the abbey of Cambuskenneth. Wallace allowed 5,000 of the vanguard to cross, then struck the bridgehead before it could become established. Virtually the whole force north of the river was annihilated and Surrey fell back, closely pursued by the jubilant Scots, as far south as the Tweed river. Although the garrisons at Stirling, Edinburgh, Roxburgh and Berwick held out, within two months the Scots had overrun Northumberland and much of Cumberland, and the English were now faced with a major task of recovery.

Stockach *(French Revolutionary Wars)*, 1799

As part of the strategy of the anti-French Second Coalition, Archduke Charles Louis, brother of the Holy Roman Emperor, marched 60,000 Austrians against General Jourdan's army of 40,000 men east of the Rhine. On 25 March 1799 at Stockach (at the head of Lake Constance and fifty-five miles south-west of Ulm) Jourdan's force was defeated with the loss of 5,000 casualties, and the French retreated to the Rhine. After crossing the river Jourdan was replaced in command by General Masséna.

Stoke *(Simnel's Rebellion in England)*, 1487

In support of Lambert Simnel, who had been crowned Edward VI in Dublin, Yorkists crossed from Ireland to England. At East Stoke in the Midlands, led by the Earl of Lincoln and reinforced by Irish and German mercenaries, they met a superior royal force under Henry VII on 16 June 1487. The rebels were routed, Lincoln was killed, other leaders were captured and Simnel was found employment in the royal kitchens.

Stollhofen *(War of the Spanish Succession)*, 1707

With the northern front in the Netherlands quiet, the Duke of Villars marched a French force of forty-five battalions to the Rhine, where between Karlsruhe and Strasbourg the Margrave of Baden-Baden commanded Imperial forces holding the Lines of Stollhofen, reputedly impregnable. In a surprise night attack on 22 May 1707, however, Villars stormed the position, put the defenders to flight and captured fifty artillery pieces. With the loss of this line of defence, the south-western part of the Holy Roman Empire was open to French attack.

Stralsund I *(Thirty Years War)*, 1628

In order to secure a Baltic port, General von Waldstein (Wallenstein) despatched an Imperial force to take Stralsund on the Pomeranian coast in February 1628. The inhabitants resisted and, having been reinforced by Swedish and Scottish mercenaries and promised supplies by the Swedish navy, prepared to withstand a siege, which Wallenstein arrived to direct personally on 5 July. Three attempts were made to carry the defences in the period 6–9 July, but although a few minor works did fall, Wallenstein was unable to capture Stralsund. At length on 28 July he returned to Prague, and a week later his army raised the siege of the port through which Gustavus Adolphus was later to bring his Protestant Swedish army into the Thirty Years War.

Stralsund II *(Great Northern War)*, 1715

Seeking to clear the Swedes from territory south of the Baltic, in 1715 a combined Danish and Prussian force of 36,000 men laid siege to Stralsund and after three months succeeded in capturing the island of Rügen. Recognizing the importance of this feature Charles XII led the Swedish garrison in an attempt to recapture it, but failed and on 10 October 1715 the besiegers took further dominating positions. Ten days later, with defeat imminent, Charles, who had been severely wounded during the fighting, escaped to Sweden by sea and shortly afterwards the garrison surrendered.

Stratton *(English Civil War)*, 1643

In south-western England Sir Ralph Hopton rallied support for the King, and on 16 May 1643, reinforced by loyal Cornishmen, four columns of his Royalist troops attacked Parliamentarians under Sir William Waller, then holding Stratton Hill in Cornwall, five miles east of Bude on the Atlantic coast. The position was carried in the late afternoon after heavy fighting, Hopton capturing 1,700 prisoners, thirteen guns and the Parliamentarian baggage train. He now overran the whole of Devon, with the exception of Barnstaple, Exeter and Plymouth, and advanced until checked by Waller with a reorganized and reinforced army at Lansdown in July.

Svistov *(Russo–Turkish Wars)*, 1877

Following the Russian declaration of war on Turkey in support of Serbia on 24 April 1877, a Russian army advanced into Moldavia and Wallachia (soon to be recognized as Romania), and on 26 June an advance guard of 15,000 men under General Dragomirov slipped across the Danube during the night. Next day they attacked the Turkish fortress of Svistov, fourteen miles east of Nikopol (Nicopolis) on the southern bank of the Danube, and after reinforcements commanded by General Skobolov had arrived, the garrison surrendered. By achieving surprise, the Russians lost less than 1,000 casualties in the assault, and they were now able to move on to Nikopol and later Plevna.

Syracuse I *(Carthaginian Invasion of Sicily)*, 387 BC

During their struggle to control Sicily, once more the Carthaginians attacked Syracuse on the south-east coast in 387 BC. With

50,000 men, and the aid of a powerful fleet, Himilco laid siege to the city, which was defended by Dionysius the Elder with a similar number of troops. An epidemic in their camp greatly reduced the strength of the besiegers, and thirty Spartan triremes arrived to assist the defenders at sea. Dionysius was then able to counter-attack both on land and at sea. The Carthaginian fleet was surprised and almost completely destroyed while many of the crews were ashore, and the siege lines were broken up when the garrison poured out of the city. Himilco escaped the carnage, later committing suicide, but this defeat did not entirely clear the Carthaginians from Sicily.

Syracuse II *(Second Punic War)*, 213–212 BC

In 213 BC 25,000 Roman troops under Marcus Marcellus and a fleet commanded by Appius Claudius laid siege to Syracuse, which was defended by pro-Carthaginian rebels led by Hippocrates. The initial assault was repulsed by strong defences, reinforced by an ingenious collection of slings and catapults devised by the Greek Archimedes. Trouble in other parts of Sicily led to withdrawal of some of the Romans, and the siege was not vigorously pursued. In 212 BC, however, the Romans took advantage of a Syracusan festival to gain possession of the upper part of the city. A counter-attack by the garrison failed, then the Romans destroyed defences which were preventing the free action of their fleet, so that the rest of Syracuse soon fell. Archimedes died during the siege, which resulted in the fall of the last important centre of resistance against Rome in Sicily.

Szentgotthard *(Ottoman Wars)*, 1664

In 1663 a Turkish army under the Grand Vizier, Ahmed Kuprili, marched into Hungary once more to threaten the Holy Roman Empire and precipitate another war. The following year, an Imperial force commanded by Count Montecuccoli, reinforced by French troops under the Duke of Lorraine, occupied a strong position at Szentgotthard on the Raba river in western Hungary, 130 miles south-west of Budapest, as a bar to the Turks. On 1 August 1664 the Turks attacked, were defeated and withdrew. Nine days later they agreed to a peace treaty, which ensured a measure of independence for Transylvania.

Szigetvar *(Ottoman Wars)*, 1566

Advancing into Hungary, Turks under Suleiman the Magnificent laid siege to Szigetvar in the south-west, ninety miles east of Agram (Zagreb), on 5 August 1566. Led by a Croatian, Miklos Zrinyi, the garrison of 3,000 defended stubbornly, and during the fighting Suleiman died, although his death was not announced. At length the Turks stormed the defences on 7 September, killing Zrinyi and most of the garrison. The death of Suleiman was then revealed. The Ottoman Empire would never again enjoy such territorial strength, military power and administrative organization.

Taginae *(Wars of the Byzantine Empire)*, 552

In 551 Emperor Justinian I sent Narses into northern Italy from the Balkans with an army of 20,000 men to recover the Italian peninsula from the Ostrogoths. In July 552 Narses encountered the main enemy force under Totila at Taginae (Tadinum), in the Apennines near the Flaminian Way, and his archers cut the Goths to pieces. When his infantry attacked, victory was complete, and among the 6,000 enemy dead was Totila. Narses then marched south, methodically freed the rest of Italy from barbarian control and restored Byzantine authority over it.

Tagliacozzo *(Imperial Invasions of Italy)*, 1268

Two years after establishing himself as King of the Two Sicilies, Charles I of Anjou was threatened by an army led by Conradin, the Holy Roman Emperor, and Frederick, Duke of Austria. Charles, aided by the Pope, met and defeated the invaders at Tagliacozzo in central Italy, forty miles north-east of Rome, capturing and beheading both enemy commanders. The death of Conradin ended the Hohenstauffen dynasty, which had dominated the Holy Roman Empire for 130 years, and this victory strengthened Charles' position in Italy and Sicily.

Talavera *(Peninsular War)*, 1809

Invading Spain along the Tagus valley from Portugal, supported by a friendly Spanish force under General Guesta, Sir Arthur

Wellesley reached Talavera, seventy miles south-west of Madrid, in July 1809. Here he experienced supply difficulties and was faced with the advance of two French armies converging from north and south, commanded respectively by Marshals Soult and Victor. Victor arrived in the area first and, without waiting for Soult to come up, attacked on 28 July with 30,000 men. The Spaniards took little part in the battle, and the bulk of the fighting was done by 16,000 British troops, who finally threw back Victor, inflicting on him losses of 7,300 men in casualties and prisoners and twenty guns. The British lost some 6,000 casualties, but Wellesley was able to withdraw into Portugal before Soult appeared. For this victory he was created Viscount Wellington.

Tanagra *(First Peloponnesian War)*, 457 BC

Alarmed by a crushing Athenian naval victory over Aegina, Sparta re-established the Boeotian League under Thebes to curb further Athenian aggression. In 457 BC at Tanagra, fourteen miles east of Thebes, supported by allied troops the Spartans met a force of 14,000 Athenians assisted by Thessalian cavalry. Both sides suffered heavy casualties, but desertion of the Thessalians gave the Spartans victory. Their losses, however, forced them to return home, and shortly afterwards the Athenians defeated the Thebans to restore their control over central Greece.

Tannenberg I *(Rise of Poland)*, 1410

At the start of the fifteenth century Teutonic Knights ruled over much of north and east Germany from their capital at Merienburg (Malbork), twenty miles south of the Gulf of Danzig. In 1410 they were challenged by a Polish force under Ladislas V, aided by Bohemian mercenaries under Jan Žižka and many Russians and Lithuanians, at Tannenberg, then in north-east Poland. On 15 July the Knights were overwhelmed with heavy loss, and they never recovered either their former glory or power.

Tannenberg II *(First World War)*, 1914

Thrusting into East Prussia against the German Eighth Army of 160,000 men, and belying the German estimates that no major advance could occur for six weeks, the Russian First (General Rennenkampf) and Second (General Samsonov) Armies allowed themselves to become separated by the fifty-mile-long complex of lakes and wooded country known as the Masurian Lakes. When General von Hindenburg, with his Chief of Staff General Ludendorff, arrived to take over command of the Germans after the Battle of Gumbinnen, he approved a plan devised by Colonel Hoffman to exploit this weakness. Accordingly, making use of their interior lines of communication and further assisted by a good railway system, von Hindenburg transferred three complete corps from the area of Königsberg, which was evidently Rennenkampf's sole objective, to meet Samsonov in the south. The Russians were unaware of this redeployment, but the Germans knew of Russian intentions through their habit of sending uncoded messages by wireless. Samsonov continued to press forward, partly in search of supplies as his commissariat arrangements had broken down, and preliminary action took place on 27 August 1914. Next day some 350,000 troops were engaged in battle near the village of Tannenberg, south-west of the Masurian Lakes, as the three German corps gradually drove in the flanks of the Russian salient in a double envelopment. Such was the Russian confusion that some troops continued to advance unaware of Samsonov's order to retire, and by 31 August the Second Army had ceased to exist: 30,000 had become casualties, 92,000 were prisoners, Samsonov had committed suicide and possibly as few as 40,000 men escaped. German casualties were some 13,000, and von Hindenberg could turn his attention to Rennenkampf, who had made no move to assist his fellow commander, knowing that the Russians now exercised no real threat to East Prussia. This psychological and physical disaster for the Russians meant that German fears of simultaneous campaigns on two fronts receded.

Taormina *(Saracen Conquest of Sicily)*, 902

Early in the ninth century Moslems from North Africa invaded Sicily and began slowly to overrun the island. Syracuse fell, although the Byzantine garrison of Taormina on the east coast, between Messina and Catania, close to Mount Etna, continued to hold out. In 902 a new Saracen assault at length captured the city, which was promptly sacked, and surviving Christians fled across the Straits of Messina to the Italian mainland. This victory brought the whole of Sicily under Moslem control, which although interrupted was not finally broken until the thirteenth century.

Tarragona *(Peninsular War)*, 1811

While British troops were fighting the French in Portugal and western Spain, in the east of the Iberian peninsula Spanish garrisons were still holding out against French troops. In May 1811 Marshal Suchet laid siege to Tarragona, near the coast and fifty miles south-west of Barcelona, and gradually forced his way towards the centre of the town despite stubborn resistance. By 21 June the French had gained a lodgement in the lower town, and a week later they overran the rest of Tarragona, when 8,000 survivors of the garrison surrendered. The siege cost Suchet 6,000 casualties, but he was able then to advance towards Valencia, which was also defying the French.

Tchernaya *(Crimean War)*, 1855

The Tchernaya river flowed north-westwards into Sevastopol harbour below and east of the Heights on which French forces held the right of the allied lines. Further east, across the river, a strong Russian force was encamped on the hill where the Ruins of Inkerman and MacKenzie's Farm were situated. On 16 August 1855, three Russian divisions descended from this vantage-point and advanced over the Tchernaya against the allied right flank. Three French divisions and one Sardinian division repulsed them for the loss of 5,000 casualties to 1,200 among the allies. This was the last major Russian attempt to dislodge the besieging armies, and within three weeks the southern part of Sevastopol, with its naval dockyard, had been evacuated by its defenders.

Telamon *(Rise of Rome)*, 225 BC

Angered by the northward expansion of Rome, Cisalpine Gauls from the Po valley marched into ancient Etruria, defeated a Roman army at Clusium, eighty-five miles north of Rome, and swept south-westwards towards the coast. Near Cape Telamon (Talamone) midway between Rome and Pisa, however, they were trapped between two Roman armies and annihilated, leaving the legions free to move north against the Gauls' homeland and conquer it.

Tertry *(Rise of France)*, 687

During a period of internal strife which affected the Frankish kingdom after the death of Clovis I, Pepin, Mayor of Austrasia, and Thierry, Mayor of Neustria, vied for power. At Tertry, fifteen miles north-east of Valenciennes in north-eastern France, supporters of the two clashed in a minor skirmish in 687. The Austrasians won and Pepin was able to hand down to his son Charles Martel control of a unified kingdom.

Teruel *(Spanish Civil War)*, 1937–8

In bitterly cold weather two Republican armies, commanded by Generals Sarabia and Menendez, attacked the city of Teruel, 138 miles east of Madrid, on 15 December 1937. Completely encircled, Colonel d'Harcourt and the garrison of 4,000 held out in part of the city, but, after a relief attempt two weeks later failed to break through, he finally surrendered on 8 January 1938. The victors were then themselves besieged in Teruel by Nationalist forces, who gained an important success north of the city on 7 February when the Republicans lost 22,000 men in casualties and prisoners. By 20 February the city was completely surrounded by Nationalist troops, except for the road to Valencia, and Sarabia used this to withdraw the remnants of his army, which had been in occupation of Teruel. Behind he left 10,000 dead and 14,500 prisoners, and the military weakness of the Republican Government had once more been exposed.

Tettenhall *(Rise of England)*, 910

When the Danes of Northumbria broke the peace with the kingdom of Wessex, Edward the Elder, son of Alfred the Great, marched his army north into modern Staffordshire and on 5 August 910 defeated the Danes at Tettenhall. As a result he was able to extend his control north to the Humber.

Teutoburgerwald (*Germanic Wars of the Roman Empire*), AD 9

Believing that tribes east of the Rhine had been effectively subdued, the Romans maintained three legions of infantry and some
800 cavalry commanded by Publius Quintilius Varus in the area of
modern Westphalia. In the autumn of AD 9 Varus marched east to
put down a local insurrection and reached the Teutoburgerwald,
between the Ems and Weser rivers, with its thick woods, numerous streams and marshes. Near modern Detmold the Romans were
suddenly attacked by a strong force of tribesmen, organized by
Arminius, chief of the Cherusci, who had been serving as an
auxiliary with Varus. Very quickly the Roman auxiliaries deserted, and for three days the legions were subjected to persistent
attack. At length the entire force of 20,000 Roman troops had been
killed, though Varus in fact committed suicide to avoid capture.
This defeat persuaded the Romans to accept the Rhine as the
northern boundary of their Empire.

Tewkesbury (*Wars of the Roses*), 1471

Seeking to rally support for the claim of her son, Prince Edward, to
the English throne, Margaret of Anjou (wife of Henry VI) advanced north from Weymouth with a Lancastrian army commanded by the Duke of Somerset. At Tewkesbury in Gloucestershire,
where the Severn and Avon rivers join, on 4 May 1471 the
Lancastrians were met by a Yorkist army under Edward IV.
Somerset attacked, but his men were driven back in confusion,
Prince Edward was killed and the Yorkists carried the day.
Somerset was captured and later beheaded, Margaret of Anjou
surrendered and, when her imprisoned husband died on 22 May,
Edward IV was secure on the throne.

Thebes (*Macedonian Conquests*), 335 BC

Believing that Alexander III, the Great, had been killed in the
Balkans, Sparta and Thebes agreed to revolt against Macedonian
rule. At Thebes in eastern Boeotia, the Macedonian garrison was
surrounded in the acropolis, the Cadmea, when Alexander suddenly appeared before the walls with a relief force. Perdiccas, a
Macedonian captain with Alexander, led a surprise assault on part

of the defences, broke through and linked up with the garrison. Thebes was thus recovered and, as an example to others, Alexander ordered the execution of 6,000 Thebans and the destruction of virtually the whole city. He then felt free to move east against the Persians.

Thermopylae I *(Greco–Persian Wars)*, 480 BC

Crossing the Hellespont (Dardanelles) with 100,000 Persians, Xerxes marched through Thrace and Macedonia, then turned towards Thessaly. To stop this advance the Greeks took up a strong defensive position at Thermopylae Pass, ten miles south of Lamia at the head of the Evvoikos Channel, in the spring of 480 BC. The Persians could make no progress until the traitor Ephialtes revealed another pass through the mountains, by which the defenders could be outflanked. As the main body of 5,000 Greeks withdrew southwards, Leonidas of Sparta and 300 men fought to the last man to cover their retreat. The Greeks now retired behind a wall built across the Isthmus of Corinth.

Thermopylae II *(Wars of the Hellenistic Monarchies)*, 191 BC

In the mistaken belief that Rome was not interested in it, Antiochus the Great of Syria invaded Greece. The Romans reacted by landing an army in Epirus, which drove the Syrians back to the area of Thermopylae Pass. Here 40,000 Romans under Manius Acilius Glabrio and Marcus Porcius Cato attacked a slightly smaller Syrian force but were able to turn its strong defensive position by overwhelming 2,000 Aetolian allies on the flank. The Syrians were then routed, and Antiochus escaped with barely 500 of his men.

Thorn *(Great Northern War)*, 1703

Once he had defeated the Saxons at Pultusk in April 1703, Charles XII of Sweden needed only to take Thorn, on the Vistula river 110 miles north-west of Warsaw, to control Poland. With 10,000 men he therefore advanced to besiege the fortress, with its garrison of 5,000 troops, in late summer of 1703. Although it put up a stout defence, lack of supplies and imminent starvation forced Thorn to surrender on 22 September. Charles now ensured that his nomineee, Stanislas Leszczynski, became King of Poland, and the Swedish army turned confidently eastwards to deal with Russia.

Timisoara *(Hungarian Revolt against Austria)*, 1849

Proclamation of a Hungarian republic by rebels on 13 April 1849 prompted Russian troops to invade from the north and an Austrian army under General Haynau to advance into Hungary from the west. At Timisoara, seventy-five miles north-east of Belgrade, rebels commanded by General Dembinski stood against Haynau's force and were utterly defeated. This broke Hungarian resistance, and four days later the remaining rebel army surrendered to the Russians. After his victory Haynau took terrible revenge, hanging nine and shooting four of the rebel generals, conduct which led the British Press to condemn him as 'General Hyena'.

Tinchebrai *(Norman Revolts against England)*, 1106

Although Henry I managed to overcome opposition in England to his succession to the throne on the death of William Rufus, his elder brother Robert, Duke of Normandy, remained defiant. Henry therefore crossed the Channel and at Tinchebrai (ten miles south-east of Vire at the base of the Cherbourg peninsula) on 28 September 1106 won a clear victory. Robert was captured and imprisoned for life, and Normandy became united with England once more.

Tippermuir *(English Civil War)*, 1644

Rallying support for Charles I in Scotland, the Marquis of Montrose with 3,000 men met a Covenanter force of over 5,000 commanded by Lord Elcho at Tippermuir, north-east of Stirling. On 1 September 1644 Montrose routed the Covenanters, who lost perhaps 2,000 dead. He then went on to occupy Perth and Aberdeen and would hold the bulk of Scotland for the King until the following year, when dwindling Royalist support forced him to flee from the country.

Tisza River *(Conquests of Charlemagne)*, 795

Disturbed by the activity of barbarian Avars in the area of eastern Bavaria and north-eastern Italy, in 795 Charlemagne despatched troops against the Avar territory. Crossing the Tisza river, a northern tributary of the Danube, they attacked the tribal stronghold, a settlement enclosed by large earthworks, and overwhelmed the defenders after bitter fighting. Fifteen cartloads of treasure were reputedly gathered, and the Avars, so long a danger to Christians in central and southern Europe, vanished from history.

Tolbiacum *(Rise of France)*, 496

Whilst the Merovingian king Clovis I was trying to unite the Franks, the Alemanni tribe made frequent attacks on his territory from the east. In 496, therefore, Clovis I advanced to meet them at Tolbiacum (Zülpich), near Cologne. The Alemanni seemed to be winning the battle, until Clovis led a charge, which caused their ranks to waver, and ultimately they were driven back over the Rhine. Clovis I now gained control of all land west of the Rhine and, possibly in thanks for this victory, became a baptized Christian.

Toledo *(Spanish Civil War)*, 1936

Having cleared Madrid of Nationalist forces, Republican militia units advanced on Toledo, forty miles south-west. They quickly took the city, with the exception of the Alcazar, which was defended by some 1,300 Nationalists under Colonel Moscardo. Unable to carry the fortress, the Republicans settled down to besiege it. Two months later two Nationalist columns advanced up the Tagus valley to the relief of the beleaguered troops. Swinging north of Toledo, some of these troops cut the road to Madrid on 26 September, then attacked the city. Next day the militiamen were routed and the fortress was relieved.

Tongres *(Gallic Wars)*, 54 BC

Forced to disperse his men over much of northern Gaul due to lack of grain during the winter of 54 BC after his invasion of Britain,

Julius Caesar exposed his scattered detachments to attack. Taking advantage of this opportunity, the Eburonian chief Ambiorix attacked one of them at Tongres (Tongeren), where after an indecisive skirmish the Roman commander, Titurius Sabinus, accepted an offer of safe passage to Namur, thirty-five miles to the south-west. When they were on the march, the 9,000 Romans were suddenly attacked and slaughtered to a man, allowing Ambiorix to press on and besiege Namur, where he was thwarted by a relief force under Julius Caesar who remained in the area to maintain order.

Torgau *(Seven Years War)*, 1760

Advancing north with 44,000 Prussians in the autumn of 1760, Frederick the Great reached Torgau, on the Elbe sixty-five miles south of Berlin, where Count von Daun had deployed 65,000 troops of the Holy Roman Empire in defensive positions to the south and west of the city. On 3 November Frederick led a force to the enemy rear, whilst General von Zieten launched a frontal assault. Unfortunately the planned co-ordination of these two attacks failed, and Frederick suffered very heavy casualties: reputedly only 600 of the 6,000 grenadiers who carried out the first assault survived the enemy fire which met them. Towards evening von Zieten managed to gain control of dominant heights, however, and during the night von Daun retired, having suffered 4,200 casualties with 7,000 of his men prisoners. Frederick's victory had been costly, for he had lost 13,120 casualties – almost one-third of his force. This battle left both sides too weak to resume serious fighting that year.

Toro *(Castilian Civil Wars)*, 1476

The death of Henry IV of Castile led to a struggle for possession of the throne. Henry had designated his sister Isabella as his successor, but this was disputed by his daughter Joanna, backed by Alfonso V of Portugal. In support of Joanna, Alfonso marched some 8,000 men into north-east Spain. On 1 March 1476 he was challenged at Toro on the Duero river, twenty miles east of Zamora, by an army under Isabella's husband, Ferdinand. The Portuguese and Castilian rebels were routed, and in 1479

Isabella and Ferdinand would unite the kingdoms of Aragon and Castile.

Toulon *(French Revolutionary Wars)*, 1793

In the south of France the port of Toulon declared itself opposed to the Revolutionary government of the National Convention and allowed British and Spanish troops to enter. On 29 August 1793 a French army of 11,500 men under General Dugommier laid siege to Toulon, and by 18 December it had captured the bulk of its landward defences. Lord Mulgrave, commander of the garrison, then evacuated all foreign troops by sea, and Dugommier marched his men into Toulon. During the siege a young artillery captain, Napoleon Bonaparte, first came to prominence through his military skill.

Toulouse I *(Moslem Invasion of France)*, 721

Having conquered all but the north-west of the Iberian peninsula, Moorish cavalry crossed the Pyrenees in 718 and swiftly overran much of southern France. In 721, however, Duke Eudes (Odo) of Aquitaine rallied the Franks and near Toulouse (sixty miles north of the Pyrenees) put the invaders to flight, killing their leader, Samh ibn-Malik. The Moors were only temporarily checked, for they would mount a more serious invasion eleven years hence.

Toulouse II *(Napoleonic Wars)*, 1814

With Spain and Portugal freed from all French control, 25,000 British, Spanish and Portuguese troops under the Marquis of Wellington advanced over the Pyrenees into southern France. Marshal Soult fell back over the Garonne river into Toulouse, and here, on 10 April 1814, he was attacked by the allied army. Mustering some 30,000 French troops inside the city, Soult threw back a premature assault by Spanish troops against the northern defences, but the British advanced successfully in the centre. Soult abandoned Toulouse and retreated eastwards, having suffered 3,000 casualties to 4,659 (about 2,000 of these Spanish) among the allies. This was the last battle of the war, for, unknown to both armies in the south, Napoleon had already agreed to peace.

Tourcoing *(French Revolutionary Wars)*, 1794

Advancing from the Austrian Netherlands (modern Belgium) into north-east France, an allied army under the Prince of Saxe-Coburg encountered a French force commanded by General Pichegru at Tourcoing, eight miles north-east of Lille. Attempting to encircle the enemy on 18 May 1794, the allies became disorganized. Although their wings made progress, French counter-attacks drove in the centre so that Saxe-Coburg was forced to withdraw after suffering some 5,500 casualties. This allowed French troops to take Charleroi the following month and ultimately led to the decisive battle of Fleurus on 26 June, in which Saxe-Coburg was driven back over the Meuse, causing effective political collapse of the anti-French coalition.

Tournai *(War of the Spanish Succession)*, 1709

When peace negotiations between the allies and French broke down, early in 1709 the Duke of Marlborough determined to march on Paris from the Spanish Netherlands with some 100,000 men. At Tournai, on the Scheldt river forty-five miles south-west of Brussels, his path was blocked by a French garrison. Unwilling to leave the city untaken in his rear, Marlborough invested it on 27 June. The Duke of Villars was unable to relieve Tournai, which surrendered on 3 September after 3,000 of the defenders had become casualties, and Marlborough moved on towards Mons, which fell following the allied victory at Malplaquet in September. The growing intensity of French resistance foiled plans to reach Paris, and political chicanery soon engineered Marlborough's removal from command. Tournai became one of the so-called fortresses occupied by the Dutch in 1715, as a guarantee against renewed French aggression.

Tours *(Moslem Invasion of France)*, 732

Sweeping over the Pyrenees once more, Moors led by Abd-er-Rahman invaded France in the summer of 732. This time Duke Eudes of Aquitaine failed to halt their progress, but Charles Martel deployed a considerable body of Frankish infantry between Tours and Poitiers. The Moors attempted to overwhelm the Franks with their cavalry but were repulsed by skilful use of swords and axes. Accounts of the battle suggest that it lasted between two and seven days, though the significance of the eventual triumph of the Franks is not in doubt. Abd-er-Rahman was killed and the Moors withdrew southwards, no more to threaten northern Europe; and at length, in 759, they retired across the Pyrenees, never to return. Martel's victory at Tours was, therefore, undoubtedly one of the most decisive in European history.

Towton *(Wars of the Roses)*, 1461

In order to reinforce his claim to the English throne, Edward IV marched an army north into Yorkshire, seeking to bring the Lancastrians to battle. Reaching Ferrybridge on the Aire river on 28 March 1461, Edward's troops overcame the enemy advance guard and next day (Palm Sunday) with an inferior force attacked 22,000 Lancastrians entrenched on a plateau near Towton, bounded on the right by the Cockbrook in flood and on the left by the high road to Tadcaster. Despite this strong position the defenders were at a disadvantage in the snowstorm which raged and, seeking to act decisively and scatter Edward's force, they charged downhill. Battle was ruthlessly joined for over six hours, during which period many hundreds were slain, until the Duke of Norfolk came up with reinforcements for Edward. The Lancastrians were then routed and, although Henry VI, his wife and their son Edward escaped, many Lancastrian nobles were captured and executed. Edward IV went on to occupy York and Newcastle, and on 28 June he was formally crowned in Westminster Abbey.

Trasimeno Lake *(Second Punic War)*, 217 BC

When Hannibal crossed the Apennines to the west of the Italian peninsula from the area of modern Bologna, the Romans planned to annihilate his force north of Rome. Gaius Flaminius occupied the heights of Arretium (Arezzo), in the centre of the peninsula eighty miles west of Ancona, with 40,000 men, allowed Hannibal to proceed south with his 35,000 Carthaginians and set off in pursuit. He hoped that in the ensuing battle he would be assisted by 4,000 men under Servilius Geminus, advancing from Arminium (Rimini) on the Adriatic coast. Hannibal was aware of

Flaminius' presence and, on reaching Lake Trasimeno, twenty miles south of Arretium and eighty-five miles north of Rome, concealed most of his troops on high ground nearby. On the morning of 21 June 217 BC, the Roman column was ambushed and virtually cut to pieces by the lake; Flaminius was killed and few of his men escaped capture or slaughter at a cost of 2,500 Carthaginian casualties (many, in fact, allied Gauls). Hannibal then turned east to deal with the comparatively small force under Geminus, and his success alarmed the Roman Senate into appointing a dictator, Quintus Fabius Maximus Verrucosus, to defend Rome.

Trebbia River I *(Second Punic War)*, 218 BC

After a strenuous march from New Carthage in Spain and crossing the Alps in November, early in December 218 BC Hannibal debouched into northern Italy with some 20,000 infantry and 6,000 cavalry, though all his elephants had succumbed to adverse conditions on the march. In a short skirmish Publius Cornelius Scipio was wounded and, against his advice, Tiberius Sempronius Longus advanced over the Trebbia river, a southern tributary of the Po, with 40,000 legionaries. Attacking the Carthaginians in a snowstorm, he was deceived by Hannibal's skilful deployment of his inferior forces and, at a critical moment in the battle, Hannibal's brother, Mago, led a telling cavalry charge. Only half the Romans managed to regain their camp at Placentia, and 10,000 Cisalpine Gauls were encouraged to join Hannibal by this example of Carthaginian strength.

Trebbia River II *(French Revolutionary Wars)*, 1799

With General Moreau's force of 25,000 men on the defensive in northern Italy, the French Directory summoned 35,000 men under General Macdonald from Naples in the hope that the combined forces would be able to defeat the 25,000 Prussian and Austrian troops under Count Suvorov and Baron von Melas which stood between them. Suvorov decided to deal with Macdonald quickly, and on 17 June 1799 his men attacked the French force on the banks of the Trebbia river. For two days the two armies fought until Macdonald retired during the night of 18–19 June, having suffered some 12,000 losses in casualties and prisoners. At a cost of

6,000 casualties Suvorov had prevented the junctions of the two French armies and the development of a potentially dangerous situation for his own army.

Trifanum *(Latin War)*, 338 BC

When Rome claimed control of Capua, captured during the First Samnite War with the aid of the cities of Latium, these former allies rebelled against Rome in the so-called Latin War. Inconclusive skirmishing occurred for three years until Titus Manlius Torquatus defeated the enemy at the town of Trifanum, near the mouth of the Liri river, and Rome annexed the whole of Latium.

Trnovo *(Bulgarian Civil Wars)*, 1218

Defeated by the Byzantine Emperor at Philippopolis, Tsar Boril of Bulgaria began to lose influence in his own country, and John Asen took the opportunity to raise a rebellion in the north. Assisted by Russian troops the rebels laid siege to the capital Trnovo (Turnovo), forty miles south of the Danube and 110 miles west of the Black Sea, and in 1218 successfully stormed the walls. Boril was captured, had his eyes put out and was deposed in favour of Asen, who ruled for the next twenty-three years as John II.

Turckheim *(Dutch War of Louis XIV)*, 1675

Entry of the Holy Roman Empire into the war against France in 1674 led to confrontation between forces under the Vicomte de Turenne and the Austrian Count Montecuccoli on the Upper Rhine the following year. As both armies were preparing to go into winter quarters, Turenne suddenly executed a forced march south of the Vosges Mountains and attacked the Imperial army at Turckheim, five miles north-west of Colmar, on 5 January 1675. The French were quickly victorious, pursued their beaten foe back to the Rhine and so recaptured Alsace in one battle.

Turin *(War of the Spanish Succession)*, 1706

When the Duke of Vendôme was recalled to take command of French forces in Flanders, the Comte de Marsin concentrated on the siege of Turin in north-west Italy, which was defended by 10,000 Imperial troops under the Duke of Savoy. After Savoy left the city on 17 June to organize relief, Count von Daun assumed command of the garrison. Eventually on 7 September Prince Eugène arrived with a relief column, which inflicted heavy loss on the French and forced them to raise the siege. Eugène suffered 1,500 casualties, but the garrison had lost almost 5,000 men through combat and disease. Only 2,000 of Marsin's troops escaped the field, 6,000 were captured and a further 2,000 became casualties. This defeat ended French hopes of conquering northern Italy.

Turnhout *(Revolt of the Netherlands)*, 1597

After seizing several places from Spanish control, in 1597 Maurice of Nassau made a forced march of twenty-four miles in nine hours to surprise Spanish troops under Archduke Albert of Austria at Turnhout, twenty-six miles north-east of Antwerp. Here on 22 August Maurice routed the Spaniards on the field and mounted a vigorous cavalry pursuit to inflict a total of 3,000 casualties on them. Maurice's brilliant use of cavalry brought success here, in engagements such as those near Dunkirk and Gertruidenburg, and cleared the Spaniards from the United Provinces, ensuring acknowledgement of their independence at the Truce of Antwerp (9 April 1609).

Ulm *(Napoleonic Wars)*, 1805

When Austria and Russia joined the Third Coalition against France in 1805, Napoleon determined to deal with the Austrians before a Russian army under General Kutuzov could join them. Accordingly he left his positions around Boulogne on 27 August, abandoned plans to invade Britain and marched south-east across the Rhine towards the Danube. Learning of the French advance, Baron Mack concentrated his army in the area of Ulm, on the Upper Danube, forty-eight miles south-east of Stuttgart, expecting Napoleon to penetrate the Black Forest. On 7 October Mack learned that Napoleon had moved further east and, crossing the Danube at Neuburg, was threatening Austrian communications with Vienna. Napoleon now advanced westwards on both banks of the river and, when his attempt to check Marshal Ney's VI Corps on the north bank failed, Mack retired to Ulm. Here he was surrounded on 17 October and three days later capitulated with his 20,000 remaining troops. In several clashes since 7 October the Austrians had lost some 50,000 men in casualties, prisoners and deserters and the French suffered 6,000 casualties. Napoleon was thus free to turn eastwards against Kutuzov. Mack was later to be court-martialled for his poor performance at Ulm and sentenced to twenty years' imprisonment.

Usti nad Labem *(Hussite Wars)*, 1426

Thoroughly alarmed by the raids of Hussites into eastern and southern Germany, Sigismund, the Holy Roman Emperor, gathered a force of some 50,000 men and brought them to battle in 1426 at Usti nad Labem, at the junction of the Elbe and Bilina rivers, forty miles north-west of Prague. Led by Holý Procop, the Hussites made good use of their mobile artillery to put the Imperial troops to flight. Reputedly one third of Sigismund's army was killed, and certainly he was now too weak to prevent the victors from pillaging freely far into Imperial territory.

Vadimonian Lake *(Rise of Rome)*, 283 BC

Probing north to deal with resistance to the expansion of Rome, in 283 BC Publius Cornelius Dolabella met a force of hostile Gauls and Etruscans near Vadimonian Lake on the Tiber river, forty-five miles north of Rome. The Etruscans were annihilated as they crossed the river, then the Gauls were driven off with heavy loss. This victory ended oppposition to Roman control of central Italy.

Valenciennes *(Franco–Spanish Wars)*, 1656

In June 1656 Valenciennes, garrisoned by Spanish troops and situated on the Scheldt river sixty miles west of Namur, was besieged by French troops under the Vicomte de Turenne. On 16 July, with the city on the point of surrender, the besiegers were suddenly attacked by 20,000 Spaniards under the renegade Frenchman the Great Condé and routed, with the loss of almost

4,500 casualties. Turenne had no option but to raise the siege, and Spanish demands at the current peace negotiations were increased, which led to a formal Anglo–French alliance and continuation of a war apparently about to end.

Val-ès-Dunes *(Rise of Normandy)*, 1047

The claim of William (the future Conqueror) to the dukedom of Normandy was challenged by a group of nobles, who invoked assistance from Henry I of France. At Val-ès-Dunes, south-west of Caen, in 1047 the rebels were defeated and William's position was secured. He then went on to build up Norman military strength, which would soon challenge France and conquer England.

Valmy *(French Revolutionary Wars)*, 1792

Faced by a Prussian army under the Duke of Brunswick, French troops fell back from the frontier into north-eastern France. As a force of 36,000 men under General Dumouriez was guarding passes through the Argonne Forest, 34,000 Prussians outflanked it to reach Valmy, close to the Marne river and 100 miles east of Paris. Realizing the threat to the capital that this manœuvre created, Dumouriez turned his men to the west and opened an artillery bombardment on 20 September 1792. The Battle of Valmy was, in fact, fought mainly by artillery, and the Prussians failed to press home either an infantry or a cavalry attack. Ten days later Brunswick retreated across the Rhine and, at the cost of a few hundred casualties, French morale had been immeasurably raised and the Revolutionary government saved. Had the French lost at Valmy, it is possible that the Revolution would have collapsed. In a wider context, the advantages of a republican over a monarchical system of government became questions of practical, as well as philosophical, debate.

Varna I *(Crusade against Turkey)*, 1444

Breaking a peace agreement with the Turks, a Christian army under János Hunyadi, Ladislas VI of Poland and Cardinal Cesarini marched south of the Danube to the Black Sea port of Varna, in order to rendezvous with the Venetian fleet. But the Venetians remained at Gallipoli and even failed to prevent the Sultan, Murad II, from returning to Constaninople from Asia Minor. Gathering an army, Murad II marched on Varna where, on 10 November, he was rashly attacked by Hunyadi. Repelling this assault, next day the Turks drove in the Christian entrenchments, killing Ladislas and Cardinal Cesarini. Although Hunyadi escaped, the crusade thus came to an ignominious end.

Varna II *(Russo–Turkish Wars)*, 1828

Crossing the Danube at several points, Russian armies advanced towards Constantinople in the summer of 1828 but were delayed by scattered Turkish strongpoints. One of these was Varna, the port on the Bulgarian coast of the Black Sea, defended by 20,000 men. Prince Menshikov detached a Russian force to take Varna, though due to strong Turkish resistance the Russians were forced to lay siege to the town in July, and not until 11 October were the walls stormed; next day the garrison surrendered. However, this delay meant that the Russian advance on Constantinople could not be resumed until the following year.

Veii *(Rise of Rome)*, 405–396 BC

The long struggle for supremacy between Rome and its northern neighbours centred on Veii, the Etruscan stronghold twelve miles north of Rome, in 405 BC. The city was besieged by the Romans in a rather desultory fashion for almost ten years, until in 396 BC the besiegers were driven back from their entrenchments. Marcus Furius Camillus immediately rallied the Romans, prosecuted a more vigorous siege and stormed Veii. This broke Etruscan power and greatly enhanced the military reputation of Rome.

Velletri *(War of the Austrian Succession)*, 1744

In the summer of 1744 serious conflict spread into Italy for the first time during the war, when Austrian troops under Prince Lobko-witz marched south towards Naples. In the face of this threat Charles VII, King of the Two Sicilies (later Charles III of Spain), allied with Spain, and a combined army gathered at Velletri, twenty miles south-east of Rome. Here the Austrians were checked on 11 August and, having secured his frontier, Charles VII withdrew from the war as Lobkowitz marched north once more.

Venice *(Italian Wars of Independence)*, 1849

Taking advantage of uprisings throughout the Austrian Empire, on 22 March 1848 Venice declared itself a republic. With the tide turning in favour of the Austrians and many of the revolutionary outbreaks now crushed, the infant republic was besieged by Field-Marshal Radetsky and an Austrian army on 20 July 1849. With no hope of relief and ravaged by artillery bombardment and disease, the starving citizens finally capitulated on 28 August, and the city would remain in Austrian hands for another seventeen years.

Vercellae *(Gallic Invasions of Italy)*, 101 BC

Once he had defeated the Teutones in 102 BC Gaius Marius could concentrate his forces to deal with the Cimbri invasion of northern Italy through the Brenner Pass. Reinforced by further troops under Quintus Lutatius Catulus, Marius attacked and routed the invaders at Vercellae, thirty-nine miles south-west of Milan, in 101 BC. This defeat ended the Gallic invasions of Italy, and Marius was acclaimed as a hero.

Verdun *(First World War)*, 1916

Believing that the French would defend Verdun, on the Meuse 140 miles east of Paris, to the last man, General von Falkenhayn launched the German Fifth Army and 1,500 guns against the French Second Army, responsible for the immediate defence of the city. Preceded by a twelve-hour bombardment, the Germans attacked on 21 February 1916 and in a relatively short time captured outlying fortifications such as Fort Douaumont, which were not heavily defended. General Pétain was ordered to take command of Verdun, and he managed to slow the rate of German advance both east of the city and in the north, where other German units tried to outflank the defences by crossing the Meuse. Although the village of Vaux, three miles east of Verdun, fell on 29 March, nearby Fort de Vaux was not taken until 6 June. In the north Hill 295 held out until 29 May, and Hill 304 was never captured. Realizing that high ground east of Verdun was the key to the city, the German Fifth Army commander, Crown Prince Frederick William, launched two major assaults against it on 23 June and 11 July. Both were beaten back, the latter by the narrowest of margins. At this stage it was clear that the Germans would not take Verdun, which had already cost them 280,000 casualties to 315,000 among the defenders. On 24 October General Nivelle, who had taken over command from Pétain, launched a counter-offensive, which ended on 18 December with all the lost ground recovered, plus a few territorial gains. The Battle of Verdun had claimed 542,000 French casualties and 434,000 German. Success, however, had been vital for French and Allied morale, and a major German breakthrough had also been averted.

Verneuil *(Hundred Years War)*, 1424

In an effort to stem the flow of English conquests in northern France, 15,000 French and Scottish troops under the Earls of Douglas and Buchan attacked less than 9,000 English commanded by the Duke of Bedford at Verneuil, fifty miles west of Paris, on 17 August 1424. Protected by palisades, the English longbowmen wrought havoc in the enemy ranks and drove them from the field. Douglas and Buchan were among an estimated 5,000 Scottish dead; the French lost 1,500 together with an unknown number of prisoners including the Duke of Alençon and Marshal Lafayette. Following this success, the English advanced rapidly to the Loire.

Verona *(Civil Wars of the Roman Empire)*, 312

Seven years after the abdication of Emperor Diocletian, the Roman Empire was torn by internal strife among rival claimants to his throne. Marching into northern Italy with 50,000 men from Gaul, Constantine I laid siege to Verona (fifteen miles east of Lake Garda) which was held by Pompeianus on behalf of another claimant, Maxentius. Pompeianus escaped to raise a relief force, but when this column approached the city, it was routed and Pompeianus killed. Verona then surrendered, and Constantine was master of northern Italy, free to march on Rome and to deal with Maxentius.

Verulamium *(Roman Conquest of Britain)*, AD 61

Having destroyed Camulodunum (Colchester) and Londinium (London), rebel Iceni tribesmen from East Anglia under their queen, Boudicca (Boadicea), advanced north-west of the Roman capital to devastate Verulamium (St Albans) in AD 61. Before the Iceni were clear of Verulamium, however, Suetonius Paulinus arrived with two legions from Wales and, choosing his ground carefully, attacked the more numerous rebels mercilessly. Not even camp-followers were spared in the slaughter, when 80,000 rebels were reputedly killed. Boudicca took poison. At a cost of 400 dead legionaries, Paulinus had suppressed the rebellion. In some part, too, he had avenged 70,000 people killed by the Iceni.

Viborg *(Scandinavian Wars)*, 1157

Civil war raged in Denmark between Sweyn III and Canute V for ten years until Canute was assassinated in 1157. A relative, Waldemar, claimed the throne, and his army met that of Sweyn at Viborg in the north of the Jutland peninsula, thirty-five miles north-west of Aarhus. Sweyn's force was defeated, and he himself killed during the pursuit. Waldemar therefore acceded to the throne and ruled for twenty-five years as Waldemar I.

Vienna I *(Ottoman Wars)*, 1529

After overcoming Hungarian forces near Budapest, Suleiman I 'the Magnificent', marched up the Danube with over 100,000 Turks towards the Habsburg capital of Vienna. Quickly Charles V, the Holy Roman Emperor, reinforced the garrison to 20,000 men before the Turkish investment commenced on 26 September 1529. Several assaults were beaten back, and at length on 16 October Suleiman I was forced to raise the siege, a failure hailed as a great victory for Christendom.

Vienna II *(Ottoman Wars)*, 1683

In 1683 a Turkish force once more laid siege to Vienna, when on 17 July 140,000 men under the Grand Vizier Kara Mustafa invested the city, from which Emperor Leopold I and his court had fled.

The garrison of some 40,000 men under Count von Starhemberg repelled several assaults, and Turkish engineers began mining operations. When this action seemed about to succeed, John III of Poland appeared with 20,000 troops and on 12 September attacked the besiegers from the rear. Although they resisted stoutly, at length the Turks were routed and forced to retreat south-eastwards. They would no more threaten central Europe, and for this failure at Vienna Mustafa was executed.

Vimeiro *(Peninsular War)*, 1808

Taking advantage of unrest which followed French occupation of Portugal, in July 1808 30,000 British troops led by Sir Arthur Wellesley landed north of Lisbon. Unchecked at Rolica on 15 August, Wellesley continued towards the Portuguese capital with a force of 17,000 men and at Vimeiro, thirty-two miles to the north-west, on 21 August encountered 14,000 French troops commanded by Marshal Junot. The French were driven back with the loss of 1,800 casualties and thirteen guns to total British casualties of 720. Wellesley was unable to follow up his victory, for Sir Harry Burrard and Sir Hew Dalrymple arrived at the moment of victory and nine days later agreed to the Convention of Cintra, whereby the French were evacuated from Portugal in British ships.

Vimy Ridge *(First World War)*, 1917

A dominant feature ten miles north of Arras was Vimy Ridge, which was a valuable tactical position for the Germans to hold. Briefly during May 1915 it was captured by the French, but not until Sir Douglas Haig's offensive in April 1917 did the Allies gain permanent control of it. Then on Easter Monday, 9 April, after three hours of hard fighting, the ridge was taken and held by the Canadian Corps of the British First Army.

Vinaroz *(Spanish Civil War)*, 1938

Having repulsed the Republican attack at Teruel, Generalissimo Franco organized a massive Nationalist offensive into Aragon and the Levante. On 9 March 1938 General Davila launched five columns against the enemy line, which gave way under pressure of ground and air attack. Republican forces fell back rapidly, and a decisive engagement took place on 15 April at the fishing village of Vinaroz, midway between Barcelona and Valencia on the Mediterranean coast. When this was captured by a division under General Vega, the Nationalists succeeded in splitting Republican Spain in two.

Vinegar Hill *(Irish Rebellion against George III)*, 1798

Faced with formation of the militant Protestant Orange Order, harsh new laws and fading hopes of political emancipation, Catholics in Ireland began to organize a rebellion early in 1798. With Ulster secure once prominent leaders were arrested, support elsewhere dwindled and only the extreme south-east of the island rose in May. To deal with an estimated 16,000 ill-organized rebels led by Father Murphy, General Lake marched an army of regular troops into Wexford County and on 21 June 1798 attacked Murphy's camp at Vinegar Hill near Enniscorthy. The rebels were swiftly overrun with 4,000 casualties, and the survivors dispersed to carry out isolated acts of disorder in roving bands. The French belatedly landed troops in August, but they were quickly mopped up. Effectively the rebellion had crumbled on Vinegar Hill, which, although hardly a major battle, would live on in Irish folklore as a gallant defence against British oppression.

Vitoria *(Peninsular War)*, 1813

Profiting from the withdrawal of French forces from the Iberian peninsula following Napoleon's setbacks in Russia and central Europe, Viscount Wellington led some 80,000 British, Portuguese and Spanish troops with ninety guns out of Portugal into northern Spain. Crossing the Upper Ebro, he outflanked a force of 66,000 French troops with 150 guns under Marshal Jourdan, who had been joined by Joseph Bonaparte, nominally King of Spain. At Vitoria, 175 miles north-east of Madrid, on 21 June 1813 Wellington launched a three-column assault on the enemy and drove them back through the town in considerable confusion. The French lost almost 8,000 men in casualties, prisoners and missing, plus practically their entire artillery and baggage trains. For 5,000 casualties

Wellington had ensured that the French would never again dominate Spain during this war and had opened the way for his army to
the Pyrenees, where by the end of October San Sebastian and
Pamplona had fallen.

Vittorio Veneto *(First World War)*, 1918

Sensing that Austrian determination was wavering, the Italian
commander General Diaz determined to attack fifty-eight enemy
divisions and 6,000 guns north of the Piave river. He planned to
attack with the Italian Fifth and Sixth Armies on the left (west) and
five other armies (including British and French units) on the right:
in all he could muster fifty-seven divisions and 7,700 guns. The
offensive was launched on 24 October 1918 and, although Italians
on the left encountered fierce opposition, within four days various
bridgeheads north of the river had linked up. On 30 October the
Italian Eighth Army on the right captured Vittorio Veneto, thirty-
eight miles north of Venice on a tributary of the Livenza river.
This proved decisive, and Austrian resistance collapsed from the
Trentino river to the Adriatic Sea, so that on 3 November the
Austrians agreed to a truce, which became effective the following
day.

Vouillé *(Rise of France)*, 507

Once he had secured his northern frontier against the Alemanni,
Clovis I turned south to deal with the Visigoths. At Vouillé, forty
miles south-west of Poitiers, the Franks met a Visigoth army under
Alaric II, who was marching to join Ostrogoths under Theodoric
the Great in Italy. Clovis' men overwhelmed the Visigoths, mainly
through effective use of their short-handled axes, and killed
Alaric. This defeat forced the Goths to abandon their capital at
Toulouse and retire over the Pyrenees into modern Spain, which
left the Frankish king in control of much of France.

Vyazma *(Second World War)*, 1941

Driving towards Moscow during the autumn of 1941 as part of
Operation Barbarossa, German troops of Army Group Centre
reached Vyazma, 120 miles west of the Soviet capital. Using a

tactic familiar throughout this campaign, Field-Marshal von Bock sent the Third and Fourth Panzer Groups north and south of the city to encircle it on 2 October, then used infantry to mop up resistance in the pocket. By 13 October 600,000 Soviet troops caught between the huge armoured pincers had either been killed, wounded or captured.

Vyborg *(Russo–Finnish Wars)*, 1918

Whilst Russia was torn by internal revolution, Finland declared itself independent, only to see much of the southern part of the new country overrun by Bolshevik troops during the civil war which followed Lenin's seizure of power. Supported by a German force, the Finnish White Army commanded by General von Mannerheim cleared the Reds from Helsinki, then on 29 April 1918 defeated them again at Vyborg, seventy miles north-west of Leningrad (Petrograd). This victory virtually ensured establishment of the republic of Finland, which was formally acknowledged the following year.

Wagram *(Napoleonic Wars)*, 1809

Reinforced by troops from Italy under his stepson Eugène de Beauharnais, Napoleon passed the bulk of his 188,000 men and 554 guns onto Lobau Island in the Danube, four miles due east of Vienna. From there during the night of 4–5 July 1809 French troops crossed to the east bank and quickly established a bridgehead in the face of weak Austrian opposition. That evening, with the Austrians retiring before him, Napoleon advanced towards the heights of Wagram ten miles north-east of the Austrian capital, where Archduke Charles Louis had 155,000 men in defensive positions, but initial French attempts to storm the heights failed. Shortly after dawn on 6 July, the Archduke launched an attack along the river bank towards Lobau Island in an attempt to sever French communications, but this was repulsed by Marshal Masséna's IV Corps. After another surprise Austrian advance early in the day had been checked by Marshal Davout with III Corps, General Macdonald's 8,000 men attacked the enemy left and, when Marshal Oudinot's II Corps supported by reserve artillery successfully pierced the centre of Archduke Charles Louis's line, the Austrians began to withdraw from the field. Although Archduke John came up with 12,500 reserves, they were too late and too few to be effective, and by nightfall the French were completely victorious. The price of success was high: 34,000 casualties, even though Austrian losses probably exceeded 40,000. The French were too exhausted to mount a pursuit that night, but four days later Charles Louis requested an armistice.

Wakefield *(Wars of the Roses)*, 1460

The compromise that Richard, Duke of York, should succeed Henry VI as King of England did not satisfy Lancastrians, who under Margaret of Anjou, the Queen, advanced into Yorkshire. Moving to confront them, Yorkists led by Richard were ambushed outside Wakefield on 30 December 1460. Very fierce fighting occurred, but with surprise on their side the Lancastrians eventually triumphed. Richard, his son and the Earl of Salisbury were all killed (Salisbury being murdered in captivity), and this battle virtually extinguished the older line of noble leaders in the war.

Warburg *(Seven Years War)*, 1760

In the summer of 1760 30,000 French troops under the Chevalier du Muy advancing on Hanover discovered 35,000 Prussian and British troops under the Duke of Brunswick in their path at Warburg, twenty miles north-west of Kassel. Here the two forces clashed on 31 July and, when British cavalry under the Marquis of Granby threatened to envelop their flanks, the French retired, having already lost 3,000 men in casualties and prisoners. This battle not only protected Hanover: it also did something to restore the reputation of the British cavalry, adversely affected by its lack of action at Minden the previous year.

Warsaw I *(Baltic Wars)*, 1656

Allied with Prussia, in 1656 Charles X of Sweden invaded Poland, determined to end John I's claim to the Swedish throne. Advancing on the Polish capital, he attacked Warsaw on 28 July. For two days the defenders fought hard but were then forced to surrender. Although obliged to retire from Warsaw the following year, at the end of the war Charles gained the Polish Baltic provinces, and John I renounced his claim to the Swedish throne.

Warsaw II *(Polish Revolt against Russia)*, 1831

By the summer of 1831 one remaining centre of resistance in the revolt against Russian control over Poland was Warsaw, where 30,000 troops under General Dembinski occupied strong defensive positions. On 6 September 60,000 Russians commanded by General Paskevich attacked and took the first line of defences, but the Poles grimly held out for a further two days. At length on 8 September the city surrendered: 9,000 Poles had died in its defence, and its capture cost the Russians 10,500 casualties. However, the revolt had been crushed.

Warsaw III *(First World War)*, 1914

In an effort to relieve pressure on Austrian troops further south, on 28 September the German Ninth Army under General von Mackensen advanced on Warsaw, then held by Russia. By 9 October the German troops had reached the Vistula river, and three days later they were within twelve miles of their goal. But the Russians had an overwhelming superiority in numbers and counter-attacked effectively at this point. Five days later the attackers began a general retreat, and by the end of the month they were back to their start line. This failure had cost the Germans 40,000 casualties and left Silesia open to Russian attack. They were too weak to exploit this opportunity and, having reorganized, von Mackenson eventually took Warsaw almost a year later, on 4 August 1915.

Warsaw IV *(Russo–Polish War)*, 1920

While the Russians were engaged in a civil war after the Bolshevik Revolution, the Poles declared themselves independent and advanced eastwards into Russia with the aid of rebel Ukrainians. In May 1920, however, the Russians launched a counter-attack, which by the end of July was within reach of Warsaw. Advised by the French General Weygand and commanded by General Piłsudski, the Polish Fourth Army attacked the Russian southern flank before Brest-Litovsk to save the new state's capital. By 25 August the Russians had been pushed back 200 miles and had lost some 70,000 prisoners. Following this success the Poles were able to achieve a favourable eastern boundary, which endured until September 1939.

Warsaw V *(Second World War)*, 1939

Seven days after the German invasion of Poland, on 8 September 1939 armoured units reached the outskirts of Warsaw. Five days later the Third Army reached the city from the north, and meanwhile aircraft and heavy artillery had been pounding the Polish capital. On 17 September, the day that Russian units marched into eastern Poland, the Germans Fourth and Fourteenth Armies encircled Warsaw. For ten further days the Poles gallantly resisted, but on 27 September they were forced to capitulate, and organized military opposition to the invaders ceased.

Warsaw VI *(Second World War)*, 1944

When Russian armoured units under Marshal Rokossovski reached the eastern suburbs of Warsaw on 31 July 1944, 40,000 members of the Polish underground rose against occupation forces in the city. With limited supplies of food and ammunition, they believed that the main Soviet armies were on the point of attacking the German defenders. But Soviet troops halted to regroup east of the Vistula and, with reinforcements rushed in, the Germans proceeded ruthlessly to crush the rebels. Fighting was savage on both sides: the Germans suffered 26,000 casualties (7,000 of them listed as missing). On 2 October the Poles surrendered with their supplies exhausted and having lost some 15,000 men. The Germans then took further terrible revenge. Much of the city was deliberately razed, and many of the prisoners were executed for crimes allegedly committed during the uprising. As a result of the siege and bloody aftermath, 200,000 civilians were estimated to have died, and Warsaw was not liberated by the Red Army until 17 January 1945.

Waterloo *(Napoleon's Hundred Days)*, 1815

Believing that Field-Marshal Blücher and his Prussian troops, following their defeat at Ligny on 16 June, were too far east to take any effective part in the coming action, Napoleon gathered 72,000 men and 246 guns in the area of La Belle Alliance on the road south of Brussels. Before him, deployed behind a low ridge at Mont St-Jean just south of Waterloo and twelve miles from Brussels, the Duke of Wellington had 68,000 allied British, Dutch, Flemish and German troops with 156 guns. In front of the ridge Wellington's men also held the farm of La Haye Sainte and on the right Hougoumont, which were to be important positions in the battle. Under cover of their artillery the French moved forward shortly before noon on 18 June 1815 but failed to make immediate progress against Hougoumont and did not take La Haye Sainte until six o'clock in the evening. Meanwhile, despite the pressure of French artillery bombardment and cavalry attacks, allied infantry squares on the ridge held firm, while Blücher's Prussians were gradually closing on the French right flank from the east. In late afternoon 31,000 Prussians attacked and captured the village of Plancenoit in the rear of La Belle Alliance and, although it was retaken by French reserves, Napoleon realized that he must gain a rapid decision in the main battle. A last desperate attack, stiffened by nine battalions of the Old Guard led by Marshal Ney, struck the allied centre at seven o'clock. When this failed and the Prussians took Plancenoit once more, the French began to retreat. In this decisive battle Wellington suffered 15,000 casualties, the Prussians 7,000 and the French a total of 44,000, including prisoners. Not only had Wellington's victory saved Brussels, but it persuaded Napoleon to abdicate for the second time four days later.

Wattignies *(French Revolutionary Wars)*, 1793

Encouraged by the relief of Dunkirk in September 1793, the French Army turned its attention to Maubeuge, on the border with the Austrian Netherlands fifty miles south-east of Lille and then besieged by 26,000 Austrians under the Prince of Saxe-Coburg. On 15 October 50,000 French troops under General Jourdan were beaten back, but during the night 8,000 of them were marched across to the right flank near the village of Wattignies. Next morning they were in a position to outflank the Austrian left and, to avoid disaster, Saxe-Coburg abandoned the siege of Maubeuge and fell back.

Wavre *(Napoleon's Hundred Days)*, 1815

After the reverse at Ligny on 16 June 1815, Field-Marshal Blücher retired towards Wavre with his Prussian troops. To guard against a flank attack by Blücher, as he moved his main body towards Brussels, Napoleon detached Marshal Grouchy with 33,000 men to protect his right flank. Probing forward, during the morning of 18 June Grouchy encountered Prussian forces in the area of Wavre. Aware that a general action was imminent near Brussels, Blücher had left General Thielmann with 15,000 men to defend the village, which Grouchy attacked fiercely throughout the day, oblivious of the fact that Blücher was marching ten miles south-west with the bulk of the Prussians to intervene decisively on the battlefield of Waterloo. On the morning of 19 June Grouchy captured Wavre, but by then his success was completely irrelevant.

Werben *(Thirty Years War)*, 1631

Marching north along the Elbe with 22,000 men after the sack of Madgeburg, the Comte de Tilly encountered 16,000 Swedish troops under Gustavus Adolphus in strong defensive positions at Werben near the junction of the Elbe and Havel rivers, sixty miles north-west of Berlin. On 22 July 1631 Tilly attacked, but he was thrown back by the accurate Swedish batteries. Six days later he tried again, only to be repulsed a second time. He then retired southwards towards Saxony, having suffered 6,000 casualties. However, the Swedish success prompted the Elector of Saxony to ally with Gustavus, and their combined armies pursued Tilly towards Leipzig.

Wexford *(Cromwell in Ireland)*, 1649

Marching into south-east Ireland after subduing Drogheda, Oliver Cromwell approached the port of Wexford at the mouth of the Slaney river, which was defended by Irish and English Royalists. The defenders could not cope with the attack by 10,000 men under Cromwell, and the walls were carried on 11 October 1649. The port was then sacked and the garrison put to the sword. The treatment meted out to defenders here and at Drogheda prompted other towns to surrender rather than risk attack, making Cromwell's pacification of the island easier and quicker to achieve.

White Mountain (*Thirty Years War*), 1620

Frederick V of the Palatinate reached Prague in late 1619 to assume the crown, which had been offered to him by the Protestants. The following summer Maximilian I of Bavaria despatched a Catholic army of 25,000 men commanded by the Comte de Tilly into Bohemia, and 15,000 Bohemians under Christian of Anhalt fell back towards their capital. Joined by Hungarians led by Bethlen Gabor, Christian entrenched his men on a chalk rise, known as the White Mountain, to the west of Prague. Here he was surprised in the morning mist of 8 November, when Tilly sent the Imperial troops up the slope under cover of an artillery bombardment. The defenders were scattered and some 5,000 became casualties or prisoners. Tilly went on to take Prague, and Frederick fled from Bohemia with his wife, thus becoming recognized as 'the Winter King', due to his short reign. His flight left Bohemian Protestants, who had embarrassed successive emperors since the execution of John Hus, at the mercy of Imperial anger. Soon Frederick's own inheritance (the Rhenish Palatinate) fell to the Catholics also, and the European confrontation initiated by events in Bohemia would not be settled until 1648.

Wiesloch (*Thirty Years War*), 1622

Once Bohemia had been restored to Catholic control, the Palatinate on the Rhine became the focus of military attention. In the spring of 1622 Count von Mansfeld, with his mercenary army employed by Frederick, the deposed King of Bohemia, crossed the Rhine from Alsace and joined with forces under the Margrave of Baden-Durlach. The main allied aim was to prevent union of an army under the Comte de Tilly and 20,000 Spaniards commanded by Gonzales de Córdoba. On 22 April Tilly came up with the Protestant rearguard at Wiesloch, fifteen miles south of Heidelberg, and drove it back, only to be checked when he attacked the main body. This encounter was in fact inconclusive, but Tilly later outflanked Mansfeld to link up with the Spaniards and pose a major threat to the Protestant forces.

Wilton *(Danish Invasions of England)*, 871

In the summer of 871, Danish invaders struck deeply into Wessex from the area of Reading, where they had already defeated the West Saxons. At Wilton, four miles west of Salisbury, they were met by another Saxon force led by Alfred, now king after Ethelred I's death. Failing to make progress, the Danes feigned retreat, lured the Saxons from their positions, then turned to scatter them. Alfred was forced to make peace and pay a large tribute, where-upon the Danes again retired eastwards. In the five years of peace which followed, Alfred built up his army for a more favourable confrontation.

Wimpfen *(Thirty Years War)*, 1622

Faced by two Catholic forces under Gonzales de Córdoba and the Comte de Tilly in the Palatinate, the armies of Count von Mansfeld and the Margrave of Baden-Durlach planned to link up with another Protestant force commanded by Christian of Brunswick north of the Neckar river. Hoping to divide the enemy, Mansfeld was to cross the Neckar near Heidelberg, while Baden-Durlach moved upstream (eastwards) to cross at Wimpfen, seven miles north of Heilbronn. This ruse failed, for both enemy armies concentrated against Baden-Durlach, to cut him off from the river near Wimpfen. Baden-Durlach deployed his outnumbered force of 14,000 men on a low hill and bravely defended it against the Catholic assault on 6 May 1622. The weight of Tilly's artillery was too great for the defenders, however, and they were driven from their entrenchments with heavy loss. Meanwhile Mansfeld had crossed the Neckar, and the Catholics now marched north to prevent his junction with Brunswick's men.

Winwaed *(Rise of England)*, 655

Following victories over two successive rulers of the kingdom of Northumbria (which comprised Bernicia and Deira), Penda, King of Mercia, exercised control over all six Anglo-Saxon kingdoms. In 655, however, Oswiu (Oswy), brother of the last Northumbrian king, rallied Bernician support against Penda. At the Winwaed stream, reputedly near Leeds, Oswiu faced combined Mercian and

East Anglian forces under Penda and defeated them. As Penda was killed during the battle, Oswiu established his own power over a united Northumbrian kingdom and extended his influence over Mercia and much of southern England.

Wissembourg *(Franco–Prussian War)*, 1870

The first battle of the war occurred on 4 August 1870 at Wissembourg, forty miles north of Strasbourg. Defended by 4,000 French troops under General Douay, the town was attacked by 25,000 men of the Prussian Third Army, which was advancing into eastern France. For six hours the garrison resisted before the Prussians stormed the defences and captured the town. Their victory cost the attackers 1,500 casualties and the French 2,300, including Douay, who was killed. The inevitable outcome of this brief battle showed how strategically unprepared the French were to resist invasion.

Wittstock *(Thirty Years War)*, 1636

In the two years after its defeat at Nördlingen, the Swedish army suffered a number of setbacks in central Germany, and in 1636 Field-Marshal Baner found himself isolated with 22,000 men in Brandenburg. Seeking to cut Baner's communications with the Baltic, 30,000 Saxon and Imperial troops under John George of Saxony took up a strong defensive position on a hill at Wittstock, fifty-eight miles north-west of Berlin. Noting the strength of the enemy position, Baner sent only part of his force towards the foot of the hill, while Scottish troops under General King made a wide flanking movement out of sight of the allied army. Believing that the men advancing to their front comprised the entire Swedish army, John George's men left their entrenchments to attack, and King struck them in the flank and rear. The allied force was scattered, losing 11,000 casualties and 8,000 prisoners to Swedish casualties of 5,000. This victory did much to restore Swedish morale and also encouraged other North German states to oppose Catholic domination.

Wolgast (*Thirty Years War*), 1628

Believing that the Catholic army of General von Waldstein (Wallenstein) was fully occupied in besieging Stralsund, Christian IV of Denmark seized Wolgast on the Pomeranian coast, thirty miles to the south-east, in the summer of 1628. Wallenstein abandoned the siege of Stralsund in August and intercepted Christian's army as it marched out of Wolgast on 2 September. The Danes were utterly defeated, only Christian and a handful of survivors reaching their ships in safety. This defeat ended Christian's participation in the war, and the following year he came to terms with the Holy Roman Emperor.

Worcester (*English Civil War*), 1651

As Oliver Cromwell advanced deep into Scotland, Charles II, who had been crowned by the Scots on 1 January 1651, led a force southwards over the border into England. Few Englishmen joined Charles, and on 3 September, with 16,000 men (mostly Scots), he was brought to battle at Worcester on the Severn, twenty-two miles north of Gloucester, by Cromwell who, having severed enemy lines of communication with Scotland, had come south at the head of 28,000 New Model Army veterans and militiamen. The Royalists were repulsed when they attacked Cromwell, then in turn were attacked as they retired by a Parliamentarian force which had marched along the Severn river. In this, the last battle of the Civil War, Charles' army was annihilated: 3,000 were killed and the bulk of the remainder captured. For six weeks Charles himself had to hide to avoid capture, but eventually he escaped to the Continent.

Wörth (*Franco–Prussian War*), 1870

After driving the French out of Wissembourg on 4 August 1870, 77,000 men of the Prussian Third Army marched ten miles south-west to Wörth, where the Comte de MacMahon had assembled 37,000 French troops to halt the invasion. MacMahon had only 101 obsolescent pieces of artillery, and under cover of their 234 rifled, breech-loading cannon the Prussians attacked at dawn on 6 August. By use of their superior small arms fire and their *mitrailleuse* machine-guns, the French succeeded in holding off the Prussians until late afternoon, before MacMahon was forced to retreat towards the Vosges. The French lost 10,000 casualties, 6,000 prisoners and twenty-eight guns, the Prussians 10,500 casualties. Failure once more to halt the invaders in this area was ominous for French survival.

Würzburg *(French Revolutionary Wars)*, 1796

Having halted the French advance at Amberg, thirty miles east of Nuremberg, in August 1796, with 45,000 Austrians Archduke Charles Louis pursued General Jourdan as he fell back to the north-west. Archduke Charles Louis was anxious to prevent this French army from joining another under General Moreau. On 3 September at Würzburg, sixty miles south-east of Frankfurt-am-Main, the Austrians caught and defeated Jourdan's force of 40,000 men, forcing it back over the Rhine, away from Moreau. In this battle the French lost 2,000 men killed and seven cannon, leaving Archduke Charles Louis to turn south and deal with Moreau unmolested.

York *(Danish Invasions of England)*, 867

Having established themselves in East Anglia, Danes under Ivar the Boneless moved north to besiege York in 867. Temporarily abandoning disputes among themselves, the Northumbrians assembled a force to repel the besiegers, which attacked in co-ordination with a sortie by the garrison. In a confused encounter the more numerous Northumbrian forces became thoroughly disorganized and were routed. This defeat ended Northumbrian power in the north, and York, which was now taken, became a Danish stronghold.

Ypres I *(First World War)*, 1914

In an attempt to penetrate the Allied line before it had become firmly established, on 14 October 1914 General von Falkenhayn launched the German Fourth and Sixth Armies against Ypres, just inside Belgium's north-western border with France, where the British Expeditionary Force (BEF) and Belgian forces came together. For nine days the Germans pressed forward, until French reinforcements arrived to halt the advance and the Belgians opened sluice gates in their front to flood the area from Diksmuide to the sea. The Allies counter-attacked on 28 October, and von Falkenhayn made one last effort to break through before the offensive came to a halt in snow and rain on 11 November. The British were left in possession of Ypres at the base of a salient which jutted six miles into the German line. This, the last battle in the west during 1914, cost the BEF 58,155 casualties (approximately eight per cent of its original strength), the French 50,000, Germans 130,000 and the Belgians almost forty per cent of their remaining troops. The Ypres salient would remain a focus of fierce military attention for most of the war.

Ypres II *(First World War)*, 1915

On 22 April 1915 the Germans discharged chlorine gas over British lines in the Ypres salient for the first time and quickly created a four-mile gap in the line. Through this General von Falkenhayn poured German forces, but General Smith-Dorrien managed to halt the advance with Canadian reserves, who withstood another gas attack on 24 April. Smith-Dorrien then ordered a withdrawal to the outskirts of Ypres and was promptly replaced by Sir Herbert Plumer in command of the Second Army. On 1 May Plumer in fact carried out the planned withdrawal, and on 25 May German attacks ceased. The defenders suffered 60,000 casualties to 35,000 among the attackers, a reversal of the usual ratio during similar offensives, probably explained by the shock use of gas. But the second major attempt by the Germans to break through to Calais and Boulogne, which would have been disastrous for the Allies, had been prevented.

Ypres III, see Passchendaele

Zallaka *(Spanish–Moslem Wars)*, 1086

After Alfonso VI of Castile and Leon had seized Toledo in 1085, the Moors of southern Spain called for assistance from north-west Africa. Yusof ibn-Tashfin therefore landed with a force of some

40,000 men at Algeciras, east of Gibraltar, in 1086 and marched north through Seville and Badajoz to challenge the Christians. At Zallaka (Zalaca) he used his cavalry to good effect on 23 October, when Alfonso's army was utterly defeated and the King barely escaped with his life. Ibn-Tashfin then ruled Spain south of Toledo for the next twenty years, except for Valencia, which remained independent under El Cid until 1099.

Zamora *(Spanish–Moslem Wars)*, 939

Reacting to the Christian counter-offensive against their territory in southern Spain, Moors under Abd-er-Rahman III laid seige to Zamora, 130 miles north-west of Madrid. When Ramiro II of the Austurias, Leon and Castile arrived with a relief force, the garrison came out and the large body of besiegers was driven off. Thousands were either killed or drowned in the moat surrounding Zamora, but this success did not materially hasten Christian re-conquest of Moslem territory.

Zenta *(Ottoman Wars)*, 1697

When the Turks began to menace south-eastern Europe in 1697, the Holy Roman Emperor, Leopold I, despatched Prince Eugène of Savoy with a strong force to deal with them. He caught a Turkish column as it was crossing the Tisza river at Zenta, eighty miles north-west of Belgrade. Allowing the enemy cavalry to reach the far bank, Eugène then attacked the infantry as they were passing over a temporary bridge. The Turks were virtually annihilated: many drowned in the river, and an estimated 20,000 became casualties to 500 Imperial troops. The victory paved the way for the Peace of Carlowitz (1699), whereby Austria gained Hungary and Transylvania, and Poland secured Podolia and the Ukraine.

Zorndorf *(Seven Years War)*, 1758

While Frederick the Great was campaigning in Austria, a Russian army overran East Prussia and then marched westwards to lay siege to Custrin (Kostrzyn) on the Oder river forty-five miles north-east of Berlin. Hastily moving back north with 15,000 men, Frederick reached Frankfurt-am-Oder on 20 August and joined with 21,000 other Prussian troops in the area to advance and challenge the Russian army of 42,000. Raising the siege of Custrin, the Russian commander withdrew north towards Stettin and occupied a strong defensive position at Zorndorf. But he deployed his force in three irregular squares, which could not adequately support one another due to marshland between them. Noting these poor enemy dispositions, on 25 August Frederick attacked the right-hand square, to face stiff opposition and to succeed only with the assistance of cavalry under General von Seydlitz. Again bitter resistance was encountered before the central square crumbled but, when darkness fell, the third square remained unbroken. By then the Prussians had suffered 13,500 casualties, the Russians 21,000 – an appalling loss rate. Both armies were too weak to resume fighting the following day, and the Russians began to retire eastwards, giving Frederick valuable time to reorganize and recover. A more determined Russian general might well have pressed the Prussians harder with greater ultimate effect.

Zurich I *(French Revolutionary Wars)*, 1799

Following its victories over French troops in northern Italy, the Second Coalition determined to free Switzerland, which had been formed into the Helvetian Republic, from French control. With 40,000 troops, mainly Austrian, Archduke Charles Louis therefore advanced from Baden on Zurich, which was defended by 25,000 men under General Masséna. In a four-day battle from 4 to 7 June, the French resisted until the Austrian superiority of numbers finally drove Masséna back and Zurich fell.

Zurich II *(French Revolutionary Wars)*, 1799

Shortly after Archduke Charles Louis captured Zurich, illness forced him to leave its defence to General Korsakov with 30,000 Russians. Late in August, planning to unite with General Korsakov and clear the French completely out of Switzerland, Count Suvorov began to move north from Italy with another Russian army. Sending a small force to harass Suvorov as he marched through the St Gotthard Pass, Masséna concentrated the bulk of his men against Korsakov. On 26 September, therefore, a second battle in less than four months was fought before Zurich, and this time

Masséna triumphed. The Russians lost 8,000 casualties and many others became prisoners. Masséna thus recovered Zurich and shortly afterwards so harassed Suvorov's line of march that the Russians withdrew eastwards. These reverses, and anger at perceived lack of support from his allies, caused Tsar Paul I to abandon the Second Coalition against France the following month.

Zusmarshdusen *(Thirty Years War)*, 1648

When Bavaria re-entered the war in support of the Holy Roman Empire in autumn 1647 after a brief period of peace, an allied force of some 40,000 French and Swedish troops under the Vicomte de Turenne and Field-Marshal Wrangel marched into the German state. The invaders surprised an Austro–Bavarian force of some 30,000 men under Count von Melander at Zusmarshdusen, fourteen miles west of Augsburg, on 17 May 1648. Leaving Count Montecuccoli with a small force to cover his retreat, von Melander began to retire eastwards. But a large baggage train and numerous camp followers slowed progress. When von Melander was fatally wounded, Montecuccoli abandoned non-military personnel and impedimenta to withdraw to Landsberg with the bulk of the army. The French and Swedish troops overran Bavaria up to the Inn river, before being checked by Field-Marshal Piccolomini, but the country was fully restored to the Elector Maximilian I under the terms of the Peace of Westphalia signed on 24 October 1648.

Zutphen *(Revolt of the Netherlands)*, 1586

In 1586 English troops under the Earl of Leicester, acting in support of Dutch rebels against Spain, laid siege to Zutphen, sixty miles south-east of Amsterdam. On 22 September they intercepted a Spanish relief column outside the town, but were driven off with heavy loss, including Sir Philip Sidney. Leicester was now forced to raise the siege, and the Dutch did not capture the town for a further five years.

List of Wars and Battles

For brevity, individuals are identified by their title at the time or, if without one, military rank: hence, 'Sir Douglas Haig' and 'Field-Marshal Kesselring'. Fuller details appear in the Index of Persons, which as far as possible shows Christian names, the highest title and military rank attained, date of death – with 'd.' (died of natural causes or committed suicide), 'k.' (killed in battle) or 'assassinated' – and a note of those aspects of the career covered in this volume. Decorations and awards are not given.

Albigensian Crusade
Muret, 1213

Alemanni Invasions of the Roman Empire
Argentoratum, 357
Châlons-sur-Marne I, 366
Pavia I, 271
Placentia, 271

American War of Independence
Gibraltar II, 1779–83

Anglo–French Wars
Bouvines, 1214
Calais II, 1558
Gisors, 1197
Ré, Ile de, 1627
Rouen I, 1204
Saintes, 1242

Anglo–Scottish Wars
Alnwick, 1092
Bannockburn, 1314
Berwick-on-Tweed, 1296
Falkirk I, 1298
Flodden, 1513
Halidon Hill, 1333
Homildon Hill, 1402
Loudon Hill, 1307

Methven, 1306
Myton, 1319
Neville's Cross, 1346
Otterburn, 1388
Pinkie, 1547
Solway Moss, 1542
Standard, The, 1138
Stirling Bridge, 1297

Aragonese Conquest of Sardinia
Alghero, 1353

Austrian Succession, War of the
Bergen-op-Zoom I, 1747
Dettingen, 1743
Fontenoy, 1745
Hennersdorf, 1745
Hohenfriedberg, 1745
Lauffeld, 1747
Mollwitz, 1741
Prague IV, 1744
Rocourt, 1746
Sohr, 1745
Velletri, 1744

Austro–Prussian War
Langensalza, 1866
Münchengrätz, 1866
Sadowa, 1866

Austro–Swiss Wars
Morgarten, 1315
Näfels, 1388
Sempach, 1386

Baltic Wars
Reval, 1219
Warsaw I, 1656

Bohemian Wars
Kressenbrunn, 1260
Marchfeld, 1278

Bulgarian Civil Wars
Trnovo, 1218

Byzantine Empire, Wars of the
Adrianople III, 972
Balathista, 1014
Constantinople I, 717–18
Constantinople II, 1453
Ravenna II, 729
Rome III, 537–8
Rome IV, 546–7
Sofia, 981
Taginae, 552

Cade's Rebellion in England
Sevenoaks, 1450

Carthaginian Invasion of Sicily
Acragas, 406 BC
Crimisus River, 341 BC
Selinus, 409 BC
Syracuse I, 387 BC

Castilian Civil Wars
Montiel, 1369
Toro, 1476

Civil Wars of the Roman Empire
Adrianople I, 323
Aquileia II, 394
Bedriacum, AD 69
Heraclea Propontis, 313
Lugdunum, 197
Margus, 285
Mursa, 351

Saxa Rubra, 312
Verona, 312

Civil Wars of the Roman Republic
Mount Tifata, 83 BC
Mutina, 43 BC

Commune Uprising
Paris III, 1871

Conquests of Charlemagne
Pavia IV, 773–4
Roncesvalles, 778
Tisza River, 795

Conquests of Ivan the Terrible
Astrakhan I, 1554–6
Kazan, 1552

Crimean War
Alma, 1854
Balaclava, 1854
Inkerman, 1854
Oltenita, 1853
Sevastopol I, 1854–5
Silistra, 1854
Tchernaya, 1855

Cromwell in Ireland
Drogheda, 1649
Wexford, 1649

Cromwell in Scotland
Dunbar, 1650

Crusade against Turkey
Varna I, 1444

Dacian Wars of the Roman Empire
Moesia, AD 89

Danish Invasions of England
Aclea, 851
Ashdown, 871
Chippenham, 878
Edington, 878
Hingston Down, 837
Hoxne, 870
Maldon, 991

Pen, 1016
Reading, 871
Wilton, 871
York, 867

Danish Invasion of Ireland
Clontarf, 1014

Danish Invasion of Scotland
Mortlack, 1010

Deposition of Isabella II
Alcolea, 1868

Dutch War of Louis XIV
Fehrbellin, 1675
Maastricht II, 1673
Mons I, 1678
Sasbach, 1675
Seneffe, 1674
Sinsheim, 1674
Turckheim, 1675

English Anarchy
Lincoln I, 1141

English Civil War
Adwalton Moor, 1643
Alford, 1645
Auldearn, 1645
Edgehill, 1642
Grantham, 1643
Inverlochy, 1645
Kilsyth, 1645
Langport, 1645
Lansdown, 1643
Lostwithiel, 1644
Marston Moor, 1644
Naseby, 1645
Newbury I, 1643
Newbury II, 1644
Philiphaugh, 1645
Preston I, 1648
Rathmines, 1649
Roundway Down, 1643
Selby, 1644
Tippermuir, 1644
Worcester, 1651

Epirot Invasion of Italy
Heraclea, 280 BC

First Balkan War
Adrianople VI, 1913
Luleburgaz, 1912
Shkodër II, 1912–13

First Barons' War
Lincoln II, 1217

First Bishops' War
Newburn, 1640

First Jacobite Rebellion
Preston II, 1715
Sheriffmuir, 1715

First Peloponnesian War
Coronea, 447 BC
Tanagra, 457 BC

First Punic War
Lilybaeum, 250–241 BC
Messina, 264 BC
Panormus, 251 BC

First Triumvirate, Wars of the
Dyrrachium, 48 BC
Ilerda, 49 BC
Munda, 45 BC
Pharsalus I, 48 BC

First World War
Aisne I, 1914
Aisne II, 1917
Aisne III, 1918
Amiens, 1918
Antwerp II, 1914
Arras II, 1917
Artois, 1915
Belleau Wood, 1918
Cambrai, 1917
Caporetto, 1917
Gorlice-Tarnow, 1915
Gumbinnen, 1914
Isonzo River, 1915
Jadar River, 1914

Kovel–Stanislav, 1916
Le Cateau, 1914
Liège, 1914
Lodz, 1914
Loos, 1915
Lys River, 1918
Marne I, 1914
Marne II, 1918
Masurian Lakes I, 1914
Masurian Lakes II, 1915
Messines, 1917
Meuse–Argonne, 1918
Mons II, 1914
Namur II, 1914
Naroch Lake, 1916
Neuve–Chapelle, 1915
Passchendaele, 1917
Piave River, 1918
Przemysl, 1914–15
Riga II, 1917
Rudnik Ridges, 1914
St-Mihiel, 1918
Somme I, 1916
Somme II, 1918
Tannenberg II, 1914
Verdun, 1916
Vimy Ridge, 1917
Vittorio Veneto, 1918
Warsaw III, 1914
Ypres I, 1914
Ypres II, 1915

Fourth Crusade
Adrianople IV, 1205
Philippopolis II, 1208

Franco–Burgundian Wars
Montlhéry, 1465

Franco–Flemish Wars
Courtrai, 1302
Mons-en-Pévèle, 1304

Franco–Norman Wars
Montfaucon, 886

Franco–Prussian War
Bapaume, 1871
Gravelotte, 1870
Le Mans, 1871
Mars-la-Tour, 1870
Metz, 1870
Paris II, 1870–71
St-Quentin II, 1871
Sedan, 1870
Spicheren, 1870
Wissembourg, 1870
Wörth, 1870

Franco–Spanish Wars
Arras I, 1654
Barletta, 1502
Cerignola, 1503
Dunes, The, 1658
Garigliano, 1503
Gravelines, 1558
St-Quentin I, 1557
Valenciennes, 1656

Frankish Invasion of Italy
Ravenna III, 756

French Revolutionary Wars
Alkmaar II, 1799
Arcole, 1796
Bergen-op-Zoom II, 1799
Fleurus III, 1794
Hondschoote, 1793
Lodi Bridge, 1796
Lonato, 1796
Malborghetto, 1797
Mantua, 1796–7
Marengo, 1800
Mondovi, 1796
Montenotte, 1796
Neerwinden II, 1793
Neuwied, 1797
Novi Ligure, 1799
Quiberon, 1795
Rivoli, 1797
Stockach, 1799
Toulon, 1793
Tourcoing, 1794
Trebbia River II, 1799

Valmy, 1792
Wattignies, 1793
Würzburg, 1796
Zurich I, 1799
Zurich II, 1799

French Wars of Religion
Arques, 1589
Coutras, 1587
Ivry, 1590
Jarnac, 1569
St-Denis, 1567

French Wars in Italy
Benevento, 1266
Fornovo, 1495
Marignano, 1515
Novara I, 1513
Pavia V, 1525

Gallic Invasions of Italy
Allia River, 390 BC
Rome I, 387 BC
Vercellae, 101 BC

Gallic Wars
Agendicum, 52 BC
Alesia, 52 BC
Avaricum, 52 BC
Bibracte, 58 BC
Gergovia, 52 BC
Sambre River, 57 BC
Tongres, 54 BC

German States, Wars of the
Lechfeld, 955
Riade, 933

Germanic Invasions of Italy
Aquileia I, 166–7

Germanic Wars of the Roman Empire
Lippe, 11 BC
Minden I, AD 16
Teutoburgerwald, AD 9

Gothic Conquest of Italy
Ravenna I, 491–3

Gothic Invasions of the Roman Empire
Adrianople II, 378
Naissus, 269
Philippopolis I, 251

Grand Alliance, War of the
Fleurus II, 1690
Marsaglia, 1693
Namur I, 1695
Neerwinden I, 1693
Steenkerke, 1692

Great Northern War
Fredrikshald, 1718
Holowczyn, 1708
Klissow, 1702
Narva, 1700
Poltava, 1709
Pultusk I, 1702
Stralsund II, 1715
Thorn, 1703

Great Peloponnesian War
Amphipolis, 422 BC
Delium, 424 BC
Mytilene, 427 BC
Plataea II, 429–427 BC

Greco–Persian Wars
Marathon, 490 BC
Plataea I, 479 BC
Thermopylae I, 480 BC

Greco–Turkish Wars
Adrianople V, 1365
Pharsalus II, 1897

Greek City-States, Wars of the
Cynoscephalae I, 364 BC
Haliartus, 395 BC
Leuctra, 371 BC
Mantinea, 362 BC

Greek War of Independence
Mesolongion, 1821–6

Hellenistic Monarchies, Wars of the
Sellasia, 221 BC
Thermopylae II, 191 BC

Huguenot Uprising
La Rochelle, 1627–8

Hundred Years War
Agincourt, 1415
Auray, 1364
Beaugé, 1421
Calais I, 1346–7
Castillon, 1453
Crécy, 1346
Formigny, 1450
Harfleur, 1415
Nájera, 1367
Orleans, 1428–9
Patay, 1429
Poitiers, 1356
Rouen II, 1418–19
Rouen III, 1449
Verneuil, 1424

Hungarian Revolt against Austria
Schwechat, 1848
Timisoara, 1849

Hussite Wars
Kutna Hora, 1422
Nemecky Brod, 1422
Prague I, 1420
Usti nad Labem, 1426

Imperial Invasions of Italy
Sant' Angelo, 998
Tagliacozzo, 1268

Imperial Succession, War of the
Mühldorf, 1322

Irish Rebellions
Aughrim, 1691
Boyne, The, 1690
Kinsale, 1601
Limerick, 1691
Londonderry, 1689
Vinegar Hill, 1798

Italian Wars of Independence
Aspromonte, 1862
Calatafimi, 1860
Custozza I, 1848
Custozza II, 1866
Gaeta, 1860–61
Magenta, 1859
Mentana, 1867
Milazzo, 1860
Novara II, 1849
Rieti, 1821
Rome VII, 1849
Solferino, 1859
Venice, 1849

Latin War
Trifanum, 338 BC

League of Cognac, War of the
Rome II, 1527

Lombard Invasion of Italy
Pavia III, 569–72

Lombard League, War of the
Legnano, 1176

Lusitanian War
Numantia 143–133 BC

Macedonian Conquests
Megalopolis, 331 BC
Pandosia, 331 BC
Thebes, 335 BC

Mongol Conquests
Kiev I, 1240
Liegnitz I, 1241
Mohi, 1241

Monmouth's Rebellion in England
Sedgemoor, 1685

Moslem Conquest of Spain
Rio Barbate, 711

Moslem Invasion of France
Toulouse I, 721

Tours, 732

Napoleon's Hundred Days
Ligny, 1815
Quatre Bras, 1815
Waterloo, 1815
Wavre, 1815

Napoleonic Wars
Abensberg, 1809
Arcis-sur-Aube, 1814
Aspern, 1809
Austerlitz, 1805
Bautzen, 1813
Berezina River, 1812
Borodino, 1812
Copenhagen, 1807
Danzig II, 1807
Dennewitz, 1813
Dresden, 1813
Eckmühl, 1809
Eylau, 1807
Friedland, 1807
Grossbeeren, 1813
Hanau, 1813
Heilsberg, 1807
Höchstädt II, 1800
Hohenlinden, 1800
Jena, 1806
Katzbach, 1813
Kulm, 1813
Landshut, 1809
Laon, 1814
La Rothière, 1814
Leipzig, 1813
Lützen II, 1813
Maida, 1806
Maloyaroslavets, 1812
Mogilev, 1812
Montebello, 1800
Montereau, 1814
Oberhollabrunn, 1805
Paris I, 1814
Pultusk II, 1806
Raab, 1809
Reims, 1814
Saalfeld, 1806
Sacile, 1809

Smolensk I, 1812
Toulouse II, 1814
Ulm, 1805
Wagram, 1809

Norman Conquest of England
Hastings, 1066

Norman Seizure
Rome V, 1084

Norman Revolts against England
Gerberoi, 1080
Tinchebrai, 1106

Norse Invasion of England
Fulford, 1066
Stamford Bridge, 1066

Norse Invasion of Scotland
Largs, 1263

Northumbrian Invasion of Scotland
Nechtanesmere, 685

Ottoman Wars
Belgrade I, 1456
Belgrade II, 1521
Harkany, 1687
Khotin I, 1621
Khotin II, 1673
Kossovo I, 1389
Kossovo II, 1448
Mohacs I, 1521
Mohacs II, 1687
Nicopolis, 1396
Peterwardein, 1716
Salonika, 1430
Shkodër I, 1478
Slankamen, 1691
Szentgotthard, 1664
Szigetvar, 1566
Vienna I, 1529
Vienna II, 1683
Zenta, 1697

Parsons' War
Kappel, 1531

Peasants' War
Frankenhausen, 1525

Peninsular War
Albuera, 1811
Badajoz, 1812
Busaco, 1810
Ciudad Rodrigo, 1812
Corunna, 1809
Fuentes de Onoro, 1811
Oporto, 1809
Pyrenees, The, 1813
Salamanca, 1812
Saragossa II, 1808–9
Talavera, 1809
Tarragona, 1811
Vimeiro, 1808
Vitoria, 1813

Percy's Rebellion in England
Shrewsbury II, 1403

Polish–Cossack War
Beresteczko, 1651

Polish Revolt against Russia
Grochow, 1831
Warsaw II, 1831

Polish Succession, War of the
Danzig I, 1733–4
Parma, 1734
Philippsburg, 1734

Portuguese Civil War
Santarem, 1834

Revolt of the Netherlands
Alkmaar I, 1573
Antwerp I, 1584–5
Gembloux, 1578
Haarlem, 1572–3
Leyden, 1574
Maastricht I, 1579
Mookerheide, 1574
Nieuwpoort, 1600
Ostend, 1601–4
Turnhout, 1597

Zutphen, 1586

Rise of England
Ashingdon, 1016
Heathfield, 633
Heavenfield, 634
Mons Badonicus, c.500
Stainmore, 954
Tettenhall, 910
Winwaed, 655

Rise of France
Soissons, 486
Tertry, 687
Tolbiacum, 496
Vouillé, 507

Rise of Normandy
Val-ès-Dunes, 1047

Rise of Poland
Tannenberg I, 1410

Rise of Portugal
Ourique, 1139

Rise of Rome
Asculum I, 279 BC
Beneventum, 275 BC
Telamon, 225 BC
Vadimonian Lake, 283 BC
Veii, 405–396 BC

Rise of Russia
Kulikovo, 1380
Novgorod, 862
Peipus Lake, 1242

Rise of Sparta
Sepeia, 494 BC

Roman Conquest of Britain
Mons Graupius, AD 84
Shrewsbury I, AD 50
Verulamium, AD 61

Roman Social War
Asculum II, 90–89 BC

Roses, Wars of the
Barnet, 1471
Bosworth Field, 1485
Hedgeley Moor, 1464
Hexham, 1464
Lose-coat Field, 1470
Mortimer's Cross, 1461
Northampton, 1460
St Albans I, 1455
St Albans II, 1461
Tewkesbury, 1471
Towton, 1461
Wakefield, 1460

Russo–Finnish Wars
Mannerheim Line, 1939–40
Vyborg, 1918

Russo–Polish Wars
Polotsk, 1579
Warsaw IV, 1920

Russo–Turkish Wars
Astrakhan II, 1569
Azov, 1696
Focsani, 1789
Kulevcha, 1829
Plevna, 1877
Plovdiv, 1878
Rimnik, 1789
Shipka Pass, 1877–8
Svistov, 1877
Varna II, 1828

Saracen Conquest of Sicily
Taormina, 902

Scandanavian Wars
Stiklestad, 1030
Viborg, 1157

Schleswig–Holstein War
Dybböl, 1864

Schmalkaldic League, War of the
Mühlberg, 1547

Scottish Rebellions
Killiecrankie, 1689
Langside, 1568

Second Barons' War
Evesham, 1265
Kenilworth, 1265

Second Jacobite Rebellion
Culloden, 1746
Falkirk II, 1746
Prestonpans, 1745

Second Macedonian War
Cynoscephalae II, 197 BC

Second Punic War
Cannae, 216 BC
Ilipa, 206 BC
Metaurus River, 207 BC
New Carthage, 209 BC
Nola, 215 BC
Syracuse II, 213–212 BC
Trasimeno Lake, 217 BC
Trebbia River I, 218 BC

Second Triumvirate, Wars of the
Perusia, 41–40 BC
Philippi, 42 BC

Second World War
Anzio 1944
Ardennes, 1944–5
Arnhem, 1944
Berlin, 1945
Falaise, 1944
Gothic Line, 1944–5
Gustav Line, 1943–4
Kiev II, 1941
Kursk, 1943
Leningrad, 1941–4
Minsk, 1941
Moscow, 1941
Normandy, 1944
Salerno, 1943
Sevastopol II, 1941–2
Smolensk II, 1941
Stalingrad, 1942–3

Second World War – cont.
Vyazma, 1941
Warsaw V, 1939
Warsaw VI, 1944

Serbo–Bulgarian War
Pirot, 1885
Slivnica, 1885

Seven Years War
Breslau, 1757
Crefeld, 1758
Gross-Jägersdorf, 1757
Hastenbeck, 1757
Hochkirch, 1758
Kolin, 1757
Kunersdorf, 1759
Landeshut, 1760
Leuthen, 1757
Liegnitz II, 1760
Lobositz, 1756
Maxen, 1759
Minden II, 1759
Olmütz, 1758
Prague V, 1757
Rossbach, 1757
Torgau, 1760
Warburg, 1760
Zorndorf, 1758

Simnel's Rebellion in England
Stoke, 1487

Spanish Civil War
Barcelona II, 1938–9
Bilbao, 1937
Ebro River, 1938
Gijon, 1937
Guadalajara, 1937
Madrid, 1936–9
Málaga II, 1937
Santander, 1937
Teruel, 1937–8
Toledo, 1936
Vinaroz, 1938

Spanish Conquest of Portugal
Alcantara, 1580

Spanish–Moslem Wars
Alacros, 1195
Alhama, 1482
Baza, 1489
Granada, 1491–2
Huesca, 1096
Las Navas de Tolosa, 1212
Loja, 1486
Málaga I, 1487
Rio Salado, 1340
Saragossa I, 1118
Simancas, 934
Zallaka, 1086
Zamora, 939

Spanish–Portuguese Wars
Aljubarrota, 1385
Montijo, 1644

Spanish Succession, War of the
Almansa, 1707
Barcelona I, 1705
Blenheim, 1704
Cremona, 1702
Denain, 1712
Donauwörth, 1704
Douai, 1710
Gibraltar I, 1704
Hochstadt I, 1703
Landau, 1702
Lille, 1708
Luzzara, 1702
Malplaquet, 1709
Oudenarde, 1708
Ramillies, 1706
Stollhofen, 1707
Tournai, 1709
Turin, 1706

Swedish–Polish Wars
Linköping, 1598
Riga I, 1621

Swiss–Burgundian Wars
Grandson, 1476
Héricourt, 1474
Laupen, 1339
Morat, 1476

Nancy, 1477

Swiss–Milanese War
Giornico, 1478

Swiss–Swabian War
Dornach, 1499

Third Macedonian War
Pydna, 168 BC

Third Samnite War
Sentium, 295 BC

Third Servile War
Mount Vesuvius, 75–71 BC

Thirty Years War
Breitenfeld I, 1631
Breitenfeld II, 1642
Dessau, 1626
Fleurus I, 1622
Frankfurt-am-Oder, 1631
Freiburg, 1644
Fürth, 1632
Höchst, 1622
Jankau, 1645
Lens, 1648
Lutter, 1626

Lützen I, 1632
Magdeburg, 1631
Mergentheim, 1645
Nördlingen I, 1634
Nördlingen II, 1645
Pilsen, 1618
Prague III, 1648
Rain, 1632
Rheinfelden, 1638
Rocroi, 1643
Sablat, 1619
Stadtlohn, 1623
Stralsund I, 1628
Werben, 1631
White Mountain, 1620
Wiesloch, 1622
Wimpfen, 1622
Wittstock, 1636
Wolgast, 1628
Zusmarshdusen, 1648

Western Roman Empire, Wars of tʰ
Aquileia III, 452
Châlons-sur-Marne II, 451
Florence, 406
Pavia II, 476
Pollentia, 402
Rome I, 410
Rome II, 455

Select Bibliography

C. Barnett, *Britain and Her Army* (1970)

Cambridge University Press, *Ancient History*

Cambridge University Press, *Medieval History*

Cambridge University Press, *Modern History*

Cambridge University Press, *New Modern History* (Vol. XIV, Atlas)

D. G. Chandler, *The Campaigns of Napoleon* (1967)

D. G. Chandler (ed.), *A Traveller's Guide to the Battlefields of Europe*, I & II (1965)

E. Christiansen, *The Northern Crusades, 1100–1525* (1980)

A. Clark, *Barbarossa: the Russian–German Conflict 1941–1945* (1965)

E. Creasy, *Fifteen Decisive Battles of the World* (1949)

E. & T. Dupoy, *The Encyclopedia of Military History* (1970)

V. J. Esposito & J. R. Elting, *A Military History and Atlas of the Napoleonic Wars* (1964)

C. Falls, *A Hundred Years of War, 1850–1950* (1962)

C. Falls, *Great Military Battles* (1964)

C. Falls, *The Great War, 1914–1918* (1959)

J. W. Fortescue, *History of the British Army*, I–XIII (1900 et seq.)

J. F. C. Fuller, *The Decisive Battles of the Western World and their influence upon History*, I–III (1953 et seq.)

M. Gilbert, *First World War Atlas* (1970)

J. Gillingham, *The Wars of the Roses* (1981)

M. Howard, *The Franco–Prussian War* (1961)

H. M. Stationery Office, *History of the Second World War* (Official History, European volumes)

Baron Jomini, *The Wars of Frederick the Great*, I & II (Eng. trans., 1865)

B. H. Liddell-Hart, *A History of the World War, 1914–1918* (1934)

B. H. Liddell-Hart, *History of the Second World War* (1970)

W. F. P. Napier, *History of the War in the Peninsula, I–VI* (1886)

Official History, *The Great War: Military Operations France and Belgium, 1914–1918*

C. W. C. Oman, *A History of the Art of War in the Middle Ages* (1924)

C. W. C. Oman, *History of the Art of War in the Sixteenth Century* (1937)

C. W. C. Oman, *A History of the Peninsular War*, I–VII (1902 et seq.)
Oxford University Press, *History of England*, I–XV
W. B. Pemberton, *Battles of the Crimean War* (1962)
K. M. Setton, *A History of the Crusades* (1962)
F. Taylor, *The Wars of Marlborough 1702–1709*, I & II (1921)
H. Thomas, *The Spanish Civil War* (1961)
Thucydides, *History of the Peloponnesian War* (Eng. trans., 1874)
Times, The, Atlas of the World, III & IV
J. Warrington (ed.), *Caesar's War Commentaries: De Bello Gallico &
De Bello Civili* (Eng. trans., 1953)
C. V. Wedgwood, *The Thirty Years War* (1938)
A. Werth, *Russia at War, 1941–1945* (1964)
E. F. M. Wood, *British Battles on Land and Sea* (1915)
P. Young, *The British Army* (1967)
P. Young & R. Holmes, *A Military History of the Three Civil Wars
1642–1651* (1974)
P. Young & J. P. Lawford (ed.), *History of the British Army* (1970)
P. Young & R. Natkiel, *Atlas of the Second World War* (1973)

Index of Persons

When a name is used by more than one person (e.g. Charles), entries are in alphabetical order of nationality.

A

Abd-er-Rahman, Moorish commander in southern France (k. 732), 227, 228

Abd-er-Rahman III, Caliph of Córdoba (912–61), 253

Abou Abdilehi (Boabdil), King of Granada (1482–92), 71

Abrogastes, anti-Roman pagan commander (d. 394), 25

Aemilianus, Publius Cornelius Scipio, grandson of Scipio Africanus, known as 'Numantinus' following capture of Numantia (133 BC), 154

Aëtius, Flavius, military commander of Western Roman Empire (k. 454), 47

Agis III, King of Sparta (338–331 BC), 125

Agricola, Gnaeus Julius, Roman governor of Britain AD 84, who crushed organized resistance, 134

Agrippa, Marcus Vipsanius, Roman naval and military commander during Wars of the Second Triumvirate, 162

Aistulf, King of the Lombards (749–56), 176

Alaric I, King of the Visigoths (395–410), 168, 182, 183

Alaric II, King of the Visigoths (484–507), 240

Albemarle, Earl of, Arnold Joost van Keppel, Dutch supporter of William III in England and military commander during War of the Spanish Succession (d. 1718), 54

Albergotti, General d', French commander during War of the Spanish Succession, 55

Albert, Archduke of Austria, Spanish commander during Revolt of the Netherlands, 149, 156, 231

Albert, Archduke of Austria, commander against Italians during mid-nineteenth century, 52

Albinus, Clodius, military commander of Roman Britain and one of four claimants to the imperial throne in 193 (k. 197), 111

Alboin, King of the Visigoths, who crossed the Alps and established a new kingdom in northern Italy centred on Pavia (d. 572), 160

Albret, Charles d', Constable of France (k. 1415), 16

Albuquerque, General Mathias d', seventeenth-century Portuguese commander instrumental in establishing John IV as king of an independent Portugal, 136

Alcidas, Spartan commander during Great Peloponnesian War, 142

Alençon, Duke of, John II, French commander during Hundred Years War, 236

Alexander I, Prince of Battenberg, Prince of Bulgaria (1879–86), 166, 204

Alexander I, Tsar of Russia (1801–25), 78

Alexander III, the Great, King of Macedonia (d. 323 BC), 123, 157, 221, 222

Alexander, King of Epirus (342–331 BC), uncle of Alexander the Great, 157

Alexander, tyrannical ruler of Pherae (369–358 BC), 52

Alexander, Earl, Field-Marshal Harold Rupert Leofric George, British and Allied commander during Second World War (d. 1969), 74

Alfonso I, the Warrior, King of Aragon and Navarre (d. 1134), 194

Alfonso IV, the Brave, King of Portugal (1325–57), 181

Alfonso V, King of Portugal (1438–81), 225

Alfonso VI, the Valiant, King of Castile and Leon (1072–1109), 157, 252

Alfonso VIII, King of Castile (1158–1214), 18, 99

Alfred, the Great, King of Wessex (871–99), laid foundations for united English kingdom, 30, 47, 48, 59, 177, 220, 248

Allenby, Viscount, Field-Marshal Henry Hynman, British commander First World War (d. 1936), 29

al-Mansur, leader of Almohad Berber sect, which replaced the Almoravids in twelfth-century Moorish Spain, 18

Alva (Alba), Duke of, Fernando Alvarez de Toledo, sixteenth-century Spanish military commander, 18

Alvensleben, General Gustav von, German commander during Franco-Prussian War, 123

Alvintzy, Baron Joseph von Barberek, Austrian commander during French Revolutionary Wars, 25, 26, 181

Amadeo I, King of Spain (1870–73), 19

Ambiorix, joint king of the Eburones with Catuvolcus and leader of anti-Roman revolt in Gaul 54–51 BC, 225

Angoulême, Duke of, Charles de Valois, royal commander against the Huguenots in France (d. 1650), 99

Anjou, Duke of, younger brother of Charles IX of France and later himself Henry III; Catholic commander during French Wars of Religion, 86

Antigonus III, King of Macedonia (227–221 BC), 198

Antiochus III, the Great, Seleucid Emperor of Syria (223–178 BC) and invader of Greece, 222

Antipater, Macedonian commander under Philip II and Alexander the Great, later regent of Macedonia (d. 319 BC), 125

Antonio, Dom, claimant to the Portuguese throne (exiled 1580), 19

Antony, Mark, rebel against First Triumvirate, member of Second
Triumvirate and associated with Cleopatra (d. 30 BC), 57, 142, 162,
163

Apraskin, Count, Field-Marshal Stepan, Russian commander during
Seven Years War, 73

Aranda, General Antonio, Nationalist commander during Spanish
Civil War, 69

Archidamus II, King of Sparta (476–427 BC), 167

Archimedes, Greek physicist and military engineer (k. 212 BC), 215

Arco, Comte d', French commander during War of the Spanish
Succession, 55

Argenteau, Count, General Florimond Claude Mercy von, Austrian
commander during French Revolutionary Wars, 135

Argyll, Duke of, Archibald Campbell, royal commander during First
Jacobite Rebellion, (d. 1761), 201

Argyll, Earl of, Archibald Campbell, supporter of Mary Stuart and
forced into exile with her in 1568 (d. 1573), 97

Argyll, Earl of, Archibald Campbell, Scottish Covenanter commander
during English Civil War, changed sides to crown Charles II in 1651,
again changed sides and executed 1661, 85, 91

Arminius, anti-Roman leader of the Cherusci Germanic tribe
(k. AD 21), 129, 221

Artaphernes, the Younger, fifth-century Persian commander under
Darius I and Xerxes, 119

Arthur, King, legendary British leader against the invading
Anglo-Saxons after the Roman departure, who supposedly checked
the invaders' advance for fifty years during the sixth century, 134

Artois, Comte d', Robert, French commander under Philip IV
(k. 1302), 49

Attila, King of the Huns, who invaded Gaul, Italy and the Balkans
(d. 453), 25, 47

Augereau, Marshal Charles-Pierre-François, Duke of Castiglione
and French commander during French Revolutionary and
Napoleonic Wars (d. 1816), 25, 59, 87

Augustulus, Romulus, Western Roman Emperor (475–6), 160

Augustus II, Elector of Saxony (1697–1733) and briefly King of Poland
during Great Northern War, 91

Augustus III, King of Poland (1733–63), 53

Aurelian (Aurelianus), Roman Emperor (270–75), 160, 166

Aurelius, Marcus, Roman Emperor (161–9), 24

B

Baden-Baden, Margrave of, Louis William I, Imperial commander
during late sixteenth and early seventeenth centuries (d. 1707), 96,
213

Baden-Durlach, Margrave of, George Frederick, Protestant commander during Thirty Years War, 247, 248

Bagration, Prince Peter Ivanovich, Russian commander during Napoleonic Wars, 131, 154, 205

Baillie, William, Scottish Covenanter commander during English Civil War, 19, 91

Bajazet I, Sultan of Turkey (1389–1402), 149

Baker, Major Henry, commander of Protestant garrison during Siege of Londonderry (killed in action, 1689), 109

Baldwin IX, Count of Hainault, Crusader and (as Baldwin I) Latin Emperor of Constantinople (1204–5), 15, 164

Baner, Field-Marshal Johan, Swedish commander during Thirty Years War (d. 1641), 249

Barbarossa, Frederick I, Holy Roman Emperor (1152–90), 101

Barclay de Tolly, General Mikhail, Russian commander during Napoleonic Wars, 205

Basil II, Byzantine Emperor (976–1025), 34, 205

Bassus, Roman defender of Rome against the Ostrogoths during sixth century, 184

Bathory, Stephen, King of Poland (1576–86), 169

Batu Khan, grandson of Genghis Khan and Mongol leader during the thirteenth century, 89

Bazaine, Marshal François-Achille, French commander during Franco-Prussian War, later imprisoned for surrendering Metz, 72, 123, 128, 196

Beauharnais, Prince Eugène de, Duke of Leuchtenberg, Napoleon's step-son, French commander during Napoleonic Wars and Viceroy of Italy, 1806–14 (d. 1824), 117, 174, 175, 189, 241

Beaulieu, Baron Jean-Pierre de, Flemish subject of the Holy Roman Emperor and Austrian commander during French Revolutionary Wars, 108, 109, 133, 135

Bedford, Duke of, John of Lancaster, English commander during Hundred Years War (d. 1435), 236

Bela IV, King of Hungary (1206–70), 93, 132

Belisarius, sixth-century Byzantine commander against the Vandals, Goths and Persians, 183, 184

Bellais, Colonel John, Royalist commander during English Civil War, 197

Benedek, Field-Marshal Ludwig von, Austrian commander-in-chief during Austro-Prussian War, 189

Bennigsen, Field-Marshal Levin Auguste Théophile, Russian commander during Napoleonic Wars, 59, 65, 78, 173

Beresford, Viscount, General William Carr, commanded Portuguese troops during Peninsular War (d. 1854), 18, 66

Bernadotte, Marshal Jean-Baptiste, Prince of Ponte-Corvo and French commander during Napoleonic Wars, King of Sweden and Norway (1818–44), 33

Berthier, Marshal Louis-Alexandre, Prince of Neuchâtel and Prince of Wagram, French commander during French Revolutionary and Napoleonic Wars (d. 1815), 108

Berwick, Duke of, Marshal James FitzJames, natural son of James II and Arabella, sister of Duke of Marlborough, French commander during eighteenth century (k. 1734), 22, 105, 164

Bittenfeld, General Herwarth von, Prussian commander during Austro-Prussian War, 140

Blois, Charles de, French claimant to the duchy of Brittany (k. 1364), 32

Blois, Comte de, Louis, crusader (k. 1205), 15

Bloodaxe, Eric, King of Norway (947–8 and 952–4), invader of England (k. 954), 209

Blücher, Field-Marshal Gebhard Lebrecht, Prince of Wahlstadt and Russian commander during late eighteenth and early nineteenth centuries (d. 1819), 88, 98, 99, 101, 105, 113, 174, 178, 244, 246

Bock, Field-Marshal Feodor von, German commander during Second World War, 138, 205, 241

Boehn, General Max von, German commander during First World War, 122

Bojna, General, Austrian commander during First World War, 165

Bonaparte, Joseph, brother of Napoleon, King of Naples 1806 and King of Spain 1808–13 (d. 1844), 116, 192, 195, 239

Bonaparte, Napoleon, French military commander, Emperor of the French 1804–14 and 1815 (d. 1821), 13, 25, 30, 32, 36, 37, 39, 42, 53, 56, 58, 59, 60, 75, 78, 81, 87, 96, 98, 99, 101, 102, 105, 108, 109, 113, 117, 119, 120, 133, 135, 136, 141, 147, 153, 154, 158, 172, 174, 175, 178, 188, 189, 205, 226, 231, 232, 239, 245, 246

Boril, Tsar of Bulgaria (1207–18), 164, 230

Boromha (Brian Boru), eleventh-century Irish leader against the Danes, 48

Bosco, Colonel del, Neapolitan commander against Garibaldi in Sicily (1860), 129

Bosquet, Marshal Pierre-Jean-François, nineteenth-century French commander (d. 1861), 85

Bossu, Comte, Admiral Jean de Henin-Lietard, Spanish naval commander during Revolt of the Netherlands, 21

Boudicca (Boadicea), rebel Iceni queen against the Romans in Britain (d. AD 61), 237

Boufflers, Duke of, Marshal Louis François, French commander during War of the Spanish Succession, 105

Bourbon, Duke of, Charles, Constable of France and French military commander during early sixteenth century, 184

Boutillier, Guy de, French garrison commander of Rouen during Hundred Years War, 186

Brandenberger, General Ernst, German commander during Second World War, 26

Brasidas, Spartan commander during Great Peloponnesian War (k. 422 BC), 23

Brennus, fourth-century Gallic leader who sacked Rome and established himself in northern Italy, 21

Browne, Count, Field-Marshal Maximilian von, Austrian commander during Seven Years War (k. 1757), 107, 171

Bruce, Robert, Robert I, King of Scotland (1306–29), 35, 60, 75, 110, 128, 142

Brune, General Guillaume, French commander during French Revolutionary Wars, 21

Brunswick, Duke of, Ferdinand, Prussian commander during Seven Years War, 50, 51, 129, 130, 242

Brunswick, Duke of, Charles William Ferdinand, Prussian commander during French Revolutionary and Napoleonic Wars (k. 1806), 87, 233

Brutus, Decimus Junius, Roman military commander (k. 43 BC), 142

Brutus, Marcus Junius, rebel Roman commander against Second Triumvirate (d. 42 BC), 163

Buchan, Earl of, John Stewart, Constable of France and Scottish commander during Hundred Years War (k. 1424), 236

Buckingham, Duke of, Humphrey Stafford, Lancastrian commander during Wars of the Roses (k. 1460), 152

Buckingham, Duke of, George Villiers, Court favourite and English commander (assassinated 1628), 99, 177

Bucquoy, Comte de, Charles-Bonaventure de Longueval, Austrian Catholic commander during Thirty Years War, 188

Bülow, Baron, General Frederick William, Count von Dennewitz, Prussian commander during Napoleonic Wars, 54, 73

Bülow, General Karl von, German commander during First World War, 144

Bülow, General Otto von, German commander during First World War, 46

Bundy, General Omar, American commander during First World War, 38

Burrard, Sir Harry, Lieutenant-General during Peninsular War (d. 1813), 238

Byng, Viscount, General the Honourable Julian Hedworth George, British commander during First World War and subsequently Governor-General of Canada (d. 1935), 208

Byrhtnoth, leader of English resistance to Danes in Essex (k. 991), 117

Byron, Baron, George Gordon, poet who died at Mesolongion (1824), 126

C

Cade, Jack, leader of Kentish rebellion (k. 1450), 200, 201

Cadiz, Marquis of, fifteenth-century Spanish commander against the Moors, 20

Cadorna, Count, General Luigi, Italian Chief of the General Staff
during First World War (d. 1928), 85

Cadwallon (Caedwalla), King of Gwynedd (k. 634), 77

Caesar, Germanicus Julius, nephew of Emperor Tiberius (AD 14–37)
and Roman military commander against Germanic tribes (d. AD 19),
129

Caesar, Julius, Roman commander, consul and dictator (assassinated
44 BC), 16, 19, 33, 41, 57, 68, 84, 162, 163, 193, 225

Calgacus, first century AD Celtic leader in Scotland against the
Romans, 134

Camillus, Marcus Furius, Roman commander, reputedly six times
military tribune and five times dictator (d. 365 BC), 234

Campbell, Sir Colin, Field-Marshal, Baron Clyde, British
commander during nineteenth century and Commander-in-Chief
India (d. 1863), 34

Camulogenus, Gallic leader against Romans (k. 52 BC), 16

Canute II, the Great, King of England (1016–21), King of Denmark
(1018–35) and King of Norway (1028–35), 30, 162

Canute V, claimant to Danish throne (1146–57) (assassinated 1157),
237

Caractacus (Caradoc), British king (AD 43–50) and rebel against
Romans, 202

Cardigan, Earl of, Lieutenant-General James Thomas Brudenell,
British light cavalry commander during the Crimean War (d. 1868),
34

Carinus, Marcus Aurelius, Roman commander (k. 285), 120

Cathcart, Earl, General William Schaw, nineteenth-century British
commander, 49

Catherine II, the Great, Tsarina of Russia (1762–96), 63, 180

Catinat, Marshal Nicolas de, French commander during War of the
Spanish Succession, 96, 122

Cato, Marcus Porcius, Roman commander during Second Punic
War, later pursued active political career (d. 147 BC), 222

Catulus, Quintus Lutatius, Roman commander and consul (d. 78
BC), 235

Cesarini, Cardinal Giuliano, Christian commander against the Turks
(k. 1444), 233, 234

Chandos, John, English commander during Hundred Years War (d.
1370), 32

Chanzy, General Antoine Eugène, French commander during
Franco-Prussian War, 102

Charlemagne (Charles the Great), King of the Franks (768–814) and
Holy Roman Emperor (800–816), 161, 185, 224

Charles I, King of England (1625–49), 15, 32, 58, 98, 110, 123, 145,
148, 163, 171, 177, 223

Charles II, King of England (1660–85), 57, 197, 250

Charles VII, the Well-served, King of France (1422–61), 64

Charles VIII, King of France (1483–98), 64

Charles IX, King of France (1560–74), 86, 190

Charles V, Holy Roman Emperor (1519–56), 140, 184, 185, 237

Charles VI, Holy Roman Emperor (1711–40), proclaimed Charles III of Spain by anti-Bourbon allies in 1707 when Archduke Charles but never reigned, 22, 35

Charles I, Count of Anjou, French thirteenth-century commander and King of the Two Sicilies (1266–85), 38, 216

Charles VII, Don Carlos of Bourbon, King of the Two Sicilies (1733–59) then King of Spain as Charles III (1759–88), 234, 235

Charles IX, Regent of Sweden (1599–1604), King of Sweden (1604–11), 107

Charles X, King of Sweden (1645–60), 242, 243

Charles XI, King of Sweden (1660–97), 61

Charles XII, King of Sweden (1697–1718), 65, 82, 91, 145, 169, 172, 214, 222, 223

Charles the Bold, Duke of Burgundy (1467–77), 71, 79, 137, 144

Charles the Fat, Holy Roman Emperor (881–7), 136

Charles (Karl Alexander), Prince of Lorraine, brother-in-law of Maria Theresa and Austrian commander during War of the Austrian Succession and Seven Years War, 44, 78, 81, 103, 170, 171, 181, 182, 206

Charles Albert, Prince of Carignano, King of Sardinia (1831–49), 52, 152, 153

Charles Edward, Prince, grandson of deposed James II of England, known as the Young Pretender (d. 1788), 51, 60, 172

Charles Louis, Archduke of Austria, brother of Emperor Francis I, Imperial commander during French Revolutionary and Napoleonic Wars, 13, 30, 58, 117, 212, 241, 251, 254

Chmielnicki, Bogdan, seventeenth-century Cossack leader, 39

Chnodomar, fourth-century King of the Alemanni, 27

Chodkiewicz, General Jan Carol, Polish commander against the Turks (k. 1621), 89

Christian IV, King of Denmark (1588–1648), 111, 112, 250

Christian, Prince, son of Christian IV of Denmark, Protestant commander during Thirty Years War, 61, 80

Christian I, Prince of Anhalt-Bernburg, commander of Bohemian Protestant forces during Thirty Years War, 247

Christian of Brunswick, Duke of Brunswick-Wolfenbüttel, Protestant commander during Thirty Years War (d. 1626), 209, 248

Chuikov, General Vassili, Soviet commander during Second World War, 210

Cialdini, Colonel Enrico, Duke of Gaeta, Piedmontese commander against the Two Sicilies (1861), 67

Clam-Gallas, Count Eduard von, Austrian commander in Italy (1859), 115, 140

Clarence, Duke of, Thomas, brother of Henry V, English commander during Hundred Years War (k. 1421), 37

Clark, General Mark, American commander during Second World War, 192

Claudius II, Roman Emperor (268–70), named 'Gothicus' after victory at Naissus (269), 143

Clausel, Comte, General Bertrand, French commander during Peninsular and Napoleonic Wars, 192

Cleombrotus I, King of Sparta (380–371 BC), 103

Cleomenes I, King of Sparta (520–490 BC), 199

Cleomenes III, King of Sparta (235–221 BC), 198

Cleon, Athenian politician and commander (k. 422 BC), 23

Clermont, Comte de, Charles de Bourbon, French commander during Hundred Years War, 64

Clermont, Comte de, Louis de Bourbon-Condé, French commander during Seven Years War and War of the Austrian Succession (d. 1771), 50

Clovis I, King of the Salian Franks (481), King of the Franks (486–511), 206, 220, 224, 240

Coehoorn, Baron Menno van, seventeenth-century Dutch military engineer, 143

Coigny, Marshal Jean-Antoine-François de, French commander during War of the Polish Succession (k. 1748), 159

Coligny, Gaspard de, Admiral of France, Huguenot leader during French Wars of Religion (assassinated 1572), 87, 190, 191

Condé, Prince of, Louis I de Bourbon, Huguenot commander during French Wars of Religion (k. 1569), 86, 87, 190

Condé, the Great, Louis II de Bourbon, Prince of Condé, seventeenth-century French commander – except 1652–9 when employed by the Spanish (d. 1686), 28, 57, 65, 103, 126, 150, 151, 182, 195, 198, 232

Conradin, Holy Roman Emperor (1254–68), 216

Constans, Flavius Junius, Western Roman Emperor (340–50), 141

Constantine I, Western Roman Emperor (311), united western and eastern empires 324–37, which split again on his death; renamed Byzantium Constantinople (330), 14, 79, 195, 196, 236

Constantius II, joint Roman Emperor (340–50), sole Emperor (350–61), 27, 141

Contades, Duke of, Marshal Louis-Georges-Erasme, French eighteenth-century commander and last duke created under the Ancien Régime (d. 1795), 129, 130

Conway, Viscount, Edward, Royalist cavalry commander during English Civil War, 148

Cope, General Sir John, royal commander during Second Jacobite Rebellion (d. 1760), 172

Córdoba, Gonzales de, Spanish Catholic commander during Thirty Years War, 61, 80, 247, 248

Córdoba, Gonzalo de, late fifteenth- and early sixteenth-century Spanish commander against the French in Italy, 36, 47, 67

Courtanvaux, Marquis de, Louis Tellier, French commander during Seven Years War, 76

Crassus, Marcus Licinius, Roman commander and member of First Triumvirate, executed by the Parthians 53 BC, 139

Crescentius, the Younger, commanded Italian forces which ousted Pope Gregory V, captured and executed 998, 194

Cromwell, Oliver, Parliamentarian commander during English Civil War, later Lord Protector of England (d. 1658), 56, 71, 123, 148, 171, 176, 246, 247, 250

Cumberland, Duke of, William Augustus, British commander during War of the Austrian Succession and royal commander during Second Jacobite Rebellion (d. 1765), 51, 61, 63, 76, 100

D

Dalrymple, General Sir Hew, British commander during Peninsular War who signed Convention of Cintra, 1808 (d. 1830), 238

Dandolo, Enrico, Doge of Venice, leader of Fourth Crusade (d. 1205), 15

Datis, fifth-century BC Persian commander against the Greeks, 119

Daun, Count, Field-Marshal Leopold von, Austrian commander during Seven Years War, 80, 91, 92, 100, 103, 124, 154, 171, 225, 231

David I, King of Scotland (1124–53), 211

David II, King of Scotland (1329–71), 147

Davidovich, Baron, General Paul, Austrian commander during French Revolutionary Wars, 25

Davila, General Fidel, Nationalist commander during Spanish Civil War, 41, 193, 194, 238

Davout, Marshal Louis-Nicolas, Duke of Auerstadt and Prince of Eckmühl, French commander during French Revolutionary and Napoleonic Wars (d. 1823), 13, 32, 59, 87, 96, 131, 241

Debeney, General Marie-Eugène, French commander during First World War (d. 1927), 23

Decebalus, King of the Dacians and leader of anti-Roman rebellion (d. 106), 130

Decius, Trajanus, Roman Emperor (249–51), 164

Dembinski, General Henryk, rebel commander during Polish uprising against Russia (1831) and Hungarian uprising against Austria (1848–9), 223, 243

de Montfort, John, fourteenth-century successful English claimant to the dukedom of Brittany, 32

de Montfort, Simon, the Elder, Count of Toulouse and Duke of Narbonne (k. 1218), 141

de Montfort, Simon, Earl of Leicester and leader of baronial rebellion against Henry III of England (k. 1265), 59, 88, 89

Demosthenes, Athenian commander during Great Peloponnesian

War (executed 413 BC), 53

Dentatus, Manius Curius, Roman commander (d. 270 BC), 39

Desaix, General Louis, French cavalry commander during French Revolutionary Wars (k. 1800), 120

Desiderius, last King of the Lombards (756–74), deposed by Charlemagne, 161

Dexippus, fifth-century Spartan commander against the Carthaginians in Sicily, 13

Diaz, General Armando, Italian commander during First World War, 165, 240

Diebitsch, Count, General Hans von, Russian nineteenth-century commander against Polish rebels and Turkey, 72, 93

Dietrich, General Sepp, German panzer commander during Second World War, 26

Diocles, Syracusan commander against the Carthaginians in Sicily (d. 408 BC), 197

Diocletian, Gaius Aurelius Valerius Diocletianus, sole Roman Emperor (284–6), joint Emperor (286–305), 120, 236

Dionysius, the Elder, tyrant of Syracuse and military commander against the Carthaginians (d. 367 BC), 215

Docturov, General Dmitri Sergeievich, Russian commander during Napoleonic Wars, 117

Dolabella, Publius Cornelius, third-century Roman commander, 232

Dolgoruky, Prince Vassili Vladimirovich, Russian commander during Great Northern War, 145

Domitian, Roman Emperor (AD 81–96), 130, 134

Donskoi, Demetrius, Grand Duke of Vladimir and Moscow during the fourteenth century, 94

Douay, General Charles Abel, French commander during Franco-Prussian War (k. 1870), 249

Douglas, Sir Archibald, Scottish commander against England (k. 1333), 75

Douglas, Earl of, Archibald, Scottish commander against English and fought with the French during Hundred Years War (k. 1424), 83, 236

Douglas, Sir James, Scottish commander against England, knighted on the field at Bannockburn (d. 1330), 142

Douglas, Earl of, James, Scottish commander against England (k. 1388), 156

Dragomirov, Mikhail, Russian commander against the Turks during nineteenth century, 214

Drusus, consul and Roman commander against the Gauls (d. 9 BC), 107

Duchêne, General Denis, French commander during First World War, 18

Dugommier, General Jean-François-Coquille, French commander during French Revolutionary Wars, 226

Dumouriez, General Charles-François, former French Minister of War and commander during French Revolutionary Wars who changed sides after the Battle of Neerwinden (1793), 146, 233

Dundee, Viscount, John Graham of Claverhouse, royal commander under Charles II and James II, who led Scottish resistance to William III (k. 1689), 90

E

Ecgfrith, King of Northumbria (670–85), 145

Edhem Pasha, Turkish commander against Greece during late nineteenth century, 163

Edmund the Martyr, King of East Anglia (executed 870), 83

Edmund II, Ironside, briefly King of England (1016), 30, 162

Edric, Edmund II's brother-in-law, deserted to the Danes but executed by them (1017), 30

Edward I, son of Henry III and King of England (1272–1307), 41, 59, 60, 89, 128, 212

Edward II, King of England (1307–27), 35, 110, 142

Edward III, King of England (1327–77), 45, 50, 75, 147

Edward IV, Duke of York then King of England (1461–83), 36, 79, 110, 138, 190, 221, 228

Edward the Elder, King of England (899–925), 220

Edward, Prince of Wales, the Black Prince, elder son of Edward III, English commander during Hundred Years War (d. 1376), 136, 143, 168

Edward, Prince of Wales, son of Henry VI (k. 1471), 221, 228

Edwin, King of Northumbria (585–633), 77

Edwin, Earl, son of Elfgar, English commander against the Norse (d. 1069), 66

Egbert, King of England (827–39), 80

Egmont, Comte d', Lamoral, Flemish commander of Spanish troops during mid-sixteenth-century Franco-Spanish Wars, executed 1568 for leading Dutch rebels, 72, 191

Eichhorn, General Hermann von, German commander during First World War, 124

Elcho, Lord, David, Earl of Wemyss, Scottish Covenanter commander during English Civil War (d. 1679), 223

El Cid, Rodrigo Diaz de Bivar, Spanish soldier of fortune and commander of Valencia (d. 1099), 253

Eliott, General George Augustus, Baron Heathfield, commander of British garrison during Siege of Gibraltar 1779–83 (d. 1790), 69

Emmich, General Otto von, German commander during First World War, 104

Enver Bey, Turkish leader and commander during early twentieth century, 15

Epaminondas, Theban general (k. 362 BC), 103, 118

Ephialtes, Malian traitor, who assisted the Persians at Thermopylae
(480 BC), 222

Erlach, Rudolph von, fourteenth-century Swiss commander against
Burgundy, 100

Essex, Earl of, Robert Devereux, Parliamentarian commander
during English Civil War (d. 1646), 58, 110, 148

Ethelred I, King of Wessex and England (866–71), 30, 177, 248

Ethelred II, the Unready, King of England (987–1016), 117, 162

Ethelwulf, King of England (839–58), 13

Eudes (Odo), Duke of Aquitaine, Frankish commander against the
Moors during eighth century, 226, 227

Eudes (Odo), ninth-century Count of Paris, 136

Eugène, Prince Eugène François, Prince of Savoy-Carignan,
Imperial commander during eighteenth century (d. 1736), 42, 51,
54, 55, 105, 106, 113, 118, 156, 157, 162, 164, 231, 253

Eugenius, pagan challenger for the Western Roman Empire
(executed 394), 25

F

Faidherbe, General Louis Léon, French commander during
Franco-Prussian War, 35, 192

Fairfax, Baron, Ferdinando, Parliamentarian commander during
English Civil War (d. 1648), 15

Fairfax, Sir Thomas, son of Baron Ferdinando, whom he succeeded,
Parliamentary commander during English Civil War and later
reconciled to Charles II, 97, 145, 148, 197

Falkenberg, Dietrich von, Hessian Protestant commander of
Magdeburg during Thirty Years War, 115

Falkenhayn, General Erich von, German commander during First
World War, 17, 235, 251, 252

Falkenstein, General Vogel von, Prussian commander during
Austro-Prussian War, 97

Fastolf, Sir John, English commander during Hundred Years War
(d. 1459), 160

Ferdinand I, King of Portugal (1367–83), 20

Ferdinand I, nominally Ferdinand IV of Naples (1759–1821) but
deposed by Napoleon then by Neapolitan rebels in 1820, King of
the Two Sicilies (1821–5), 179

Ferdinand II, Holy Roman Emperor (1619–37), 188

Ferdinand III, Holy Roman Emperor (1637–57), as Archduke
Ferdinand commanded Imperial Catholic forces during Thirty
Years War, 86, 150

Ferdinand II, King of Aragon (1479–1516), also Ferdinand V of
Castile on marriage to Isabella I in 1469 but deposed on her death in
1504, 20, 37, 71, 109, 116, 225, 226

Feversham, Earl of, Louis Duras, royal commander during

Monmouth Rebellion and later held several diplomatic
  appointments (d. 1709), 197
Finck, General Friedrich von, Prussian commander during Seven
  Years War, 124
Flamininus, Titus Quinctius, Roman commander and tribune (d.
  174 BC), 52, 53
Flaminius, Gaius, Roman consul and commander (k. 217 BC), 228, 229
Foch, Marshal Ferdinand, French commander and Allied Supreme
  Commander during First World War (d. 1929), 22, 122, 128
Forster, General Thomas, Jacobite commander in 1715 (d. 1738),
  171
Francis I, King of France (1515–47), 121, 161
Francis II, King of the Two Sicilies (1859–61), 67
Franco, Generalissimo Francisco, overall Nationalist commander
  during Spanish Civil War, 36, 115, 116, 238
François, General Hermann von, German commander during First
  World War, 74, 123
Franz Joseph, Emperor of Austria (1848–1916), 206
Frederick I, the Handsome, Duke of Austria and joint Holy Roman
  Emperor with Louis IV (1325–30), 137, 140
Frederick II, the Great, King of Prussia (1740–86), 44, 73, 78, 80,
  81, 82, 91, 92, 94, 95, 103, 105, 108, 124, 132, 154, 170, 171, 185,
  186, 206, 225, 253, 254
Frederick V, the Palsgrave, Elector Palatine and King of Bohemia
  1619 (d. 1632), 112, 165, 188, 247
Frederick, Duke of Austria, Imperial commander in Italy (executed
  1268), 216
Frederick of Toledo, Don, natural son of the Duke of Alva and
  Spanish commander during Revolt of the Netherlands, 20, 74
Frederick Charles, Prince, nephew of William I, Prussian
  commander against Denmark, Austria and France during
  nineteenth century, 57, 102, 128, 140, 189
Frederick William, the Great Elector of Brandenburg (1640–88), 61
Frederick William III, King of Prussia (1797–1840), 87
Frederick William, Crown Prince of Prussia and briefly Emperor
  before death in 1888, Prussian commander during Austro-Prussian
  War, 189
Frederick William, Crown Prince of Prussia, German commander
  during First World War, 236
French, Sir John, Field-Marshal Denton Pinkstone, Earl of Ypres,
  British commander during First World War and later Viceroy of
  Ireland (d. 1925), 100, 110, 147
Frossard, General Charles-Auguste, French commander during
  Franco-Prussian War, 208
Fulvia, wife of Mark Antony and leader of revolt against Octavian (d.
  40 BC), 162
Fuscus, Cornelius, Roman commander (killed by Dacian rebels AD
  87), 130

G

Gabor, Bethlen, Prince of Transylvania, Hungarian Protestant commander during Thirty Years War (d. 1629), 247

Galliéni, General Joseph Simon, military governor of Paris during First World War (d. 1916), posthumous Marshal, 121

Galway, Earl of, Massue de Ruvigny, Henri de, Frenchman who served under William III as English commander during War of the Spanish Succession (d. 1720), 22

Gambetta, Léon Michel, French statesman and resistance leader during Franco-Prussian War, 128

Garibaldi, Giuseppe, Italian patriot and commander during the nineteenth-century struggle for independence (d. 1882), 31, 45, 125, 129, 185

Geminus, Servilius, third-century Roman commander against the Carthaginians, 228

Genghis Khan, thirteenth-century Mongol conqueror of much of Asia and invader of Europe, 89, 104

Genseric, Vandal invader of Italy (k. 455), 183

George II, King of Great Britain (1727–60) and last British monarch to command personally in the field, 51, 55

George V, King of Hanover, fought on Austrian side during Austro-Prussian War and deposed by Prussia (1866), 97

George Frederick, Prince of Waldeck, commander of Prussian troops during the War of the Grand Alliance, 61, 62

Gérard, Comte, Marshal Etienne-Maurice, French commander during Napoleonic Wars, 135

Ginkel, General Godert de, Dutch supporter of William III who commanded English troops during War of the Grand Alliance and War of the Spanish Succession (d. 1703), 32, 106

Glabrio, Manius Acilius, Roman consul and commander against the Syrians during second century BC, 222

Glendower, Owen, Welsh rebel leader against Henry IV, reconciled in 1415 but died 1416, 202, 203

Goeben, General August von, Prussian commander during Franco-Prussian War, 35, 192

Goetz, Count Johann von, Austrian cavalry commander during Thirty Years War (k. 1645), 86

Gonzaga, Francesco, Marquis of Ferrara, commanded forces of the League of Venice during late fifteenth century, 64

Goring, Baron, George, Royalist commander during English Civil War (d. 1657), 97, 123

Gough, General Sir Hubert de la Poer, British commander during First World War (d. 1963), 29, 208

Gouraud, General Henri, French commander during First World War (d. 1946), 122

Grammont, Comte de, French commander during War of the Austrian Succession, 55

Granby, Marquis of, John Manners, British cavalry commander during War of the Austrian Succession and Seven Years War (d. 1770), 242

Gregory V, Pope (996–9), first German holder of the office, briefly deposed 998, 194

Gregory VIII, Pope, (1073–85 but deposed 1080), 184

Grey, Sir Edmund, Earl of Kent, Lancastrian commander during Wars of the Roses who changed sides in 1460 (d. 1489), 152

Grouchy, Marquis, Marshal Emmanuel de, French commander during Napoleon's Hundred Days (d. 1847), 246

Guderian, General Heinz, German commander during Second World War, 90, 138

Guesclin, Bertrand du, Constable of France, Comte de Borja, French supporter of Charles de Blois's claim to Brittany during fourteenth century (d. 1379), 32, 136, 143

Guiscard, Robert, Duke of Apulia, Norman mercenary who sacked Rome (d. 1085), 184

Guise, Duke of, François de Lorraine, French commander against the English during sixteenth century, 45

Gurko, General Osip, Russian commander against the Turks and later Governor-General of St Petersburg during nineteenth century, 167, 201

Gustavus Adolphus (Gustavus II), King of Sweden (1611–32), 43, 64, 67, 112, 115, 175, 180, 213, 246

Guthrum, Danish commander against English and sometime King of East Anglia (d. 890), 47, 48, 59

H

Haakon IV, King of Norway (1204–63), 98

Haig, Earl, Field-Marshal Douglas, commander of British troops on Western Front during First World War (d. 1928), 22, 28, 29, 110, 127, 159, 238

Hannibal, third-century BC Carthaginian commander, historically famed for the use of elephants in battle (d. *c.*183 BC), 46, 127, 128, 148, 149, 150, 228, 229

Harcourt, Colonel Rey d', Nationalist commander of Teruel during Spanish Civil War, 220

Hardrada, Harold II, King of Norway (1015–66), 66, 211

Harold II, King of England (1066), 66, 76, 77, 210, 211

Hasdrubal, son of Hamilcar and brother of Hannibal, Carthaginian commander during third century BC (k. 207 BC), 127, 148

Hasdrubal, son of Hanno, Carthaginian commander during third century BC (d. 221 BC), 157, 158

Hassan, Abdul, fifteenth-century Moorish leader in Spain, 20

Hawley, General Henry, British commander during Wars of the Spanish and Austrian Succession and the Second Jacobite Rebellion (d. 1759), 61

Haynau, Baron, General Julius von, Austrian commander against
Hungarian rebels (1848–9), 223

Heinrici, General Gotthard, German commander during Second
World War, 40

Henriques, Alfonso, recognized as independent King of Portugal
(1143), 157

Henry I, King of England (1100–1135), 211, 223

Henry III, King of England (1216–72), 88, 107, 191

Henry IV, King of England (1399–1413), 83, 202, 203

Henry V, King of England (1413–22), commander during Hundred
Years War, 16,76, 186, 202

Henry VI, Lancastrian King of England (1422–61), deposed during
Wars of the Roses and briefly recovered Crown in 1470 (d. 1471),
36, 77, 138, 152, 190, 200, 228, 242

Henry VII (Henry Tudor), King of England (1485–1509), 42, 43,
138, 213

Henry I, King of France (1027–59), 233

Henry III, King of France (1574–89), whose murder ended the Valois
royal line but not the Wars of Religion, 28

Henry IV, King of Castile (1454–74), 225

Henry IV, Holy Roman Emperor (1056–1106), 184

Henry I, Duke of Saxony and Holy Roman Emperor (916–36), 101,
179

Henry of Flanders, Latin Emperor of Constantinople as Henry I
(1205–16) in succession to his brother Baldwin I, 164

Henry, Prince of Nassau, brother of William the Silent and Dutch
rebel commander (k. 1574), 137

Henry of Navarre, Huguenot leader during French Wars of Religion
and Henry IV, King of France (1589–1609), 28, 50, 85, 86

Henry, Prince of Prussia, brother of Frederick the Great, Prussian
commander during Seven Years War, 80

Henry of Trastamara, rebel leader against Pedro the Cruel during
Castilian Civil War, proclaimed Henry II of Castile and Leon
(1369), 136

Hiller, Baron, General Johann, Austrian commander during
Napoleonic Wars, 96

Himilco, Carthaginian commander (d. 387 BC), 13, 215

Hindenburg, Field-Marshal Paul von, German commander during
First World War, 74, 93, 108, 123, 180, 218

Hippocrates, Commander of Syracusans against the Romans during
Second Punic War, 215

Hippocrates, Athenian commander during Great Peloponnesian War
(k. 424 BC), 53

Hirtius, Aulus, Roman consul and commander during Wars of the
Second Triumvirate (k. 43 BC), 142

Hitler, Adolf, German Führer and overall military commander
during Second World War (d. 1945), 210

Hoche, General Louis-Lazare, French commander during French

Revolutionary Wars and suppressor of royalist uprisings (d. 1797), 147, 174

Hohenlohe, Prince of, Frederick Louis, Prussian commander during Napoleonic Wars, 87

Holk, Count, Field-Marshal Heinrich, Imperial Catholic commander during Thirty Years War, 112

Honorius, Flavius, Western Roman Emperor (395–423), 182

Hopton, Sir Ralph, Baron Hopton, Royalist commander during English Civil War (d. 1652), 98, 187, 214

Horn, Count, Field-Marshal Gustaf Karlsson, Count of Björneborg, Swedish Protestant commander during Thirty Years War, 150

Horne, General, Henry Sinclair, Baron Horne of Stirkoke, British commander during First World War, 113

Hoth, General Hermann, German panzer commander during Second World War, 210

Hötzendorf, Baron Field-Marshal Franz Conrad, Austrian commander during First World War, 85, 165

Houchard, General Jean-Nicolas, French commander during French Revolutionary Wars, 83

Humbert, General Georges, French commander during First World War, 23

Huntly, Earl of, George Gordon, persistent Scottish rebel against English during sixteenth century (d. 1562), 165

Hunyadi, János, fifteenth-century Hungarian commander against the Turks and sometime Regent of Hungary (d. 1456), 38, 92, 233, 234

Hurry (or Urry), Sir John, Scot, who changed sides three times during English Civil War (executed 1650), 32

Hutier, General Oskar von, German commander during First World War, 180

I

ibn-Tashfin, Yusof, eleventh-century Moorish commander in Spain, 252, 253

Irles, General Campo d', Austrian commander during French Revolutionary Wars, 119

Isabella I, Queen of Castile (1474–1504), became Isabella II of Aragon in 1479 through marriage to Ferdinand II, 225, 226

Isabella II, Queen of Spain (1833–70), 19

Ivan IV, the Terrible, Tsar of Russia (1533–84), 31, 88, 169

Ivar the Boneless, Danish leader in East Anglia and conqueror of Northumbria during ninth century, 251

J

James II, King of England, James VII of Scotland (1685–8), 43, 90, 106, 109, 197

James IV, King of Scotland (1488–1513), 62

James V, King of Scotland (1513–42), 207

Jilinsky, General Ivan, Russian commander during First World War, 124

Joan of Arc, briefly (1429–30) French commander during Hundred Years War (executed 1431), 155, 156, 160

Joanna of Castile, daughter of Henry IV of Castile and unsuccessful claimant to succeed him in 1474, 225

Joffre, Marshal Joseph Jacques Césaire, French commander during First World War (d. 1931), 17, 110

John, King of England (1199–1216), 43, 186

John I, King of Castile (1379–90), 20

John II, the Good, King of France (1350–64), 168

John I, King of Portugal (1385–1433), 20

John IV, King of Portugal (1640–56), 136

John I, John Casimir, King of Poland (1648–68), 39, 242, 243

John III, John Sobieski, King of Poland (1674–96), successful commander against the Turks (1673 and 1683), 89, 238

John II, John Asen, successful Bulgarian rebel and Tsar of Bulgaria (1218–41), 230

John, Archduke, brother of Emperor Francis II, Austrian commander during Napoleonic Wars, 82, 174, 189, 242

John of Austria, Don, sixteenth-century Spanish naval and military commander, Governor-General of the Spanish Netherlands 1576–8 (d. 1578), 67

John of Austria, Don, the Younger, Spanish commander against France mid-seventeenth century, 57

Jones, Colonel Michael, Parliamentary garrison commander of Rathmines during English Civil War, 176

Joseph II, Holy Roman Emperor (1765–90), 63, 180

Joubert, General Barthélemy-Catherine, French commander during French Revolutionary Wars (k. 1799), 153, 181

Jourdan, Comte, Marshal Jean-Baptiste, French commander during French Revolutionary and Napoleonic Wars (d. 1833), 62, 212, 239, 245, 251

Joyeuse, Duke of, Anne, Catholic commander during French Wars of Religion (k. 1587), 50

Julian, sometime Roman governor of Britain, Spain and Gaul, Emperor (361–3), 27

Julianus, Calpurnius, first-century Roman commander against the Dacians, 130

Junot, Marshal Andoche, Duke of Abrantès, French commander during Peninsular War, 238

Justinian I, the Great, Byzantine Emperor (527–65), 216

K

Kaidu, grandson of Genghis Khan and thirteenth-century Mongol leader in eastern Europe, 104

Kalkreuth, Count, Field-Marshal Friedrich Adolph von, Prussian commander during Napoleonic Wars, 53

Kaloyan (Yoannitsa), thirteenth-century Tsar of Bulgaria (d. 1207), 15, 164

Kesselring, Field-Marshal Albert, German commander during Second World War, 193

King, General James, Baron Eythin and Kerrey, served in Swedish Army and commanded Protestant troops during Thirty Years War (d. 1652), 249

Kleist, Field-Marshal Paul von, German commander during Second World War, 90

Kluck, General Alexander von, German commander during First World War, 100, 101, 121, 122

Kluge, Field-Marshal Gunther von, German commander during Second World War, 95, 151

Konev, Marshal Ivan Stepanovich, Soviet commander during Second World War, 40

Königsmarck, Count, Field-Marshal Johann Christoph von, Swedish commander during Thirty Years War, 170

Korsakov, General Alexander, Russian commander during French Revolutionary Wars, 254

Kray, Baron, General Paul Kray von Krajowa, Austrian commander during Napoleonic Wars, 81, 82

Krüdener, General Nicolas, Russian commander against the Turks during nineteenth century, 167

Kuprili, Ahmed, Grand Vizier of Turkey (1661–76), 215

Kuprili, Mustafa, Grand Vizier of Turkey (1687–91), 204

Kutuzov, Prince, Field-Marshal Mikhail Larivonovich Golenichov, Prince of Smolensk, Russian commander during late eighteenth and early nineteenth centuries, 32, 42, 154, 231, 232

Kyriel, Sir Thomas, English commander during Hundred Years War and Lancastrian supporter during Wars of the Roses (executed 1461), 64

L

Labienus, Titus, Roman commander in Gaul and supporter of Pompey during Wars of the First Triumvirate (k. 45 BC), 16, 68, 162

Ladislas V, King of Poland (1377–1434), 217

Ladislas VI, King of Poland (1434–44), 233, 234

Laevinus, Publius Laverius, third-century BC Roman commander, 78

Lafayette, Marshal Gilbert Motier de, French commander during Hundred Years War (d. 1462), 236

La Haye, General, French commander during French Revolutionary Wars, 135

Lake, Viscount, General Gerard, Viscount Lake of Delhi and Leswarree, British commander during French Revolutionary Wars (d. 1808), 238

La Marmora, Marquis of, General Alfonso Ferrero, Sardinian commander during Crimean War and Italian commander during Wars of Independence, 52

La Motte-Fouque, Baron Heinrich de, Prussian commander during Seven Years War, 96

Langdale, Baron Marmaduke, Royalist commander during English Civil War (d. 1661), 171

Lannes, Marshal Jean, Duke of Montebello, French commander during French Revolutionary and Napoleonic Wars, 13, 30, 33, 66, 87, 96, 135, 154, 173, 188, 195

Laudon, Baron, Field-Marshal Gideon Ernst von, Austrian commander during Seven Years War, 94, 96, 105

Lazar I, Prince of Serbia (k. 1389), 92

Lefebvre, Marshal François-Joseph, Duke of Danzig, French commander during Peninsular and Napoleonic Wars, 13, 53, 195

Lehwald, General Hans von, Prussian commander during Seven Years War, 73

Leicester, Earl of, Robert Dudley, Baron Denbigh, English commander in the Netherlands (d. 1588), 255

Leman, General Gérard, Belgian commander of Liège during First World War, 104

Leo I, the Great, Pope (440–61), 25

Leo III, Byzantine Emperor (717–41), 176

Leonidas I, fifth-century BC King of Sparta, 222

Leopold I, Holy Roman Emperor (1658–1705), 237, 253

Leopold I of Habsburg, Duke of Austria, brother of fourteenth-century claimant to Imperial throne Frederick the Handsome, 137

Leopold III of Habsburg, Duke of Austria (k. 1386), 198

Leopold William, Archduke, brother of Emperor Ferdinand III and Austrian commander during Thirty Years War (d. 1654), 44, 103

Leslie Alexander, Earl of Leven and Balgonie, Lord-General of the Scottish Army during First Bishops' War, Parliamentary supporter during English Civil War and field-marshal in Swedish Army during Thirty Years War (d. 1661), 147, 148

Leslie, David, Baron Newark, Scottish commander on Parliamentary side during English Civil War, served in Swedish Army during Thirty Years War (d. 1682), 56, 163, 171

Leszczynski, Stanislas, Louis XV's father-in-law, twice unsuccessful claimant to the Polish throne during eighteenth century who became Duke of Lorraine, 53, 82, 223

Licinius, Lucinianus, Eastern Roman Emperor (307–24), 14, 79

Ligonier, Sir John, born Jean Louis in France, served in English Army during Wars of the Spanish and Austrian Succession, became field-marshal and earl (1766); (d. 1770), 100

Lincoln, Earl of, John de la Pole, commander of rebel force supporting Lambert Simnel against Henry VII (k. 1487), 213

Linsingen, General Alexander von, German commander during First World War, 93

Lobkowitz, Prince George Christian, Austrian commander during War of the Austrian Succession, 234, 235

Longinus, Gaius Cassius, rebel commander against the Second Triumvirate (d. 42 BC), 163

Longus, Tiberius Sempronius, third-century BC Roman commander against the Carthaginians, 229

Lorraine, Duke of, Charles V, mid-seventeenth-century French commander against the Turks, 76, 131, 204, 215

Louis IX, King of France (1226–70), died on North African crusade and later canonized, 191

Louis XI, King of France (1461–83), 137

Louis XII, King of France (1499–1515), 64, 67, 152

Louis XIV, King of France (1643–1715), 35, 114, 195

Louis IV, Duke of Upper Bavaria and Holy Roman Emperor (1314–47), 137, 140

Louis II, King of Bohemia and Hungary (1506–26), 131

Louis, Prince of Nassau, brother of William the Silent and Dutch rebel commander (k. 1574), 137

Louis Ferdinand, Prince of Prussia, nephew of Frederick the Great, Prussian commander during Napoleonic Wars (k. 1806), 188

Löwendal, Count Marshal Ulrich-Frédéric-Valdemar von, commander of French troops during War of the Austrian Succession (d. 1755), 40

Lucan, Earl of, Patrick Sarsfield, Jacobite commander in Ireland who later joined French Army (k. 1693), 32, 106

Lucas, General John P., American commander during Second World War, 24

Lucius, brother of Mark Antony and leader of rebellion against Octavian in 41 BC, 162

Ludendorff, General Erich, German commander during First World War (d. 1937), 17, 23, 74, 113, 122, 191, 208, 218

Luxembourg, Duke of, Marshal François Henri de Montmorency-Bouteville, French commander during seventeenth century, reputedly undefeated in a major battle (d. 1695), 62, 133, 143, 146, 211

Lysander, Spartan general and statesman (k. 395 BC), 75

M

Macdonald, Marshal Etienne-Jacques-Joseph-Alexandre, Duke of Tarentum, French commander during French Revolutionary and Napoleonic Wars, 88, 229, 241

Mack, Baron Karl Mack von Lieberich, Austrian commander during Napoleonic Wars, later imprisoned for surrendering Ulm, 231, 232

Mackay, General Hugh, commander of English and Scottish troops under William III (k. 1692), 90

Mackensen, General August von, German commander during First World War, 70, 108, 243

MacMahon, Comte de, Marshal Marie-Edmé-Patrice-Maurice, Duke of Magenta, French nineteenth-century commander and later President of France, 115, 116, 159, 196, 206, 250, 251

Magnentius, Flavius Magnus, Roman rebel leader against Constantius II, usurped Western Roman Empire (350–53), 141

Mago, brother of Hannibal and Carthaginian commander during Second Punic War (d. 203 BC), 148, 229

Malcolm II, King of Scotland (1005–34), 138

Malcolm III, King of Scotland (1057–92), 22

Manchester, Earl of, Edward Montagu, Parliamentary commander during English Civil War later reconciled to Charles II and promoted general (d. 1671), 123, 148

Manfred, usurper King of the Two Sicilies (k. 1266), 38

Mannerheim, Baron, Field-Marshal Carl Gustav von, Finnish commander during First and Second World Wars, 241

Mansfeld, Count Ernst von, mercenary general during Thirty Years War, 54, 61, 80, 111, 165, 188, 209, 247, 248

Manstein, Field-Marshal Erich von, German commander during Second World War, 200

Manteuffel, General Hasso von, German commander during Second World War, 26

Mar, Earl of, John Erskine, Jacobite commander during First Jacobite Rebellion, went into exile with Old Pretender and created duke by him (d. 1732), 201

Marcellus, Marcus Claudius, third-century BC Roman commander reputed to have killed Gallic king Britomartus in single combat (k. 208 BC), 149, 150, 215

Mardonius, son-in-law of Darius I and Persian commander against the Greeks (k. 479 BC), 166

Margaret of Anjou, wife of Henry VI and organizer of Lancastrian forces during Wars of the Roses after his deposition, 152, 190, 221, 242

Maria II, Queen of Portugal (1834–53), 194

Marius, Gaius, Roman commander against the Numidians, Cimbri and Teutones (d. 86 BC), 235

Marlborough, Duke of, John Churchill, English commander who

deserted James II for William III, subdued southern Ireland and
commanded during War of the Spanish Succession until his
dismissal in 1711 (d. 1722), 42, 55, 105, 113, 118, 156, 175, 197,
227

Marmont, Marshal Auguste-Frédéric-Louis-Viesse de, Duke of
Ragusa, French commander during Peninsular War, 48, 98, 101,
158, 192

Marsin, Comte de, Marshal Ferdinand, French commander during
War of the Spanish Succession, 42, 230, 231

Martel, Charles, illegitimate son of Pepin II, Mayor of Austrasia, and
undisputed King of the Franks (714–40), 220, 227, 228

Mary I, Queen of England (1553–8), 45

Mary II, eldest daughter of James II, joint sovereign of England with
her husband William III (1689–94), 90, 106

Mary Stuart, Queen of Scots (1542–87), effectively succeeded by her
son in 1567, 97, 165, 166, 207

Maslama, eighth-century Moslem commander, who besieged
Constantinople, 48

Masséna, Marshal André, Duke of Rivoli and Prince of Essling,
French commander during Napoleonic Wars (d. 1817), 44, 66, 96,
108, 117, 134, 181, 212, 241, 254, 255

Matilda (Maud), daughter of Henry I and claimant to the English
throne after his death (d. 1167), 106, 211

Maunoury, General Michel Joseph, French commander during
First World War, 121

Maurice, Prince, nephew of Charles I and younger brother of Prince
Rupert, Royalist commander during English Civil War, 187

Maurice of Nassau, son of William the Silent, Prince of Orange,
Dutch commander during late sixteenth and early seventeenth
centuries, 149, 156, 231

Maxentius, Marcus Aurelius Valerius, Roman rebel against
Constantine I (k. 312), 195, 196, 236

Maximilian I, Duke, later Elector of Bavaria, founder of the Catholic
League and Catholic commander during Thirty Years War (d.
1651), 66, 247, 255

Maximilian Emmanuel, Elector of Bavaria and Imperial commander
during War of the Spanish Succession, 81

Maximinus, Galerius Valerius, claimant to the Roman Empire
during the civil wars of the early fourth century (d. 314), 79

Maximus, Petronius, Western Roman Emperor (454–5), 183

Maximus, Quintus Fabius, third-century BC Roman commander,
199

Mayenne, Duke of, Charles de Lorraine, Catholic commander
during French Wars of Religion, 28, 85

Mazepa, Ivan, eighteenth-century anti-Russian Cossack leader, 82

Melander, Count, General Peter von, Hessian commander of
Austrian and Bavarian troops during Thirty Years War (k. 1648),
255

Melas, Baron, Field-Marshal Michael F. Benedict von, Austrian commander during French Revolutionary Wars, 120, 229

Melo, General Francisco de, Spanish commander during Thirty Years War, 182

Menendez, General Leopoldo, Republican commander during Spanish Civil War, 220

Menshikov, Prince Alexander Danilovich, Russian commander during Great Northern War, 82

Menshikov, Prince Alexander Sergeievich, nineteenth-century Russian commander against the Turks and during Crimean War, 21, 84, 234

Mercy, Baron, Field-Marshal Franz von, Bavarian commander of Imperial troops during Thirty Years War (k. 1645), 65, 125, 150

Mercy, Count, Field-Marshal Claude Florimund, Austrian commander during War of the Polish Succession (k. 1734), 159

Metellus, Lucius Caecilius, Roman commander during First Punic War, blinded in a fire 241 BC (d. 221 BC), 157, 158

Miaja, General José, Republican commander during Spanish Civil War (d. 1958), 114

Middleton, General Troy H. American commander during Second World War, 26

Miguel, Dom, usurper King of Portugal (1828–34), 194

Milan I, King of Serbia (1882–9), as Prince Milan fought Russians during Russo-Turkish War earlier in the century, 166, 204

Militiades, Athenian commander and politician (d. 489 BC), 119

Mitchell, Colonel William, later brigadier-general and airpower theorist, commander of American air component on Western Front during First World War, 191

Model, Field-Marshal Walther von, German commander during Second World War, 26

Modesto, General Juan, Republican commander during Spanish Civil War, 58

Mohammed II, the Conqueror, Sultan of Turkey (1451–81), 37, 38, 48, 49, 202

Mohammed IV, Sultan of Turkey (1648–87), 76, 131

Mohammed V, Sultan of Turkey (1909–18), 15

Mohammed ben Yacoub, Sultan of Granada (1199–1213), 99, 100

Mola, General Emilio, Nationalist commander during Spanish Civil War (d. 1937), 114

Moltke, Count, Field-Marshal Helmuth Carl Bernhard von, German Chief of the General Staff (1857–88); (d. 1891), 158

Moncey, Marshal Adrien, Duke of Conegliano, French commander during Peninsular War, 195

Monmouth, Duke of, James Scott, natural son of Charles II, commanded English, Dutch and French troops before instigating Protestant rebellion against James II (executed 1685), 197

Montagu, Marquis of, John Neville, Marquis of Montagu and Earl of Northumberland, brother of Warwick 'the Kingmaker', first

Yorkist then Lancastrian commander during Wars of the Roses
(k. 1471), 78, 79

Montecuccoli, Count Raimund, Austrian commander of Imperial
forces during Dutch War of Louis XIV (d. 1681), 195, 215, 255

Montgomery, Viscount, Field-Marshal Bernard Law, British and
Allied commander during Second World War (d. 1976), 26, 230

Montmorency, Duke of, Anne, Catholic commander during French
Wars of Religion (k. 1567), 190, 191

Montrose, Marquis of, James Graham, Royalist commander during
English Civil War, made field-marshal on escape to Continent by
Emperor Ferdinand III but captured and executed on return to
Scotland in 1650, 19, 32, 85, 91, 163, 223

Moore, Sir John, British commander during Peninsular War
(k. 1809), 49, 155

Moray, Earl of, James Stuart, regent in Scotland for infant James VI
and commander of forces against James' deposed mother, Mary
(assassinated 1570), 97

Morcar, Earl of, commander of English troops against the Norse
(1066), later rebelled against William I and died in prison c. 1090, 66

Moreau, General Jean Victor, French commander during French
Revolutionary and Napoleonic Wars (k. 1813), 81, 82, 153, 229,
251

Mortier, Marshal Adolphe-Edouard-Casimir-Joseph, Duke of
Treviso, French commander during Peninsular and Napoleonic
Wars (d. 1835), 158, 195

Moscardo, General José, Nationalist commander during Spanish
Civil War, 73, 224

Mountjoy, Baron, Charles Blount, Earl of Devonshire, commanded
royal troops in Ireland early in seventeenth century after service on
the Continent (d. 1606), 91

Mulgrave, Earl of, General Henry Phipps, Earl of Mulgrave and
Viscount Normanby, British commander during French
Revolutionary and Napoleonic Wars, later pursued a political
career (d. 1831), 226

Münnich, Count, Burkhard Christoph von, Russian commander
during War of the Polish Succession, 53

Münzer, Thomas, leader of peasant uprising in Thuringia (executed
1525), 64

Murad I, Sultan of Turkey (1359–89), 15, 92

Murad II, Sultan of Turkey (1421–51), 193, 234

Murat, Marshal Joachim, Grand Duke of Cleves and Berg (1806)
and King of Naples (1808–15), French commander during
Napoleonic Wars and Hundred Days (executed 1815), 78, 154

Murphy, Father John, leader of Irish rebellion (1798), and executed
same year, 238

Murray, Lord George, Scottish commander during Second Jacobite
Rebellion, later fought in Sardinian Army (d. 1760), 61, 172

Mustafa, Kara, Grand Vizier of Turkey (executed 1683), 237, 238

Muy, Comte de, Marshal Louis-Nicolas-Victor de Felix, French commander during Seven Years War, 242

N

Napoleon III, Emperor of the French (1852–70), 125, 158, 196, 206

Narses, Byzantine commander against the Ostrogoths and Franks, who effectively ruled Italy (554–67) on behalf of Byzantium, 216

Neipperg, Count, Field-Marshal Wilhelm von, Austrian commander during War of the Austrian Succession, 132

Nemours, Duke of, Gaston de Foix, French commander in early sixteenth century (k. 1512), 47, 177

Nero, Gaius Claudius, Roman consul and commander during Second Punic War, 127, 128

Nevers, Duke of, fourteenth-century French commander against the Turks, 149

Neville, Baron Ralph de, English commander against the Scots (d. 1367), 147

Nevski, Alexander, thirteenth-century Khan of Novgorod and Russian conqueror of Kiev, 161

Newcastle, Earl of, William Cavendish, later Duke of Newcastle, Royalist commander during English Civil War (d. 1676), 15, 123, 197

Ney, Marshal Michel, Duke of Elchingen and Prince of the Moskva, French commander during Napoleonic Wars (executed 1815), 36, 54, 105, 174, 232, 245

Nicholas I, King of Montenegro (1910–17), 202

Nicholas II, Tsar of Russia (1894–1917), 93

Nicholas, Grand Duke, uncle of Tsar Nicholas II, Russian commander during First World War, 124

Niel, Marshal Adolphe, French commander during Italian Wars of Independence, 206

Nivelle, General Robert George, French commander during First World War (d. 1924), 17, 28, 29, 236

Noailles, Duke of, Marshal Adrien Maurice, French commander during War of the Austrian Succession, 54, 55

Norbanus, Gaius, Roman consul and commander during Social War (d. 82 BC), 139

Norfolk, Duke of, John Howard, Yorkist commander during Wars of the Roses and supporter of Richard III (k. 1485), 190, 228

Northumberland, Earl of, Henry Percy, supporter of Richard II then Henry IV, but rebelled against him (k. 1408), 202

O

Octavian (Octavianus Gaius Julius Caesar) Roman commander and member of Second Triumvirate, in 27 BC took title 'Augustus' and became the first Roman Emperor (d. AD 14), 142, 162, 163

Odoacer, leader of the Heruli tribe, which deposed Romulus Augustulus and ended the Western Roman Empire in 476, ruled Italy as province of Byzantium (476–93), 160, 176

Olaf II, King of Norway (995–1030), later canonized, 212

Omar Pasha, Turkish commander during Crimean War, 155

Orange, Prince of, Major-General William Frederick Henry, commander of Anglo-Dutch force during Hundred Days, 174

Orestes, father of Romulus Augustulus (k. 476), 160

Ormonde, Duke of, General James Butler, Royalist commander during English Civil War, proclaimed Charles II in Ireland (d. 1688), 176

Osman II, Sultan of Turkey (1618–22), 89

Osman Pasha, nineteenth-century Turkish commander, 167

Ostermann-Tolstoy, Count, General Alexander Ivanovich, Russian commander during Napoleonic Wars, 94

Oswald, King of Bernicia (632), King of Northumbria (633–41), 77

Oswiu (Oswy), King of Northumbria (655–70), 248, 249

Otho, Marcus Salvius, Roman commander and claimant to imperial throne (d. AD 69), 37

Ott, General Karl, Austrian commander during Napoleonic Wars, 134

Otto I, the Great, Holy Roman Emperor (936–73), 101

Otto III, Holy Roman Emperor (983–1002), 194

Ottokar II, the Great, King of Bohemia (1253–78), 93, 119, 120

Oudinot, Marshal Nicolas-Charles, Duke of Reggio, French commander during Napoleonic Wars (d. 1847), 73, 241

Oudinot, General Nicolas, son of Napoleonic general, French conqueror of short-lived Roman Republic (1849), 185

Overkirk (Ouwerkerk), Field-Marshal Hendrik, Count of Nassau, Dutch commander during War of the Spanish Succession, 157

P

Paches, Athenian commander during the Great Peloponnesian War, 142

Pagondas, commander of Boeotian and Theban troops during the Great Peloponnesian War, 53

Palafox, General José de, Spanish commander during Peninsular War, 195

Pansa Caetronianus, Gaius Vibius, consul and Roman commander (k. 43 BC), 142

Pappenheim, Count Gottfried Heinrich zu, Bavarian Catholic commander during Thirty Years War (k. 1632), 43, 112, 115

Parma, Duke of, Alessandro Farnese, Spanish commander during Revolt of the Netherlands (d. 1592), 23, 113

Paskevich, Field-Marshal Ivan Feodorovich, Count of Erivan and Prince of Warsaw, nineteenth-century Russian commander against Turks and during Crimean War, 203, 243

Patton, General George S. Jr., American commander during Second World War, 26, 60

Paul I, Tsar of Russia (1796–1801), 255

Paulinus, Gaius Suetonius, Roman governor of Britain (AD 59–62) and suppressor of Iceni rebellion, 237

Paulov, General P. Ya., Russian commander during Crimean War, 84

Paulus, Field-Marshal Friedrich von, German commander during Second World War, 209, 210

Paulus, Lucius Aemilius, Roman commander during Third Macedonian War, 173

Pausanias, Spartan commander of Greek forces against the Persians (d. *c*.470 BC), 166

Pedro I, King of Aragon and Navarre (1094–1104), 83, 194

Pedro II, King of Aragon (1196–1213), 141

Pedro IV, King of Aragon (1336–87), conqueror of Sardinia, 20

Pedro I, the Cruel, King of Castile and Leon (1350–69), 136, 143

Pelopidas, Theban commander during the Wars of the Greek City-States (k. 364 BC), 52

Pembroke, Earl of, William Marshal, Earl of Pembroke and Striguil, English commander under Henry II, Richard I, John and Henry III, for whom he led a force during the First Barons' War (d. 1219), 107

Pembroke, Earl of, Aymer de Valence, English commander under Edward I and Edward II (d. 1324), 111

Pembroke, Earl of, Jasper Tudor, Duke of Bedford, Lancastrian commander during Wars of the Roses and later held high political office (d. 1495), 107, 138

Penda, pagan King of Mercia (k. 655), 77, 248, 249

Pepe, General Guglielmo, commander of Neapolitan rebels against Ferdinand IV in 1820, 179

Pepin II, Mayor of Austrasia (679–714) during Frankish power struggle in France, 220

Pepin III, the Short, son of Charles Martel and father of Charlemagne, King of the Franks (752–68), 177

Percy, Baron, Henry Percy of Alnwick, English commander against the Scots under Edward III (d.1352), 147

Percy, Sir Henry, Hotspur, English commander during late fourteenth and early fifteenth centuries but rebelled against Henry IV (k. 1403), 83, 156, 202

Percy, Sir Ralph, grandson of Hotspur, Lancastrian commander during Wars of the Roses (k. 1464), 77, 78

Perdiccas, Macedonian commander during fourth century BC, who virtually ruled Alexander the Great's empire after his death (assassinated 321 BC), 221

Perseus, King of Macedonia (179–168 BC), 173

Pershing, General John Joseph, American commander during First World War (d. 1948), 191

Pescara, Marquis of, Fernando de Avalos, Imperial commander during the sixteenth century in Italy, 161, 177

Pétain, Marshal Henri Philippe, French commander during First World War, 17, 127, 235

Peter I, the Great, Tsar of Russia (1682–1725), 33, 145, 169

Peter I, King of Serbia (1903–21), 187

Peterborough, Earl of, Charles Mordaunt, English commander during War of the Spanish Succession, 35

Philip II, Philip Augustus, King of France (1180–1223), 43, 70, 186

Philip IV, the Fair, King of France (1285–1314), 49, 134

Philip VI, King of France (1328–50), 50

Philip II, King of Spain (1556–98), 18

Philip V, King of Spain (1715–46), 35

Philip V, King of Macedonia (229–179 BC), 52, 53

Philip, Landgrave of Hesse, sixteenth-century Protestant commander against Charles V, 140

Philippa, Queen, wife of Edward III of England, who interceded on behalf of the six burghers of Calais (d. 1369), 45

Piccolomini, Field-Marshal Ottavio d'Arragona, Duke of Amalfi, Austrian commander during Thirty Years War, 45, 255

Pichegru, General Charles, French commander during French Revolutionary Wars, 227

Picton, Sir Thomas, British commander during French Revolutionary and Napoleonic Wars and Hundred Days (k. 1815), 174

Piłsudski, General Jozef, twentieth-century Polish statesman and commander, 243

Plumer, Viscount, Field-Marshal Herbert Charles Onslow, British commander during First World War, 159, 252

Pompeianus, fourth-century Roman rebel leader against Constantine I (k. 312), 236

Pompey (Gnaeus Pompeius), the Great, first-century BC Roman commander, member of First Triumvirate and later challenger for undisputed control over the Republic (assassinated 48 BC), 84, 140, 162, 163

Pompey, Gnaeus, son of Pompey the Great, rebel leader against Julius Caesar (executed 45 BC), 141

Pompey, Sextus, son of Pompey the Great, rebel leader against Julius Caesar and later involved in Wars of the Second Triumvirate (executed 35 BC), 141

Potiorek, Field-Marshal Oskar, Austrian commander during First World War, 86, 187

Prittwitz, General Max von, German commander during First World
War, 74

Procop, Holý, the Bald, Tabor priest and Hussite rebel commander
(k. 1434), 232

Putnik, General Voivode, Serbian commander during First World
War, 187

Pyrrhus, King of Epirus (307–272 BC) whose costly success at
Asculum gave rise to the term 'Pyrrhic victory', 29, 38, 39, 78

Q

Quast, General Ferdinand, German commander during First World
War, 113

Quosdanovich, General Peter Vitus von, Austrian commander
during French Revolutionary Wars, 109

R

Radagaisus, Ostrogoth leader against Western Roman Empire
(executed 406), 62, 63

Radetski, General Fedor, Russian nineteenth-century commander,
201

Radetsky, Count, Field-Marshal Joseph, Austrian nineteenth-
century commander, 52, 152, 235

Radziwill, Prince Michael, commander of Polish rebels against
Russia (1831), 72

Ramiro II, King of the Asturias, Leon and Castile (930–50), 203, 253

Rawlinson, Baron, General Henry Seymour, British commander
during First World War (d. 1925), 23

Raimond VI, Count of Toulouse, thirteenth-century Albigensian
commander, 141

Rennenkampf, General Pavel, Russian commander during First
World War, 73, 74, 123, 124, 218

Reschid Pasha, nineteenth-century Turkish commander against
Russia, 93

Reynier, Comte, General Jean-Louis-Ebenezer, French
commander during Napoleonic and Peninsular Wars, 116

Richard I, King of England (1189–99), 70, 186

Richard III, King of England (1483–5), 42

Richelieu, Cardinal, Armand du Plessis, commander of royal troops
besieging La Rochelle (1627–8), 99, 177

Roatta, General Mario, commander of Italian troops supporting
Nationalists during Spanish Civil War, 73

Robert, Duke of Normandy, the Conqueror's son, who thrice
rebelled against him and opposed his brother's accession to the

English throne as Henry I, thus spending his last twenty-eight years in prison (d. 1134), 68, 223

Roderick (Rodrigo), last Visigoth King of Toledo in Spain (k. 711), 180, 181

Rohan, Duke of, Henri, Protestant commander during Thirty Years War (k. 1638), 179

Rokossovski, Marshal Konstantin, Soviet commander during Second World War, 40, 95, 244

Roland, medieval paladin (k. 778), 185

Rommel, Field-Marshal Erwin, German commander during Second World War (d. 1944), 151

Rudolph I, Holy Roman Emperor (1273–91), 119

Rufus, William (William II), King of England (1087–1100), 22, 223

Rundstedt, Field-Marshal Karl von, German commander during Second World War, 151

Rupert, Prince, grandson of James I and nephew of Charles I, Count Palatine and Duke of Bavaria, Royalist commander during English Civil War, later achieved high military and naval office (d. 1682), 58, 59, 123, 145

Rurik, ninth-century leader of Scandinavian invaders of Russia, Varanger Prince of Novgorod (d. 879), 153

S

Sabinus, Titus, Roman commander in Gaul (k. 54 BC), 225

Sackville, Lord George, so known until 1770 when assumed name of 'Germain' and later became George Sackville Germain, Viscount Sackville, eighteenth-century British commander (d. 1785), 130

St-Priest, General, exiled Frenchman and Russian commander during Napoleonic Wars, 178

St-Ruth, Marquis de, Charles Chalmont, French commander of troops supporting Irish rebellion (k. 1691), 32

Saldanha, Duke of, João Carlos, royal commander during Portuguese Civil War in 1834, 194

Salinator, Marcus Livius, third-century Roman consul and commander, 127

Salisbury, Earl of, Thomas de Montacute, English commander during Hundred Years War (k. 1428), 155

Salisbury, Earl of, Richard Neville, Yorkist commander during Wars of the Roses (assassinated 1460), 242

Samh-ibn-Malik, Moorish commander in Spain and southern France (k. 721), 226

Samsonov, General Alexander, Russian commander during First World War, 218

Samuel, Tsar of Bulgaria (976–1014), 34, 205

Sarabia, General Hernandez, Republican commander during Spanish Civil War, 220

Savoy, Duke of, Victor Amadeus II, Imperial commander during Wars of the Grand Alliance and the Spanish Succession, 122, 231

Saxe, Comte de, Marshal Maurice, French eighteenth-century commander, 40, 63, 100, 182

Saxe-Coburg, Prince of, Frederick Josias, Austrian commander during the late eighteenth century, 62, 146, 180, 227, 245

Saxe-Weimar, Duke of, Bernard, Protestant commander during Thirty Years War (d. 1639), 112, 150, 178, 179

Saxony, Elector of, John George I (1611–56), Protestant commander during Thirty Years War, 246, 249

Scapula, Publius Ostorius, Roman governor of Britain (AD 47–52), and captor of Caractacus, 202

Scarlett, General the Hon. Sir James Yorke, British heavy cavalry commander during Crimean War, later Adjutant-General (d. 1871), 34

Scholick, General, Austrian commander during Wars of Italian Independence, 206

Schomberg, Duke of, Frederick, commander of Anglo-Dutch force in Ireland (k. 1690), 43

Schwarzenberg, Prince Karl von, Austrian commander during Napoleonic Wars, 25, 56, 94, 99, 101, 135, 158

Schwerin, Count, Field-Marshal Kurt von, Prussian commander during War of the Austrian Succession and Seven Years War, 171

Scipio, Metellus Pius, Roman commander and supporter of Pompey against Julius Caesar during first century BC, 163

Scipio, Publius Cornelius, father of Scipio Africanus, Roman commander during Second Punic War (k. 209 BC), 229

Scipio Africanus, Publius Cornelius, first-century BC Roman commander against the Carthaginians (d. *c.*183 BC), 84, 148

Selim II, Sultan of Turkey (1566–74), 31

Serrano, Francisco, rebel Portuguese leader in Civil War (1868), 19

Sérurier, Count, Marshal Jean-Mathieu-Philibert, French commander during French Revolutionary Wars (d. 1819), 119

Severus, Septimus, Roman Emperor (193–211), 111

Seydlitz, General Friedrich Wilhelm von, Prussian commander during Seven Years War, 94, 186, 254

Shrewsbury, Earl of, John Talbot, English commander during Hundred Years War (k. 1453), 46, 160

Sidney, Sir Philip, brother of Earl of Leicester, who fought during Revolt of the Netherlands (k. 1586), 255

Sievers, General, Russian commander during First World War, 124

Sigismund, King of Hungary (1387–1437) and Holy Roman Emperor (1410–37), 95, 146, 170, 232

Sigismund III, King of Poland (1587–1632) and King of Sweden (1592–8), 107, 179

Silesia, Duke of, Henry II, thirteenth-century Polish commander (k. 1241), 104

Simnel, Lambert, crowned Edward VI in Ireland and challenger to
  Henry VII in England (d. 1525), 213
Skobolov, General Mikhail Dmitrievich, nineteenth-century
  Russian commander against the Turks, 214
Smith-Dorrien, General Sir Horace Lockwood, British commander
  during First World War, 100, 252
Soimonov, General F. I., Russian commander during Crimean War,
  84
Solchaga, General José, Nationalist commander during Spanish
  Civil War, 69
Soltikov, Count, Field-Marshal Peter, Russian commander during
  Seven Years War, 94
Somerset, Duke of, Edmund Beaufort, English commander during
  Hundred Years War and Lancastrian leader during Wars of the
  Roses (k. 1455), 187
Somerset, Duke of, Edmund Beaufort, Lancastrian commander
  during Wars of the Roses (executed 1471), 221
Somerset, Duke of, Edward Seymour, Earl of Hertford, English
  commander against the Scots (executed 1552), 165
Somerset, Duke of, Henry Beaufort, Lancastrian commander
  (executed 1464), 79
Soubise, Prince of, Marshal Charles de Rohan, French commander
  during Seven Years War, 186
Souham, Count, General Joseph, French commander during
  Napoleonic Wars, 88
Soult, Marshal Nicolas-Jean de Dieu, Duke of Dalmatia, French
  commander during French Revolutionary and Napoleonic Wars
  (d. 1851), 18, 32, 49, 87, 154, 155, 173, 217, 226
Spartacus, Thracian slave and leader of anti-Roman uprising
  (k. 71 BC), 139, 140
Spinola, Marquis of, Ambrogio, Spanish commander during Revolt
  of the Netherlands and Thirty Years War (d. 1630), 61, 156
Stalin, Marshal Josef Vissarionovich, Generalissimo of Soviet armed
  forces during Second World War and Secretary-General of the
  Central Committee of the Communist Party (d. 1953), 90
Stambolov, Stefan, nineteenth-century Bulgarian commander
  against the Serbs, 204
Stanley, Baron, Thomas, Earl of Derby, English commander during
  Hundred Years War, supported Richard III but neutral at
  Bosworth and reconciled to Henry VII (d. 1504), 42
Starhemberg, Count Ernst Rüdiger von, seventeenth-century
  Austrian commander against the Turks, 238
Steinau, Field-Marshal von, Saxon commander during Great
  Northern War, 172
Steinmetz, General Karl Friedrich von, Prussian commander during
  Franco-Prussian War, 208
Stephen II, Pope (752–7), 176
Stephen of Blois, grandson of William the Conqueror, King of

England (1135–54), 106, 211

Stilicho, Flavius, Roman commander against the Ostrogoths and effective ruler of Western Roman Empire (395–408), 63, 168, 182

Stuart, Sir John, Count of Maida, British commander during French Revolutionary, Peninsular and Napoleonic Wars (d. 1815), 116

Subotai, thirteenth-century Mongol invader of eastern Europe and southern Russia, 89, 132

Suchet, Marshal Louis-Gabriel, Duke of Albufera, French commander during Peninsular War (d. 1826), 219

Suffolk, Duke of, William de la Pole, English commander during Hundred Years War and Lancastrian supporter during Wars of the Roses (executed 1450), 155

Suleiman I, the Magnificent, Sultan of Turkey (1520–66), 38, 131, 216, 237

Suleiman II, Sultan of Turkey (1687–91), 131

Suleiman Pasha, nineteenth-century Turkish commander against the Russians, 167, 201

Sulla, Lucius Cornelius, first-century BC Roman commander and statesman (d. 78 BC), 139

Sulpicius, Publius, third-century BC Roman commander against Epirots, 29

Sulpicius, Quintus, fourth-century BC Roman commander against Gauls, 21

Surrey, Earl of, Thomas Howard, Duke of Norfolk, sixteenth-century English commander (d. 1554), 62

Surrey, Earl of, John de Warenne, English commander under Edward I, fought for and against Henry III in his dispute with the barons (d. 1304), 212

Suvorov, Count, Field-Marshal Alexander Vassilievich, Count Rimniksky, eighteenth and early nineteenth-century Russian commander, 153, 180, 229, 230, 254, 255

Sviatoslav I, Prince of Kiev (945–75), 14

Sweyn (Sven) I, Forkbeard, King of Denmark (958–1014), 138

Sweyn III, King of Denmark (1147–57) but actually one of three claimants to the throne, 237

Syagrius, last Roman governor of Gaul (k. 486), 206

T

Tallard, Comte de, Marshal Camille, French commander during War of the Spanish Succession, 42

Tavannes, Marshal Gaspard de Saulx de, Catholic commander during French Wars of Religion, 86

Theodoric I, King of the Visigoths (419–51), 47

Theodoric, the Great, King of the Ostrogoths (471–526), 176, 240

Theodosius I, the Great, Roman Emperor (378–95) on whose death the Empire divided into West and East under his sons, 25

Theresa, Maria, wife of Holy Roman Emperor Francis I, Queen of Hungary and Bohemia and Empress of Austria (1740–80) whose accession precipitated the War of the Austrian Succession, 40, 132, 205, 206

Thielmann, Baron, General Johann A. von, Prussian commander during Hundred Days, 246

Thierry III (Theoderic), Mayor of Neustria (673–9) during Frankish power struggle in France, King of the Franks (679–90), 220

Tiberius, Roman Emperor (AD 14–37), 129

Tilly, Comte de, John Tzerklaes, Catholic commander during Thirty Years War (k. 1632), 43, 80, 111, 112, 115, 175, 209, 246, 247, 248

Timoleon, fourth-century BC Corinthian commander sent to aid Syracuse against Carthage and became *de facto* ruler of Sicily (d. *c*.334 BC), 51

Timoshenko, Marshal Semën K., Soviet commander during Second World War, 118

Todleben, Count, Franz Eduard Ivanovich, Russian engineer prominent during the nineteenth-century in the Crimean War and against the Turks, 167, 200

Tolmides, Athenian commander during Great Peloponnesian War, 49

Torstensson, Field-Marshal Lennart, Count of Ortala, Swedish commander during Thirty Years War, 44, 86

Torquatus, Titus Manlius, fourth-century BC Roman consul and commander, 230

Tostig, half-brother of Harold II, who deserted to the Norse (k. 1066), 211

Totila, sixth-century Ostrogoth leader against the Romans (k. 552), 184, 216

Trémouille, Louis de la, sixteenth-century French commander in Italy, 152

Trochu, General Louis Jules, French commander during Franco-Prussian War, 158

Turenne, Vicomte de, Marshal Henri de la Tour d'Auvergne, French commander during Thirty Years War and Dutch War of Louis XIV (k. 1675), 28, 57, 65, 125, 126, 195, 204, 230, 232, 233, 255

Tyrone, Earl of, Hugh O'Neill, Baron of Dungannon, leader of several rebellions against Elizabeth I of England (d. 1616), 91

U

Ulibarri, General, Republican commander during Spanish Civil War, 194

V

Vadomair, fourth-century Alemanni leader against the Romans, 47

Valdez, General, Spanish commander during Revolt of the
Netherlands, 104

Valens, joint Roman Emperor (364–78), 14

Valentinian I, joint Roman Emperor (364–75), 47

Valentinian III, Western Roman Emperor (425–55), 183

Vandamme, Count, General Dominique-Josephe-René, Count d'
Unebourg, French commander during Napoleonic Wars, 40, 94

Varela, General José Enrique, Nationalist commander during
Spanish Civil War, 114

Varro, Gaius Terentius, consul and Roman commander during
Second Punic War, 46

Varus, Publius Quintilius, Roman commander against Germanic
tribes (d. AD 9), 129, 221

Vatutin, Marshal Nikolai, Soviet commander during Second World
War, 95

Vauban, Marquis de, Marshal Sébastien le Prestre, seventeenth-
century French engineer, 114

Vega, General Camilo Alfonso, Nationalist commander during
Spanish Civil War, 238

Vendôme, Duke of, Marshal Louis Joseph, French commander
during War of the Spanish Succession, 105, 113, 156, 157, 175, 230

Vercassivellaunus, son-in-law of Vercingetorix, Gallic leader against
Romans during first century BC, 19

Vercingetorix, Arvernian leader against Julius Caesar during Gallic
Wars (executed 46 BC), 19, 33, 68

Verrucosus, Quintus Fabius, Roman dictator during Second Punic
War and defender of Rome, 229

Victor, Marshal Claude-Victor-Perrin, Duke of Belluno, French
commander during Peninsular and Napoleonic Wars (d. 1841), 39,
66, 135, 217

Victor Amadeus III, Duke of Savoy and King of Sardinia (1773–96),
133

Victor Emmanuel II, King of Sardinia (1848) and first King of Italy
(1861–78), 31, 125, 206

Villalba, Colonel José, Republican defender of Malaga during
Spanish Civil War, 116

Villars, Duke of, Marshal Claude, French commander during War
of the Spanish Succession, 54, 81, 213, 226

Villeroi, Duke of, Marshal François de Neufville, French
commander during War of the Grand Alliance and War of the
Spanish Succession, 51, 143, 175

Viriathus, Lusitanian rebel leader against the Romans (assassinated
140 BC), 153, 154

Vitiges, sixth-century Gothic leader against the Romans, 183

Vitellius, Aulus, Roman Emperor (briefly AD 69), 37

W

Waldemar (Valdemar) I, the Great, King of Denmark (1157–82), 237

Waldemar II, the Victorious, King of Denmark (1202–41), 178

Waldstein, General Albrecht Wenceslaus von, known as Wallenstein, Duke of Mecklenburg and Prince of Friedland, Catholic commander during Thirty Years War (assassinated 1634), 54, 66, 67, 111, 112, 213, 250

Wallace, Sir William, Scottish rebel leader against Edward I (executed 1305), 60, 128, 212

Waller, Sir William, Parliamentary commander during English Civil War (d. 1668), 48, 187, 214

Warwick, Earl of, John Neville, known as 'the Kingmaker' after recrowning Henry VI following his brief release from imprisonment, supported Yorkists then Lancastrians during Wars of the Roses (k. 1471), 36, 110, 138, 152, 190

Weidling, General Kurt, German commander who surrendered Berlin during Second World War, 41

Welles, Sir Robert, Lancastrian commander during Wars of the Roses (executed 1470), 110

Wellington, Duke of, Field-Marshal Arthur Wellesley, British commander during Peninsular and Napoleonic Wars and Hundred Days, later held high military and political office including Prime Minister (d. 1852), 18, 33, 34, 44, 48, 66, 155, 173, 174, 192, 217, 226, 238, 240, 245

Wenceslas (Wenzel) II, King of Bohemia (1278–1305), 120

Werneck, General, Austrian commander during French Revolutionary Wars, 147

Werth, General Johann von, Bavarian Catholic commander during Thirty Years War, 125, 178, 179

Weygand, General Maxime, French adviser to Poland in 1920 and French commander during Second World War, 243

William I, the Conqueror, King of England (1066–87), 68, 76, 211, 233

William III, Prince of Orange and grandson of Charles I, King of England (1689–1702), 31, 43, 90, 106, 133, 143, 145, 146, 198, 211

William the Silent, William I, Prince of Orange and Stadholder of Holland, Zeeland and Utrecht, leader of Dutch revolt against Spain (assassinated 1584), 23, 68, 104

Wills, General Charles, English commander during War of the Spanish Succession and royal commander during First Jacobite Rebellion (d. 1741), 171

Wiltshire, Earl of, James Butler, Lancastrian commander during Wars of the Roses (executed 1461), 138

Wimpffen, General Emmanuel Felix de, French commander during Franco-Prussian War, 196

Windischgrätz, Prince, Field-Marshal Alfred von, Austrian
   commander during Hungarian revolt 1848–9, 196
Wittgenstein, Prince, Field-Marshal Louis Adolph, Prince of Sayn,
   Russian commander during Napoleonic Wars, 118
Worcester, Earl of, Thomas Percy, English commander under
   Richard II but rebelled against Henry IV (executed 1403), 203
Wrangel, Field-Marshal Karl Gustaf, Count of Sylfnitzbourg,
   Swedish commander during Thirty Years War, 255
Wrede, Prince, Field-Marshal Karl Philipp von, Bavarian
   commander during Napoleonic Wars, 75, 76
Würmser, Count, Field-Marshal Dagobert Sigmund von, Austrian
   commander during French Revolutionary Wars, 109, 119

X

Xerxes, son of Darius I, King of Persia (486–465 BC), 119, 222

Y

York, Archbishop of, Thurstan (1114–40), 211
York, Archbishop of, William Melton (1317–40), 142
York, Duke of, Richard Plantagenet, Yorkist commander during
   Wars of the Roses and named as his successor by Henry VI
   (k. 1460), 242
York and Albany, Duke of, Field-Marshal Frederick Augustus,
   second son of George III and British commander during French
   Revolutionary Wars (d. 1827), 21, 40

Z

Zhukov, Marshal Gregori Konstantinovich, Soviet commander
   during Second World War, 40, 139, 210
Zieten, General Johann Joachim von, Prussian commander during
   Seven Years War, 171, 225
Zimisces, John, tenth-century Byzantine commander, 14
Žižka, Jan, Hussite rebel leader against the Holy Roman Emperor
   (d. 1424), 95, 146, 170, 217
Zrinyi, Miklos, Croatian defender of Szigetvar against the Turks
   (k. 1566), 216
Zwingli, Ulrich, Swiss Protestant reformer (k. 1531), 88

Postscript

The advent of nuclear weapons brought a new dimension to military thinking in Europe. For over forty years after the close of the Second World War, fear of Mutually Assured Destruction (MAD) restrained the Western Powers and the Soviet bloc from overt clashes. 'Incidents' such as the Berlin Air Lift, when the Soviets cut off land access to the city (1948–9), and the Soviet 'invasion' of Prague (1968) did occur. But war was avoided. The influence of multi-national organisations like the European Community and North Atlantic Treaty Organisation (NATO) has further reduced the prospect of inter-state hostilities. Disintegration of Yugo-slavia during the 1990s into confrontations involving its republics seeking independence and Servia's programme of ethnic cleansing in Kosovo brought intervention by NATO. The concept of 'peace-keeping' by armed forces and police action to contain domestic violence signal that disagreements in the Balkans and Europe as a whole, if unresolved at the conference table, will in future not lead to conflicts like the Seven Years' War or French Wars of Religion. Moreover, the increasing use of aerial precision-guided weapons and the evolution of more sophisticated military technology has further reduced the likelihood of massed armies ever again recreating the battlefields of Jena or Waterloo.

John Sweetman
2004